Praise for "That None Should Perish"

This may be one of the most important books to be written in this last decade of the twentieth century. It will convict and encourage you. It will stir you to faith and action. It will bring you to your knees. Above all, it will give you the missing keys to unlock the demonic prison doors of sin and misbelief which holds millions of city dwellers in bondage till today.

Dr. Ed Murphy, author of *The Handbook for Spiritual Warfare*

Ed Silvoso makes the incredible credible. Can whole cities be evange-lized? Yes! Is prayer really capable of bringing this to pass? Yes! Are there practical steps that anyone can take to defeat Dark Powers and set the captives in your neighborhood free? You bet! This book sounds the call to seize the moment. It gives you reason to hope!

David Bryant
Founder and President
Concerts of Prayer International

FOREWORD BY C. PETER WAGNER

ED SILVOSO

THAT
NONE
SHOULD
PERISH

HOW TO REACH ENTIRE CITIES FOR CHRIST THROUGH PRAYER EVANGELISM

Regal

A Division of Gospel Light
Ventura, California, U.S.A.

Regal Books
From Gospel Light
Ventura, California, U.S.A.
Printed in the U.S.A.

Scripture taken from the New American Standard Bible, © 1960, 1962, 1963, 1968, 1971, 1972, 1973, 1975, 1977 by The Lockman Foundation. Used by permission.

The following Bible versions are also used:
KJV—King James Version.
Scripture quotations marked (NIV) are taken from the Holy Bible, New International Version®. NIV®. Copyright © 1973, 1978, 1984 by International Bible Society. Used by permission of Zondervan Publishing House. All rights reserved.

© 1994 Copyright by Ed Silvoso
All rights reserved.
This book is also available in Spanish (1-56063-849-4) and Portuguese (1-56063-850-8). Published by Editorial Unilit, Miami, FL.

Library of Congress Cataloging-in-Publication Data
Silvoso, Ed.
    That none should perish / Ed Silvoso.
        p. cm.
    ISBN 0-8307-1690-4 (trade)
    1. Evangelistic work—United States. 2. City churches—United States. I. Title.
    BV3793.S47   1994   94-17579
    269'.2—dc20   CIP

18 19 20 21 22 23 24 25 26 27 28 / 08 07 06 05 04 03

Rights for publishing this book in other languages are contracted by Gospel Light Worldwide, the international nonprofit ministry of Gospel Light. Gospel Light Worldwide also provides publishing and technical assistance to international publishers dedicated to producing Sunday School and Vacation Bible School curricula and books in the languages of the world. For additional information, visit www.gospellightworldwide.org; write to Gospel Light Worldwide, P.O. Box 3875, Ventura, CA 93006; or send an e-mail to info@gospellightworldwide.org.

Dedicated to my number one team—
Ruth, loving and devoted wife
and our daughters
Karina, loyal helper and confidante
Marilyn, wise counselor and enabler
Evelyn, faithful intercessor and encourager
Jesica, close friend and partner

Contents

Section I: The Principles

Section II: The Strategy

Appendices

Foreword

THE WORD IS BECOMING CLEARER AND CLEARER. THE HOLY SPIRIT is saying to the churches: *Take the cities for God, and bring them into My Kingdom.*

I believe that the primary target for God's spiritual armies in the 1990s is the cities of the world, not that other evangelistic targets are passé or unimportant. We must continue our aggressive efforts to evangelize nations and people groups and individuals and religions and rural populations, reaching unsaved souls wherever they may be found. But let's be clear: Nothing is more important in our day than reaching our cities.

I am not alone in this conviction. Many other Christian leaders around the world are also hearing the trumpet call for the cities. Research, publications and training focused on urban populations is exploding as never before. Pastors, missionaries, teachers and other Christian workers are responding in large numbers to God's call to the cities.

But what is the best way to evangelize a city?

Ed Silvoso, in my opinion, has the most viable and strategic answer to this question. Ed thoroughly understands the traditional methodologies for urban evangelism that we have been applying and refining over the years. His strategy makes full use of citywide crusades, friendship evangelism, door-to-door witnessing, open-air preaching, films, literature distribution, humanitarian aid, community development and whatever other way has been devised to communicate the gospel.

However, not only Ed Silvoso, but, numerous other Christian workers who have been called to the cities in general are saying to each other: "The methods we have been developing are excellent. We have a solid, biblical theology of evangelism. Why, then, are we not seeing more fruit and fruit that remains?"

Over many years, this question has been burning in the heart and soul of Ed Silvoso. His passion has been to provide an answer that will not be just an interesting theory or a robust exhortation, but also a practical way forward that will bring our urban evangelistic efforts more in line with what we have always hoped they would be and what we clearly know is God's will. God's will is *that none should perish*, the biblical phrase from 2 Peter 3:9, which Ed is using as the title of this book.

That None Should Perish is the first book that weaves into the warp and woof of a plan for urban evangelism two primary elements that have been largely missing from similar plans. One is a methodological component, and the other is a spiritual component.

The methodological component is *saturation church planting*. I frequently say that the most effective evangelistic methodology under heaven is planting new churches. This is not just a personal opinion or an application of what we see in the book of Acts, but it is also a scientific fact. Extensive research in evangelism and missiology has confirmed its validity beyond any doubt. As you will see in this book, multiplying new churches is a central feature of Silvoso's design.

The spiritual component is what many of us have been calling *strategic-level spiritual warfare*. Ed Silvoso recognizes that because it is primarily the god of this age who blinds people's minds against the gospel (see 2 Cor. 4:3,4), the real battle for our cities is a spiritual battle. As the war in the heavenlies is won through truth encounters and power encounters and allegiance encounters mediated by the Holy Spirit and based on Jesus' death on the cross, much of what has been obstructing the communication of the gospel to the unsaved in the past will be removed.

Spiritual warfare is essential if we desire to see more fruit, and church planting is essential if that fruit is to remain.

That None Should Perish will show you clearly and concisely how both can be done for the glory of God.

C. Peter Wagner
Fuller Theological Seminary
Pasadena, California

Introduction

WHEN OUR LORD SENT HIS PERSONAL MESSAGES TO THE SEVEN churches in Asia Minor through His servant John, He closed each message with the admonition to hear what the Holy Spirit was saying to the churches. That exhortation is still valid today. Each generation of Christians must tune in to the particular emphasis the Spirit chooses for that specific age of the Church.

Today, at the end of the twentieth century, what is the Spirit saying to the churches? My observation is that the Spirit is delivering a dual emphasis—prayer and evangelism. And He is doing it in such a way that it reads like one message delivered in stereo.

During the past 10 years, prayer has begun to emerge as one of the central parts—if not *the* central part—of the life of the Church worldwide.

In the United States, God has anointed David Bryant to launch Concerts of Prayer International, an organization that is bringing together thousands of Christians of all denominations throughout the United States and beyond. It seems that every major city in English-speaking North America has had at least one concert of prayer.

Dr. Paul Cedar, president of the Evangelical Free Church of America and dean of the Billy Graham School of Evangelism, has instilled thousands with a sense of awe in God's presence as they gather in "solemn assemblies." He is touching the lives of countless leaders by challenging them, by deed and by word, to a lifestyle of prayer.

Dr. Neil Anderson, president and founder of Freedom in Christ Ministries, has taught thousands how to reclaim, through prevailing prayer, the spiritual identity and freedom entrusted to them. By prevailing prayer, I mean the kind of holy insistence in prayer that characterized the pleas of the widow in the parable of the unjust judge (see Luke 18:1-8). Dr. Anderson has brought, through prayer, a much-needed practical dimension to the age-less truth of God's Word, especially in light of the increasing level of evil buffeting the Church in the last days.

Dr. Joe Aldrich, president of Multnomah School of the Bible, has been led of God to launch "Pastors' Prayer Summits," a concept so radically new that for most pastors it is necessary to see one in action before they can truly believe it is really possible. Dr. Aldrich and his associates have brought together thousands of pastors all over the United States and Canada for four days of prayer. Nothing else. No special speakers, no talented musicians, no program or agenda. Just prayer. Four days in the presence of Jesus. Thousands of pastors have been transformed in these summits. They in turn have become channels to bring healthy change to entire congregations, many of which are now transforming their communities through the quiet but very real power of prayer.

The same prayer emphasis can be seen overseas. Beginning in Korea, it has expanded all over the world. Dr. David Yonggi Cho, pastor of the Yoido Full Gospel Church of Seoul, Korea, has challenged and taught an entire generation of leaders about the necessity of praying "at least three hours a day." Rev. Omar Cabrera, leader of an emerging indigenous cluster of congregations numbering more than 80,000 members in Argentina, pioneered the concept of all-night vigils of prayer in a context of spiritual warfare. I remember participating in one of those vigils attended by more than 12,000 people. We met in an open field on a winter night to pray. And pray we did! A similar prayer/spiritual warfare emphasis has begun to spread to churches all over Argentina, creating a spiritual awakening never experienced before. The spiritual breakthrough sweeping that nation today has spilled over to many Latin American countries and beyond, but the main thrust remains the same: prayer.

All of this has been elevated to a higher level of intensity by the resurgence of militant intercession at the beginning of this decade. For instance, Cindy Jacobs, a godly and uniquely gifted woman, has been called by God to launch Generals of Intercession. Cindy and her associates have identified and marshaled "generals" of intercession in key parts of the world, which, in turn, has created a worldwide network of militant intercessors who, day and night, watch over the nations in prayer. This has added a divine militancy to the prayer movement. Learning how to pray with God-given authority has set thousands of people free.

Dr. C. Peter Wagner, professor of church growth at Fuller Theological Seminary, has brought together one of the most dynamic prayer-ministry coalitions ever assembled, under the umbrella of the Prayer and Spiritual Warfare Track, of which he is the international coordinator. When one reads the names of all the organizations that have joined hands to mobilize the Church to pray, it looks like the Who's Who of modern Christendom. Combining his zeal for missions with a sharp mind and an extraordinary ability for networking, Dr. Wagner is being used by God to motivate, train and mobilize the largest army of praying Christians ever mustered to storm the gates of hell in order to set captives free. There can be no doubt that prayer, prevailing prayer and prayer in a context of spiritual warfare, is a central part of the message the Spirit is giving to the churches today. The rediscovery of spiritual warfare as the context for prevailing prayer has resulted in effectively positioning the Church for the other part of the Spirit's message to churches today.

The other part of the message is evangelism. There is an equally intense, God-given, Holy Spirit-inspired sense of urgency to fulfill the Great Commission by the year 2000. This is so much so that a worldwide movement embodying the largest network of Christian ministries ever assembled in the history of Christianity has emerged—the AD 2000 and Beyond Movement.

This movement, through its diverse ministry tracks, has created avenues for the majority of today's Christian ministries to work together. This coming together has already reached the stage of critical mass. When it comes to the evangelization of the world in our generation, it seems that the issue is no longer "if" but "how soon."

All over the world there is a compelling sense of urgency to take the gospel to every person on the face of the earth *now*. But unlike the old days, the emphasis is not on the method, nor on the messenger, but on prayer. And this is where these two parts come together in a unified message bearing the title "prayer evangelism."

For instance, at a recent meeting of the U.S. Lausanne Committee, of which I am honored to be a member, it was unanimously decided to call the Church to prayer, repentance and reconciliation so that the Church will be able to fulfill its God-given mandate to pray for every American (more than 240 million people) to come to the saving knowledge of the truth. In this statement, we see prayer and evangelism combined in an attempt to emulate the Early Church and how it went about fulfilling the Great Commission in its generation. The Holy Spirit declares through His servant Luke in Acts 19:10, "All who lived in Asia heard the word of the Lord, both Jews and Greeks." This statement represents the most extraordinary accomplishment in

Christendom: A group of frightened, perplexed, monocultural Jews had succeeded in taking the words of their Master to *everyone* in myriad multicultural cities scattered all over Asia. A tremendous feat!

In this book, I have tried to recapture the biblical principles and the historic perspective that allowed the Early Church to take the gospel from the Upper Room to *every* living room in Asia Minor in a very short period of time.

I will share how God has led me and my ministry team, along with many of the pastors in Resistencia, Argentina (population 400,000), to the rediscovery of prayer evangelism, although at the time the name was not known to us. This, in turn, has resulted in the evangelization of an entire city and the growth of the Church there, far beyond what any other approach had produced before.

Today, those same principles are being implemented in scores of cities in several continents. The strategies and models are still very much "in progress," but the results so far are most encouraging. By no means am I saying that what happened in Resistencia is without flaws or shortcomings. In fact, the Resistencia prototype, when first developed, was very primitive and in great need of refinement. However, the prototype worked and made it possible for a large modern city to hear the gospel in the truest biblical sense. Because of that development, the Church-at-large is beginning to see that the actual evangelization of our cities today is not just a possibility but a clear probability and, as such, a definite must. This is "Plan Resistencia's" greatest contribution to the Church-at-large.

Furthermore, the model presented in this book is not new. The Early Church discovered and used it with a high degree of success. Unfortunately, it was lost during the Dark Ages. Later on, when the Reformation pointed the way back to the Scriptures and there was hope of a rediscovery, it was neutralized again by the Enlightenment through its elimination of the supernatural from our worldview. It was not until the Spirit began to bring back the current emphasis on prayer that much of what was then lost has begun to be recovered.

But what is new to many is the *implementation* of those principles in an exclusive context of prevailing prayer. Again, prayer and evangelism come together, and thus form *prayer evangelism*.

In this book, I present prayer as the main vehicle to take the gospel to every creature. I discuss the heavenly places as the battleground where the Church must face and defeat the forces of evil. I present a biblical and practical overview of spiritual strongholds—Satan's secret weapon—and how to pull them down so that the Church can fulfill its worldwide mission. I also challenge the Church to exercise the spiritual authority it has been given in the area of prayer and intercession. All of this is presented against the backdrop of "Plan Resistencia" and subsequent plans currently under implementation.

I trust that as you read this book, the two-part message of prayer and evangelism being spoken by the Spirit to the Church today will become even more clear to you as you begin to see it in a tangible context.

I also pray that as you put these principles into practice, you will perfect them further so that you, and those who will eventually learn from you, will obtain even greater results.

Ed Silvoso
Harvest Evangelism
San Jose, California

Section I

The Principles

1

Can We Reach a City for Christ?

PRINCIPLE: Cities are central to God's redemptive strategy. The Great Commission begins with a city—Jerusalem—and culminates when another city—the new Jerusalem—becomes God's eternal dwelling with His people. In order to fulfill the Great Commission, we must reach every city on earth with the gospel.

IS IT POSSIBLE TO REACH AN ENTIRE CITY FOR CHRIST? THIS WAS one of the first and most persistent questions I asked myself as a new believer. Acknowledging that God wishes that none should perish and that Christ gave Himself in ransom for all (see 1 Tim. 2:4,5; 2 Pet. 3:9), I constantly wondered what it would take for the Church in a given city to take the good news to *everyone* there.

I received the Lord when I was 13 and living in my native Argentina. The best decision I made as a new Christian was to have a weekly appointment with God. Every Thursday, at 7:00

P.M. sharp, I rode my bicycle to the western shore of the Parana River in my hometown of San Nicolas. During that precious hour, I poured out my heart to God, trying to understand the loneliness I felt as a born-again Christian high schooler in a spiritually skeptical town of almost 100,000 souls. Week after week, I attempted to reconcile the overwhelming joy of my salvation with the pain caused by the lack of response to the gospel among my friends and relatives. If Jesus was indeed the only way, why was it that no one else wanted to find Him?

In preparation for my weekly time with God, I regularly read books on revival. My heart swelled and my spirit rose within me as I learned, in the infancy of my faith, about God's mighty work in England, Wales, Bavaria and the United States. Yet that high tide of joy was inevitably followed by an equally powerful undertow of disappointment as the bleakness of Argentina's spiritual situation relentlessly hounded me.

"Why is it," I asked God, "that all the revivals I read about happened north of the equator? Is Argentina God's ugly duckling?"

Week after week, as I watched the sun set on the Argentine pampas (vast, flat grasslands), I begged God to send us a touch of revival, and as part of that, to allow Christians to reach an entire city for Christ. Only the extraordinary fervency of my newly found faith was capable of carrying me through the wilderness of disappointment that lay between those weekly meetings. Nevertheless, I was determined to find the way to see a city reached for Christ.

At the time of my conversion my pastor was Carlos Naranjo, who, years earlier, was an elder in a very separatist Plymouth Brethren assembly in Buenos Aires. His wife was healed of a terminal illness at a Pentecostal crusade, where Carlos had taken her out of desperation. Consequently, he was rejected by his local assembly and was labeled a heretic by many of his Christian friends.

Soon after that, Carlos came to San Nicolas to supervise the building of a small factory. As he witnessed to friends, employees and neighbors, many came to Christ, and a local church was born. My parents, my sister and I were "prayed into the Kingdom" by this enthusiastic cluster of new believers. True to his Brethren tradition, Carlos Naranjo began to train other laypeople for the ministry. I was picked to be a youth evangelist. I was only 14 when this happened, but it did not stop me from canvassing the streets of San Nicolas weekend after weekend. However, at the end of each year, I could count my converts on the fingers of one hand. The disappointment I felt became part of the central focus of my weekly conversations with God.

When I was 17, I formed my first evangelistic team. It happened as a result of my daily time of prayer with Ruth, who at the time was my girlfriend and now is my wife. She lived in Cordoba, 500 kilometers away from San Nicolas, and we only saw each other twice a year. To mitigate the pain of our separation, we agreed to have a daily time of prayer and fellowship "in the Spirit," as we called it. At 10:00 sharp every night, she knelt down in the hills of Cordoba and I knelt down in the pampas of San Nicolas. This was a very sacred time for me. I faithfully kept that appointment. Short of the Second Coming, nothing could keep me from it. Even if Saint Paul had come calling on me, I would have made him wait until I was done. It was the closest thing Ruth and I had to personal contact every day.

In the summer of 1963, our church held meetings every day of the week. Each night after church, the youth gathered at my parents' house for fellowship. Every night at 10:00 I sneaked out to have my time with Ruth and the Lord. I was able to do it undetected for a few days, but eventually my friends noticed my absence. They asked where I went every night at 10:00. When I told them I went to pray with Ruth, they insisted on joining me. Because my meeting with Ruth was "in the Spirit" and not in person, I did not mind. So they joined me, but instead of praying just 15 minutes, our meetings extended into the wee hours of the

---

THE DREAM OF SEEING AN ENTIRE CITY REACHED FOR CHRIST WAS VERY FRESH IN MY MIND AS WE TACKLED THOSE TINY HAMLETS. IN MY MIND I WAS BILLY GRAHAM, AND WE WERE GOING TO REACH EVERYBODY THERE WITH THE GOSPEL.

---

night. We prayed, we sang, we praised God, we quoted Scripture, we ministered to each other. After a few weeks of this, we were truly "charged up" spiritually, eager to do something for God.

We met with our pastor, and he pointed out four nearby hamlets that had no strong Christian witness. He asked us to kneel down, and he prayed for us. "Go," he said, "and the Lord will be with you."

I remember in my youthful naïveté thinking, *Maybe we will find the way to reach an entire city for Christ.* This is how my first evangelistic team came into being. I, the evangelist, was 17 years old. My associate preacher was 15. The music director, my sister, was 14, and the director of follow-up was 13. Working under him was "the youth" of the group. Only one person was older than me—Jose Lobos, who was 19 years old. We called him "Grandpa."

None of us had a vehicle, so we carried everything by hand—

the bulky P.A. system, the car battery to power the equipment, the boxes of Bibles and gospel tracts, the musical instruments. Everything! As often as we could, we tried to get a ride on a bus. But what bus driver in his right mind would let us board his bus? We had to be very creative in order to lure him to stop for us. To that effect, I positioned the two nicest looking girls in our group on one side of the street while the rest of us stood on the opposite side, pretending to wait for the bus headed in the other direction. As soon as the unsuspecting bus driver stopped, a stampede took place and all of us crossed in front of the bus. We must have looked like a caravan of U-Haul trucks—*minus* the trucks! By then I had collected the bus fare from all of my team members. As they boarded, each one told the driver, "The last guy has my fare." I was the last guy, and that was my way of making sure the bus did not leave without me.

The dream of seeing an entire city reached for Christ was very fresh in my mind as we tackled those tiny hamlets. To me they looked like New York or Los Angeles. In my mind I was Billy Graham, and we were going to reach everybody there with the gospel.

And indeed we did! We made sure that *everyone* heard the gospel. We even led a satanist to Christ. I remember wondering how many crowns a converted warlock would fetch at the Judgment Seat of Christ. In spite of these victories, we did not see mass conversions.

Again, my question was, "Why not, Lord? Why not here in Argentina?"

When I turned 20, I was drafted into the army. I dreamed of leading the entire battalion, 900 strong, to the Lord. During the time of my enlistment, I saw a small stream of converts. When discharge day came, I asked permission to give the farewell speech, hoping to see a mass movement of conversions. I witnessed a trickle of responses, but the rushing river I hoped for never materialized.

Pursuing the Dream

Eventually, I took a job as a hospital administrator in a newly built facility in San Nicolas. I enjoyed the hustle and bustle of working with doctors, nurses and patients as we watched our hospital grow. During my second year in this job, Ruth and I got married and settled in a house that I had built especially for her. As much as I liked my job as a hospital administrator, the real joy came "after hours" when I would rush home, eat a quick dinner and drive with Ruth in my newly acquired 1947 Chrysler to evangelistic meetings. The main reason I chose this mammoth vehicle as my first car was because of its payload. It could hold all of my evangelistic paraphernalia: 16 collapsible chairs, a small pulpit, Ruth's guitar and accordion, two boxes of Bibles and gospel tracts, and a variable number of "ministry associates." The car was constantly "overbooked," which resulted in some of my associates riding on the laps of their fellow "ministers."

One of those crusades took us to a small town nearby, where the local brethren invited us to hold an open-air campaign. Amazingly, we saw 92 decisions of faith made in that campaign! Afterward, I was asked to be the preacher for this emerging congregation. In my desire to reach everybody with the gospel, we held church meetings four times a week and two evangelistic meetings on Sundays. Even though we saw some growth, and the entire village heard the gospel, we did not see a book-of-Acts kind of evangelistic explosion. I remember wondering if maybe the long hours spent at my hospital job were a contributing negative factor.

A year later, Ruth and I—already enjoying the presence of our first daughter, Karina—decided that I should quit my hospital administration job to answer the call of a full-time pastorate in the beautiful city of Mar del Plata, Argentina's French Riviera. Having no secular job to take up my time, we worked hard and saw our church grow. The dream to see a city reached was always in the forefront of my thoughts and prayers. I bought a map of Mar del Plata and marked on it the location of every church. I prayed for those churches regularly. I networked as much as possible with their pastors. We saw some results but nothing spectacular. After about a year, Luis Palau, Ruth's brother, invited us to join his newly formed evangelistic team, and we moved to Mexico City.

Luis's enthusiasm for evangelism was incendiary. He loved cities, he loved sinners and he loved preaching to the multitudes. Quite often, he and I would talk into the wee hours of the night about reaching entire cities for Christ. Ruth and I felt very privileged to be a part of Luis's emerging team. His team formed part of Overseas Crusades, a mission that had a solid reputation for discipleship and a healthy disposition to mass evangelism. Dr. Dick Hillis, Overseas Crusades' founder, had worked very closely with Billy Graham, first in Asia and later on in Latin America. Along with godly men such as Keith Benson and Dr. Ed Murphy, Dr. Hillis and Overseas Crusades provided a solid environment for Luis's aggressive, and many times innovative, evangelistic thrusts. We enjoyed setting up crusades for Luis, producing TV and radio programs, arranging presidential prayer breakfasts. In the process, we saw significant numbers come to the Lord. But still, no city was fully reached.

In the early 1970s, Ruth and I took some time off from the Palau team to take the graduate course at Multnomah School of the Bible in Portland, Oregon. Afterward, we went on to attend the School of World Mission at Fuller Theological Seminary in Pasadena, California.

My time at Multnomah was the closest I have ever come to "a-road-to-Emmaus" kind of experience. The intensive course work required in-depth study of the entire Bible, from Genesis to Revelation. We went through the Bible book by book, chapter by chapter and verse by verse under the guidance of gifted Bible teachers. We even wrote our own commentary as we went along. The school was indeed true to its motto: "If you want Bible, then you want Multnomah."

I could not believe I had every waking hour of the day to read and study the Bible! This was a real treat for someone like me, who, since conversion days, had always been forced to "create" time for Bible study at the end of a busy day of other responsibilities. Every day I looked forward to delving into the Scriptures with overwhelming joy burning inside of me. Often at night I had trouble "checking out" as my heart insisted on chewing a little bit longer on the biblical truths found during the day.

Later, at the School of World Mission in Pasadena, I had the privilege of sitting under the teaching of godly and brilliant missiologists such as Donald McGavran, Ralph Winter, Arthur Glasser, Alan Tippet and Peter Wagner. This became the most exhilarating spiritual-intellectual experience of my entire life. These men were representatives of the most dynamic combination of theory and practice in a missiological context to be found anywhere among world-class thinkers. I was so excited as I walked to and from school that I developed the habit of singing out loud. There was so much joy in me that a Korean neighbor eventually received the Lord because of the happiness I projected as I walked by her window every morning.

The biblical foundation obtained at Multnomah, combined with the missiological stimulation I was receiving at Fuller, brought home with greater force than ever my youthful dream to reach entire cities for Christ. Because of my association with Luis Palau and his team, I knew that we were on the cutting edge of God's movement in Latin America. We did see many cities open up to the gospel for the first time. Luis even led to Christ the president of one nation. This was unheard of before. Also, our team pioneered the use of secular radio and television to saturate entire cities with the gospel. I truly believed that mass evangelism, the way we practiced it in the Palau team, was the best tool to reach the world for Christ in our generation.

Enter C. Peter Wagner, associate professor of church growth, who had just received his Ph.D. from the University of Southern California. In the course of his teaching, Dr. Wagner led the class through a factual critique of mass evangelism. As he presented his research on major evangelistic thrusts in various regions of the world, he concluded that most of them did not translate into church growth! According to Wagner, on an average, such crusades produced at best a mere 5 percent numerical growth in church membership. This represented a poor return on the amount of money and effort invested. In a few other cases, Wagner's research revealed that mass evangelism resulted in a *decrease* in church membership. (Palau was not included in Wagner's research because his ministry was just in the beginning stages.)

I cannot adequately describe the tension and the perplexity that Dr. Wagner's lectures produced within me. I enjoyed each one of them because of his keen intellect and unusual ability as a communicator. Besides, he had been a missionary in Bolivia and his presentations were always peppered with stories and illustrations from Latin America. All of this was medicine to my soul because of the severe homesickness I felt for Argentina. As he systematically exposed the minimal impact of mass evangelism, I finally came to the conclusion that our crusades were not as effective as we had first believed. However, I also knew they were not as irrelevant as Dr. Wagner's conclusions seemed to suggest.

This tension constantly challenged me to find a way to reconcile these opposing conclusions. I finally found the answer while preparing an assignment for Dr. Wagner's class. I drew up a plan to evangelize an entire city by combining the effective aspects of mass evangelism with the church growth principles taught at the School of World Mission. This is how "Plan Rosario" (named after a city in Argentina) came into being. Shortly after that, Ruth and I found ourselves settling down in Rosario for our experiment in "city taking."

With a population of 700,000, Rosario was popularly known as the "Argentine Chicago," and, in Christian circles, as the "cemetery for evangelists." It was also the center for spiritism in central Argentina. We knew we had a massive challenge ahead of us, but we didn't really know how big it was to be.

Overall, "Plan Rosario" was a very positive experience. Many local churches participated, and the results—by church growth standards—were 10 times better than the average. Next, we went to Uruguay, where we tried the same approach on a national scale. We evangelized simultaneously in five major cities. The results were even better than in Rosario, and by using radio and television extensively, the whole country was blanketed with the gospel. The number of public decisions of faith was three times higher than in Rosario, and the percentage of incorporation into churches was 20 percent higher. The fact that all this happened in Uruguay was also very significant because the country prided itself in being a nation of atheists. In fact, the leading newspaper in Montevideo used to spell "Dios" ("God" in Spanish) with a small d. Scores received Christ and a great majority of the people heard the gospel. I knew then that we were finally on the right track in our search for a way to evangelize entire cities.

A Direct Hit by the Enemy

Everything looked promising except for one serious problem. Since my days in Rosario, my health had begun to deteriorate. My muscles were weakening. My speech was slurred, and I suffered from double vision and shortness of breath. By 1978, I had developed a severe case of a very serious illness, myasthenia gravis. This is an incurable disease similar to multiple sclerosis and in the same family of illnesses as Lou Gehrig's disease. I knew money could not buy a cure because multimillionaire Aristotle Onassis, Jackie Kennedy's second husband, died of it. My health deteriorated to the point that it was necessary for us to move back to the United States to be near Children's Hospital in San Francisco, where an experimental treatment was in progress.

I FULLY EMPATHIZED WITH MOSES,
WHO WAS ABLE TO SEE THE PROMISED
LAND BUT NOT ALLOWED TO ENTER IT.
I HAD COME SO CLOSE TO SEEING THE
DREAM OF MY YOUTH FULFILLED, AND
NOW THAT IT WAS WITHIN REACH
I WAS BEING BENCHED.

I remember fully empathizing with Moses, who was able to see the Promised Land but not allowed to enter it. I had come so close to seeing the dream of my youth fulfilled, and now that it was within reach I was being benched. That was my perspective, but not necessarily God's. My illness was, as I later learned, partly the result of spiritual warfare. It was a direct hit by the enemy.

He was exploiting an area of my life where I had given him an entrance, mainly through ignorance.

I later came to realize that my "Head Coach" was doing more than benching me. He was sending me to the locker room to learn basic principles related to suffering, spiritual warfare and intercession. These elements were not an important part of "Plan Rosario." Like Peter in Luke 22:31,32, I was being turned over to Satan to learn some valuable and painful lessons. In the process, God would teach me that reaching entire cities for Christ did not depend on formulas or methods, but rather on the application of biblical principles and a deeper walk with Him.

After a thorough and lengthy examination at the hospital in San Francisco, the doctors told me, "We are not sure that we can help you, but you can certainly help us." As a former hospital administrator, I quickly recognized the true meaning of that. It was medical lingo for, "Would you agree to become a guinea pig?"

Myasthenia gravis is a very humbling disease. Your mouth drools. You choke on your own saliva, especially at night. Your speech is impaired. Your breathing is laborious to an extreme. You can't run or do anything strenuous. Because your body attacks itself through malfunctioning antibodies, your muscles deteriorate and soon become useless. Your entire body aches and soon comes to resemble a huge "sore thumb." Anything it touches triggers a shock of pain. Your energy is so low and so limited that you learn to map out the shortest route from your bed to the bathroom. That is how much difference a few feet makes for one who has myasthenia gravis!

I remember staring at the ceiling for hours on end until I had memorized every inch of it. My survival training in the army had taught me that the best way to endure was to take things one step at a time. However, it was extremely discouraging to realize that often, at the end of a full day, I hadn't been able to take even a single step.

I was very grateful for the excellent and helpful medical treatments I received. However, some of the procedures were as painful as the illness itself. At one time or another I was receiving 16 injections a day. That adds up to 480 injections a month! I also took 42 pills daily, in addition to 1,500 milligrams of cortisone and occasional chemotherapy by mouth. Once or twice a week I was hooked to a machine that performed a plasmapheresis. It slowly drained out all of my blood and disposed of everything except the red and white cells, which were in turn pumped back in along with human albumin to make up for the volume of lost fluid. Because this treatment removed all antibodies from my blood stream, for 48 hours I was totally vulnerable to infection.

I also had to undergo a thymectomy, which is a major surgical procedure. My sternum bone was split in two, the rib cage was retracted and the tissue under the sternum was removed. The most discouraging fact to accept was that none of these procedures was capable of providing a cure for me—they were simply done to keep me alive.

Some nights I felt so weak that I honestly believe the choice was mine whether to live or die. Two things kept me going: one was my wife and our four beautiful daughters (at the time ages one through nine); the second was the memories of Uruguay and Rosario, and the realization of how close we had come to developing a workable model for reaching entire cities for God.

A Leap of Faith

Eventually the day came when my doctor told me I had, at most, two years to live. I remember that day in 1980 vividly. It happened at Stanford Medical Center, where I was being treated at the time. My doctor took a piece of chalk and drew a horizontal line on the blackboard, saying, "This line represents your health now. You are tenuously holding your own. However, anytime in the next two years *this* will happen," and he drew a straight line downward. As he did so, the chalk hit the interior border of the chalk holder and broke. One of the pieces dropped to the floor, rolled toward me and stopped a few inches from my feet. Then I caught myself thinking, *This chalk represents my life. I still have some momentum, but sooner or later I will come to a halt.*

At that moment, Ruth and I decided to really take a leap of faith. We resigned from the Palau Team in order to concentrate whatever time I had left, on our quest to find a way to reach cities for Christ. It was an extremely difficult decision because of our love for Luis and the team we had helped develop. We then tried to join a couple of missionary organizations that had ministries in South America. In both cases we were turned down, mostly on account of my health. The president of one agency said to me, "We would love to have you, but we cannot add you on to our medical program because of your illness. At the same time, we do not feel it is right we take you on without medical insurance. We are sorry." I still remember the frustration welling within me as I heard that. I was upset that a deeply spiritual matter was being decided by the fine print on an insurance policy.

Our time was quickly running out. We had only 30 days of insurance left with the Palau Team, and my medical bills were very high. One night I prayed decisively for supernatural guidance. During the night, I had a dream in which I saw myself and a group of my friends launching a new missionary organization. I saw four men around the table, all of them longtime friends: Daniel Craig, Dr. Ed Murphy, Dick Anderson and Norm Nason. The name of the organization we were launching was "Harvest Evangelism."

The next morning, the phone rang. It was Daniel Craig calling from Los Angeles. He had heard that I was leaving the Palau team and wanted to know what he could do to help in the transition! Then and there I *knew* that God wanted us to start a new missionary organization. On August 30, 1980, Harvest Evangelism was officially and legally born.

Because my health was poor and our resources were depleted and time was running out, we decided to concentrate on building a retreat center in my native city of San Nicolas. Our hope was that when I was gone it would become a training center to reach cities for Christ. Part of the reason for choosing the location was that it was close to 109 small cities, towns and hamlets within a 100-mile radius that had no local church.

In between medical treatments in the United States, I made trips to Argentina to organize and direct the construction of the center. I would have every hospital treatment possible done in the United States, sometimes only hours before boarding the plane. I would pack up my pills, and then stay in Argentina as long as I was physically able. Upon my return to the States, I would literally crash at the hospital, feeling very much like Humpty Dumpty and hoping that the doctors would be able to put me back together again.

The main building in our training center is a prayer chapel that my friends Bob and Joan Archibald financed in memory of a daughter lost to leukemia. It has six concentric doors on three sides that provide a 270-degree view of the countryside. Most of the 109 unchurched towns are located inside that 270-degree vector.

On March 24, 1983, we dedicated the retreat center. Carlos Naranjo, the man who first trained me for the ministry, officiated at the ceremony. We met in the newly built chapel. Part of the celebration included a retreat for pastors and leaders from surrounding areas. We challenged them to reach each one of the 109 unchurched towns with the gospel. Part of me was able to see it as done through the eyes of faith. However, when I looked into the mirror, my natural eyes saw something totally different. The combination of prayer and medical treatment had stretched the initial prognosis from two to four years, but I was barely hanging on. My body was ready to quit anytime.

The dedication of the center in San Nicolas was thus a happy but nostalgic occasion. I knew we had reached a key objective. The vision had been implanted in the hearts of godly Christian leaders. However, I again found myself looking at the Promised Land from across a flooded Jordan River. I could not swim and no boats were in sight. I remember wondering if this was the end of the road for me. Would I ever see an entire city evangelized?

A Change in the Winds

Then, dramatic events began to unfold. First, something changed in "the heavenlies" over Argentina. A business owner and lay preacher by the name of Carlos Annacondia held a three-month crusade in La Plata, where it was reported that 40,000 people made public professions of faith in Christ. That was something totally unheard of at the time. At first, we questioned the verac-ity of the report. However, Annacondia next moved on to Mar del Plata, where close to 90,000 decisions were reported. He then went to San Justo, where almost 70,000 people publicly repeated the sinner's prayer. From then on it became a flood of decisions as city after city was shaken by the ministry of this unknown lay preacher.

Can you imagine what happened to a cozy, well-organized congregation of 50 when a deluge of new converts descended on the impeccable premises after an Annacondia crusade? The average congregation in pre-Annacondia Argentina had a very quiet and tranquil life. The pastor was able to forecast with reasonable accuracy the number of baptisms, births and even funerals for the coming year. He was always able to take his day off. Church services were absolutely predictable. A person could be 100 miles from the church building, look at his watch and guess exactly what was going on at that specific moment. That is how quiet and orderly things used to be. All of that was shattered forever in post-Annacondia Argentina.

When a flood of new converts came to this kind of church, the church quickly ran out of everything, from toilet paper to paper cups, from folding chairs to Sunday School teachers. Some traditional churches went into shock. I heard of one congregation where three elders were complaining in a huddle on the patio behind the church. When asked what was going on, one of them replied, "It was much better before. Now all of those undisciplined people step on the grass. There is always a line for the bathroom. Meetings are becoming noisy and at times boisterous. Some even smoke on the church sidewalk. Sunday School lessons are constantly interrupted. The new people don't even know how to look up verses in the Bible." Although this kind of response was a rare exception, it clearly illustrates the severe shock some churches could experience.

But other churches were ready to scrap tradition and make radical changes in order to cope with the avalanche of new converts. One of these was the church of Pastor Alberto Scataglini in La Plata. He went so far as to remove the pews from the church so more people would fit inside the building.

In this context, I was approached by pastor friends requesting training for their laypeople. One way to cope with this kind of growth is to "move everyone up the ladder one rung." The church janitor becomes a Sunday School teacher on account of the residual biblical knowledge accumulated through the years. The Sunday School teacher moves up to Sunday School superintendent. The superintendent takes a position as associate pastor of Christian education, and so on. Some of my friends did that as a stopgap measure. Having heard of our plans for a training center, they came for help.

I was flattered by the request to become a key trainer, but I was also down to my last ounce of energy. Myasthenia gravis was written all over my body. Oh, how I wanted to respond to that need!

Divine Intervention

This desire led to the second event that would dramatically change my life—an introduction to intercessory prayer. Harvey Lifsey, president and founder of Christian Dynamics, an evangelistic and discipleship organization at the time based in Southern California, had come to Argentina to teach on prayer. He and my dear friend Mario Gentinetta, an intercessor himself, challenged me to entreat God regarding my illness. We decided to set aside three days for intercession for the purpose of finding out from God if my illness was an illness unto life or an illness unto death. I did not mind pressing forward if that was what God wanted. However, my greatest emotional challenge was not the illness itself, but some of the prayers offered for my healing.

Time and again, since the onset of my illness, I had been given what others considered genuine prophetic words emphatically announcing my healing, yet nothing happened. Sometimes I would get a phone call inquiring what I had felt the night before at 2:00 A.M. The caller was *sure* that God, or an angel, had touched my body and that I was now healed. I remember saying to myself, *Do you really want to know what I felt last night at 2:00 A.M.? I felt pain all over my body and perplexity all over my soul, and now your call is turning that perplexity into confusion.* I never said it, but I kept it inside of me where it began to turn into a mild form of cynicism.

When someone who has a public ministry contracts a prolonged illness, there is a demand for periodic medical bulletins. I grew tired of telling the plain truth because it was so discouraging, and most people *did not want* to hear it. I sensed it in my spirit as I watched their body language. I heard it with my own ears as I caught echoes of their remarks to others. I was grieved by the implication that maybe hidden sin was the real reason God was not answering the prayers of the saints on my behalf. I was also greatly annoyed by extreme "health-food nuts," who blamed my lack of improvement on the fact that I had refused their advice to take 20 grams of vitamin C every day, and by others who proposed coffee enemas as a cure for every ailment under the sun. Sure! In reality, my most pressing problem was lack of clear direction. What was it God wanted me to believe Him for?

Harvey, Mario and I began our three-day intercession thrust on a Monday. We pleaded with God that if it pleased Him, by Wednesday at bedtime He would make His will known to me. Monday and Tuesday went by with no word from God. Finally, on Wednesday at midnight I was heading for the training center after dropping Harvey off at his hotel. As the car sped on the one-mile homestretch, I asked God if He was going to speak to me that night. At that very moment a powerful presence of God literally inundated the car. It was so real that I began to pray, praise and worship Him in a way unknown to me.

As soon as I parked the car at the training center, the Holy Spirit took over and led me through hours of prayer in a Romans chapter 8 fashion—He prayed for me and through me. "In the same way, the Spirit helps us in our weakness. We do not know what we ought to pray for, but the Spirit himself intercedes for us with groans that words cannot express" (Rom. 8:26, NIV). He led me to specific passages in the Bible and spoke to me from each one of them. I had never experienced anything like this! It was the most amazing experience of my life.

At the end of that amazing night, I *knew* that my illness was an illness unto life. I also knew that God had chosen to heal me through a *process* rather than instantaneously. All of this was confirmed by my prayer partners.

"Our prayer has been answered," Harvey said, "but because of the spiritual warfare going on in the heavenlies, God's answer is being delayed as the messenger of God battles against evil forces."

None of this made sense to me at the time. It would take the next eight years for most of it to unfold. As far as I was concerned, however, I had received from God a clear sense of direction. My perplexity immediately disappeared, and I was healed of my incipient cynicism.

The following six months turned out to be the worst period of my entire illness. I had to be hooked up to the plasmapheresis machine to survive. One of those days, the machine broke down and I almost died. On another occasion, the oral chemotherapy caused a reaction that almost cost me my life. Although that period was extremely difficult, I did not mind it. I knew that God's promises are tested by trials. I did not mind a good fight if I knew where the enemy was. Now I knew which way God's wind was blowing. When people offered to pray for my healing—obviously moved by my miserable state—I would tell them, "Please, don't pray for my healing. Just join me in thanking God that one day I will be healed as He promised me."

Sure enough, after six months, some elements of my treatment were no longer necessary. Over a period of four years, I was able to discontinue the injections (a big PTL there!), the chemotherapy, the cortisone, the oral medication and the plasmapheresis. Also, as my health improved, our team grew accordingly. God allowed us to launch *El Puente*, a Christian newspaper, in Argentina. A television studio in Buenos Aires quickly followed. Finally, a church-planting team was formally established.

Growing Ministry

In 1987, Dr. David Yonggi Cho asked us to organize his visit to Argentina. Seven thousand pastors and leaders from all over Argentina and neighboring countries attended the four-day seminar. We worked very hard to make it a truly interdenominational event. It was a resounding success with all denominations benefiting from it. As I like to say, "from the juiciest charismatics to the crunchiest evangelicals," everybody was there and went away blessed. Dr. Cho's visit catapulted us to national prominence. Hosting his seminar put a big platform under our feet. We received immediate visibility all over the nation. Our newspaper, guided by Marcelo Laffite, and the TV ministry, under Bill Kennedy's leadership, expanded this further. All of a sudden, our dreams, modestly started at the retreat center in San Nicolas, began to materialize on a national scale. Requests for help began to come from all over the nation.

Enter Chuck Starnes. Chuck and his lovely wife, Sandy, had joined our team in 1987, just in time to direct the logistical aspects of Dr. Cho's visit. Following Dr. Cho's seminar, Chuck felt led to visit Resistencia, population 400,000, in northern Argentina, to assess the potential for a citywide outreach. Chuck also had a passion for seeing an entire city evangelized. His command of the Spanish language was limited at the time, but his passion for the lost and his love for the Church were contagious. He was determined to follow God at any cost. This more than

---

WHAT WE DID NOT KNOW AT THE TIME WAS HOW LITTLE WE KNEW ABOUT SPIRI-TUAL WARFARE. IN RETROSPECT, I CAN SEE THAT WE WERE FOOLISHLY OVERCONFIDENT BECAUSE WE HAD BB GUNS TUCKED UNDER OUR BELTS, NOT REALIZING THAT THE NOISE BEHIND THE BUSH AHEAD OF US WAS MADE BY A MAD, CHARGING RHINO!

---

made up for his imperfect Spanish. He was instrumental in dis-cerning that Resistencia was the place where we should try our battery of ideas and spiritual insights on "city taking." Chuck is the one who laid down the foundation for "Plan Resistencia."

We chose Resistencia for a number of reasons. First, we were invited by several pastors who had been meeting regularly. Second, the city had an unusually low percentage of believers (1.5 percent of the total population), which made it an excellent testing ground for our principles. Third, Resistencia is a key city in northern Argentina. Like Ephesus in the book of Acts, Resistencia is a "mother of cities" all over the Argentine Chaco. Fourth, the city was under the spell of a satanic principality called "San La Muerte" (Spanish for "Saint Death"). Its roots go back to the founding of the city.

Resistencia was designed to be a military outpost on the west-ern bank of the Parana River to defend the wealthy city of

Corrientes across the river. Most soldiers at the time were recruit-ed from among the prison population of Argentina and many "agreed" to serve in the army because it was the only way out of that miserable life. The military outpost was no match for the large Indian population, and the soldiers' greatest fear was not so much death, but death by torture at the hands of the Indians. This fear, along with local fetishism and African/Brazilian voodoo, gave birth to the cult of San La Muerte. Those who made a pact with San La Muerte were promised a painless death, which met the deepest felt need of the desperate soldiers. As a city grew around the military outpost, these beliefs and practices were passed on to its inhabitants. Even though the people of Resistencia are well educated and there is a prosperous middle class, in 1988 the entire population was touched in one way or another by this local cult.

We saw all this as a definite plus since we had been learning about spiritual warfare and were eager to try our newly acquired knowledge. What we did not know at the time was how *little* we knew about spiritual warfare. In retrospect, I can see that we were foolishly overconfident because we had BB guns tucked under our belts, not realizing that the noise behind the bush ahead of us was made by a mad, charging rhino!

I remember the day we met with the pastors to officially sug-gest the outline for "Plan Resistencia." We were as nervous as high school freshmen on a first date. We felt awkward and weren't sure how to proceed. I was asked to preach. We met in a storefront church with a tin roof. The subtropical climate of Resistencia and the low tin roof raised the temperature inside the building to over 100 degrees. At the same time, I sensed the spir-itual temperature was equally high. The presence of God *was* *there*. Intense and extensive prayer had preceded our gathering.

I spoke from 2 Peter 3:9, "The Lord is not slow in keeping his promise, as some understand slowness. He is patient with you, not wanting anyone to perish, but everyone to come to repentance" (NIV). I reached the pinnacle of my presentation when I described my dream about an entire city hearing the gospel. I spoke about 500 neighborhood prayer cells interceding for each section of the city; about celebrations of unity when different congregations in the city would come together to minister to the needs of the lost; about the day when every home in the city would be visited and every inhabitant would hear God's voice; about thousands of sinners saved by, and washed in, the blood of Jesus; of angels celebrating nonstop because sinners, lots of them, were coming to Christ day after day.

At that moment, the pastors—all of them—stood up and began to clap enthusiastically. A spontaneous explosion of joy, orchestrated by the Holy Spirit, had occurred. They were not clapping for me. They were clapping for the Chief Shepherd, Jesus. In typical Acts 2:17 fashion, the old pastors saw it through the lens of their dreams, and the young ones through their visions. All of a sudden, God had spoken and everybody knew that He was ready to pour out His Spirit upon Resistencia. It was a sacred time. That was the day "Plan Resistencia" was born.

Actually, "Plan Resistencia" is a misnomer. Rather than a "plan," with its implication of sequential steps and strategic components, it was an acknowledgment of God's love for the lost in the city and the Church's commitment to the biblical principles of unity, holiness and prayer. To that end, it was most appropriate that the pastors responded through such a spontaneous outburst of joy in the Spirit, thus eliminating the possibility of us presenting an actual plan. Like young couples on their wedding day, we knew nothing about the details of the future, but we were committed to God and to each other for the sake of His Church and the lost in the city.

We challenged the pastors to establish a perimeter of godliness in the city. The original group of pastors responded. They did this by meeting regularly for prayer, intercession and accountability. This was an auspicious beginning in a city where we were told 68 of the 70 existing congregations were the result of church splits. As the pastors met, God met with them. The Holy Spirit began to work in their lives and soon a deep bond of love had enveloped them completely. At one of those meetings, one of the pastors said, "I want you to know that I love you, guys. You have become an integral part of my life. I don't think I can do it alone as I used to. I need you! I wonder if we could have the Lord's Supper today?" Never before had the Lord's Supper been celebrated outside of a local church, and it had always been for the benefit of the members of that church. Radical new ground was being broken.

Another pastor responded by saying, "If we are going to have the Lord's Supper, I need to wash your feet. I have been so aloof and so proud in the past. I must wash your feet." This act of sincere humility was quickly reciprocated by others in the group. Everyone seemed to be saying, "I want to do it first."

Lacking the elements—since it was a totally unexpected idea—they used crackers and orange juice, which one of them bought at the small market next door. It didn't matter. Never before had the cleansing blood of Jesus flowed in a more palpable way, nor was His body ever more tangible than when those sincere pastors passed around the cup with the orange juice and broke the crackers after having washed each others' feet.

The feast did not stop there. Somebody suggested that they take an offering and give it to one of them who was facing financial difficulties. An open Bible was passed around in lieu of an offering plate, and less than $50 was collected. This amount was insignificant as far as money goes. However, like the fish Jesus cooked by the seaside to feed his hungry disciples, the money collected was a genuine expression of God's provision. More than giving money, they had given themselves to each other. That was the day when the foundation for unity was truly laid down in Resistencia.

The circle quickly expanded and soon more than half the pastors in the city had agreed to reach the entire city for Christ.

The Plan Implemented

In chapters 6 through 11, I will describe in great detail the plan and its implementation. In essence, Plan Resistencia was the implementation of Paul's instructions to Timothy as recorded in 1 Timothy 2:1-8: That the Church consistently and systematically pray for everybody in the city—and especially for those in authority—with the clear intent of seeing all of them saved. This is to be done with holy hands, for which it is necessary to first rid the Church of division and dissension. This was to be done by following Paul's outline in Ephesians, where the Church is exhorted to restore unity by dealing with ethnic disunity (see chapter 2), church disunity (see chapter 3), ministerial disunity (see chapter 4), marital disunity (see chapter 5) and family and workplace disunity (see chapter 6), before engaging "the spiritual forces of wickedness in the heavenly places" (6:12).

For the time being, allow me to touch on the plan's highlights. It was agreed that there is only one Church in the city that meets in many different congregations. As such, the pastors must see themselves as undershepherds serving under the only Chief Shepherd—Jesus Himself—and the various congregations in town must see themselves as part of, and interdependent on, the other congregations.

The main reason for the Church's presence on earth is to have its members conformed to the image of God's Son and, as a result of that, to take the gospel to *everyone* in the city who still does not know Him, because God "desires all men to be saved and to come to the knowledge of the truth" (1 Tim. 2:4). To do this effectively, the Church must deal with the longstanding issues of disunity, expressed through wrath and dissension, that on one hand "give the devil an opportunity" (Eph. 4:27) against the Church, and, consequently, prevent the world from believing that Jesus is "the Christ, the Son of the living God" (Matt. 16:16) "who gave Himself as a ransom for all" (1 Tim. 2:6).

All of this happens in the context of active spiritual warfare where the Church constantly struggles against rulers, against the world forces of this darkness, against the spiritual forces of wickedness in the heavenly places (see Eph. 6:12). The essence of this struggle is twofold. On one hand, the Church must "put on the full armor of God, that [it] may be able to stand firm against the schemes of the devil" (Eph. 6:11). This has to do with God's provision, which the Church must appropriate. God has provided the armor; now the Church must wear it. This is the defensive mode.

On the other hand, the Church must also invade Satan's territory, mainly through intercessory prayer, "With all prayer and petition pray at all times in the Spirit, and with this in view, be on the alert with all perseverance and petition for all the saints, and pray on my behalf, that utterance may be given to me in the opening of my mouth, to make known with boldness the mystery of the gospel" (Eph. 6:18,19).

In doing this, the Church "[brings] to light what is the administration of the mystery which for ages has been hidden in God, who created all things; in order that the manifold wisdom of God might now be made known through the church to the rulers and the authorities in the heavenly places" (Eph. 3:9,10), exposing them as usurpers and liars. This, in turn, "[opens the eyes of the unsaved] so that they may turn from darkness to light and from the dominion of Satan to God, in order that they may receive forgiveness of sins and an inheritance among those who have been sanctified by faith in Me" (Acts 26:18). This is the offensive mode.

To do this, pastors in Resistencia began to pray together regularly. They exchanged pulpits. They sent love offerings to needy congregations. They brought their people together to celebrate their newfound unity in Christ. They partook of the Lord's Supper together. Peter and Doris Wagner, and later, Cindy Jacobs, taught scores of leaders and pastors on intercession and spiritual warfare. Hundreds of intercessors were recruited, equipped and deployed all over the city to secure and expand God's "beachhead" in the city.

Satan's perimeter was infiltrated by 635 neighborhood prayer cells (called "lighthouses") scattered throughout the city. Little by little, every home in the city was prayed for. Answered prayers gave the Church favor in the eyes of the people. "Spiritual IOUs" began to pile up in 635 neighborhoods. This favor was enhanced, first when the Church built 16 water tanks in slums with no running water, and later on when large donations of medicine and equipment were made to the public hospital.

All Out Spiritual Warfare

Satan's perimeter began to be shaken when the pastors and their most trusted intercessors proclaimed the Lordship of Christ by serving an eviction notice on San La Muerte in the central plaza where a monument honors him. At that moment, open spiritual warfare began. Pastors and leaders suffered all kinds of attacks. San La Muerte's priests declared war on the Church. However, God was in control, and He showed it. At the height of the conflict, San La Muerte's high priestess died in strange circumstances—the mattress she was sleeping on caught fire and burned her to death. Nothing else burned except her, the bed and the idol of San La Muerte *in the room next door!* The fear of God fell upon the city.

Taking advantage of the extensive and intensive prayer ministry of more than 600 neighborhood prayer cells, two major outreaches were executed. First, in one day the entire city (approximately 63,000 homes) was visited with a good news package, which was made available by Dick Eastman of Every Home for Christ Crusade through Rino Bello, its director in Argentina. The week before, the city was blitzed through TV with the announcement that the following Saturday "This package of good news is coming to your home." When homes were visited the following Saturday, many people were waiting for it. Prayers were freely and generously offered all over the city on behalf of the sick, broken marriages, rebellious children and financial troubles. Even demons were cast out. Eventually every home in the city was blessed.

That same night, the people of Resistencia were invited to go to a covered stadium to thank God for His blessings. Many people had to be turned away because the basketball stadium was not big enough to accommodate the multitudes that responded to the invitation. The mayor was there to thank us. The media covered the event. The slogan for the outreach was, "Resistencia, it is God's time for you." That day it seemed the entire city knew that.

The second event consisted of a series of simultaneous crusades. First, 34 small neighborhood crusades. Then, three months later, 10 larger area crusades. Finally, a citywide crusade. By working out of the more than 600 lighthouses, the idea was to expand from the micro to the macro picture. By the time of the citywide crusade, the city was totally open, and Satan was raving mad.

On opening night, we discovered that the local witches and warlocks had occupied a corner of the field. They looked mean, and they acted mean. Satan had launched an all-out counterattack. A satanic altar had been built and incense was being burned. Some of the people in the audience got sick, others fainted. It was an unexpected and blatant attack. Resistencia was indeed a city under the influence of San La Muerte, very much like Ephesus was under the influence of Artemis.

We positioned our top intercessors under the platform along with a ring of 70 others around the podium. The rest, approximately 100 more, mixed in with the crowd. When we stood up to preach, we were able to feel the curses and hexes coming our way from the satanists' corner. When it got too hot for comfort, we would stomp on the platform. That was the signal for our spiritual SWAT team to redouble their intercessory efforts. It was spiritual warfare indeed.

In anticipation of an Ephesus-type response, a 100-gallon drum was set up to the left of the platform for the new converts to dispose of satanic paraphernalia. As people came forward, they dumped all kinds of occult-related items into it. Before praying for the people, gasoline was poured on the contents of the drum, a match was struck and every evil thing inside went up in flames. Many times, spontaneous deliverances occurred when a specific fetish was burned and the spell was broken.

Thousands of people came to the Lord. The challenge of following through with them in their new faith was made easier by the hundreds of lighthouses spread out all over the city. They did the follow-up. The mayor acknowledged Jesus Christ as his

Savior. Later on, two of the candidates for governor prayed to receive Jesus into their hearts. Also, medical doctors, journalists, one senator, aldermen, politicians and lawyers responded. At one point, we found ourselves inside the Provincial Court of Appeals with seven appellate judges, five of whom confessed Christ as their personal Savior. The city had indeed heard the voice of God!

Turning the Guns on the Enemy

When this evangelistic phase was over, the pastors moved on to establish God's perimeter where Satan's used to be. In military terms, when raiding the enemy's camp you transform his stronghold into your stronghold by occupying it and turning the guns around. Satan's stronghold on the Church had been division, fed by deep mistrust. In the past, when evangelistic campaigns ended, there had been bitter disputes over the distribution of decision cards. Mistrust was perpetuated amid charges of "sheep stealing." This time the pastors turned the guns around. Instead of aiming at division and mistrust, they went for unity and trust, and they decided to use the baptism of the new believers as the occasion. Rather than individual baptisms in separate local churches, they chose to have a mass baptism.

On the appointed day, they invited all of the new converts to a covered arena. They positioned eight portable swimming pools in the center court arranged in the shape of a cross. The veteran believers occupied the bleachers on all four sides, while the new believers stood by the swimming pools along with the pastors. The chairman of the ministerial association led the new believers in a prayer of renunciation of Satan and allegiance to Jesus. Following that, they all got inside the swimming pools along with the pastors, who baptized them in the name of Jesus Christ. No distinction or mention was made of the individual congregation the new believer might choose to attend later. *Everyone* was baptized into the only Church in Resistencia, the Church of Jesus Christ.

Six months later, a church census was taken. To everybody's delight, the church had grown 102 percent. Beyond those

---

THE PASTORS OF RESISTENCIA HAD FINALLY GIVEN THE CHURCH-AT-LARGE A UNIQUE GIFT: A MODEL FOR EFFECTIVE EVANGELISM. THEY ALLOWED GOD TO PROVE TO THEM THAT CITIES CAN AND MUST BE ENTIRELY REACHED FOR CHRIST.

---

encouraging numbers were blessings that cannot be quantified: the dismantling of the strongholds of disunity and apathy; the healing of old festering wounds among denominations; the training and deploying of intercessors; the newly found respect for the Church in the city; the favor gained in the eyes of the government and the media. However, even more significant was the development of a viable prototype to reach entire cities for Christ. The pastors of Resistencia had finally given the Church-at-large a unique gift: a model for effective evangelism. By agreeing to turn their churches into a laboratory and themselves into spiritual guinea pigs, they allowed God to prove to them, and through them to the Church-at-large, that cities can and must be entirely reached for Christ.

Resistencia is not a perfect example. It is simply a prototype—

but a prototype that worked in spite of the mistakes we made. Like a baby, seconds after birth, it needs to be cleaned up, nurtured and cared for. The beauty of it is that Resistencia was not a stillbirth but a live birth. An article published in the March 1993 issue of the *El Puente* newspaper implies that in the two years since the plan ended, the Church grew another 400 percent, bringing the cumulative growth to over 500 percent, and the total number of congregations to 200, an increase of 130 new ones. Those figures are not the result of a scientific survey but rather the opinion of the reporting journalist. However, even if only one fourth of this is correct, it will still set Resistencia apart as one of the most successful models for contemporary citywide evangelism. At the time of this writing, 16 other cities in three continents are applying many of the principles pioneered in Resistencia.

This book attempts to present what we understand to be the scriptural principles required for effective citywide evangelism as practiced by the Early Church. Rediscovering and subsequently implementing those principles is what made "Plan Resistencia" possible.

In Section I of this book, I discuss the biblical rationale for prayer evangelism, the location and the dynamics of the battlefield, the nature of spiritual strongholds and how to destroy them, and the authority delegated to the believer and how to exercise it in prayer. In so doing, I have strived to present and discuss the principles of prayer and love for the lost, unity in the Church, personal and corporate holiness, and spiritual warfare.

In Section II, I focus on the methodology used to apply those principles, first in Resistencia, and later on in many cities on different continents. By presenting first the biblical principles and then the methodology, I have strived to avoid the common mistake of confusing the principles with the methods. God has given us principles, not methods. Biblical principles are supracultural and timeless. The choice of the method to implement those principles depends on man's constantly varying perspective and circumstances. The degree of success of that method is also in direct proportion to the degree in which the implementers yield to the Holy Spirit.

With the passage of time, we have learned much more than what we knew when "Plan Resistencia" was first launched. We are still far from knowing it all. However, what we know we gladly share with you, the reader.

On the day I left Resistencia, the plane took off toward the east, flying over the Parana River, which 700 kilometers further south washes the beaches of my native San Nicolas. This is the river that quietly listened to my youthful conversations with God week after week. Thirty years had gone by, and, finally, I had seen an entire city reached for Christ. I knew it then, and I know it now: That was not the end but the beginning of a new phase. "Plan Resistencia" was the laboratory. Now we must perfect the prototype and make it available to the nations.

As the plane left Resistencia behind, I thanked God for giving me life to see this day. I thanked Him for the pastors of Resistencia who dared to try. I thanked Him for friends like Peter and Doris Wagner, and Cindy Jacobs, who jumped in and joined us in our very messy trench at the most crucial time in the battle for Resistencia. I thanked God for my team that patiently and courageously followed me as I led them into battle, chasing the dream of my youth. I thanked God for Ruth, my wife, and for Karina, Marilyn, Evelyn and Jesica, our four daughters, who faithfully stood by me on good days and on bad days, of which there were plenty.

My prayer is that the principles contained in this book will bless you, and through you, your city and eventually your nation.

I pray that as you implement them, they will be further perfected for the glory of God and the fulfillment of the Great Commission in our generation.

2

Prayer Evangelism

PRINCIPLE: *Prayer is the most tangible trace of eternity in the human heart. Intercessory prayer on behalf of the felt needs of the lost is the best way to open their eyes to the light of the gospel.*

THE GREAT COMMISSION BEGAN WITH A CITY: JERUSALEM. "BUT you shall receive power when the Holy Spirit has come upon you; and you shall be My witnesses both in Jerusalem, and in all Judea and Samaria, and even to the remotest part of the earth" (Acts 1:8). At a time when the vast majority of the world population resided in rural areas, Jesus chose a city as the starting point of His disciples' mission. Just as the Great Commission began with a city, it will most likely end when the last city in the remotest part of the earth is evangelized.

Cities are important to God. He feels strongly about cities, and their demise saddens Him. In the Old Testament, God dispatched prophets to plead with city dwellers for repentance, and He greatly rejoiced when cities like Nineveh repented, in spite of Jonah's frustration. Jesus Himself wept openly over Jerusalem.

Later on, when He wrote His seven epistles, recorded in
Revelation chapters 2 and 3, He called the churches by the name
of the city in which they ministered. Furthermore, in the book of
Revelation, the struggle between God and the devil is centered
around two great cities: Jerusalem and Babylon.

Jesus commanded His disciples not to leave Jerusalem until
they had been endued with power from on high. Acts 1:8 implies
that once power descended on them, they were not to proceed on
to Judea and Samaria until Jerusalem had been evangelized. As
Jesus spelled out this strategy—first Jerusalem and from there,
fanning out in evergrowing circles all the way to the ends of the
earth—I can imagine Peter fighting the urge to suggest a change
of venue. "Lord," he might have said, "what about *beginning* in
the uttermost parts of the earth and slowly working our way back
to Jerusalem? By then things will have cooled considerably
around here."

Definitely there would have been some logic to Peter's suggestion. Jerusalem was the most difficult city in which to start a new
religion, least of all the Christian religion! Jerusalem was where
Jesus was publicly crucified as a criminal. It was a very popular
verdict, which the populace, manipulated by the Jewish chief
priest, demanded through what amounted to a riot. If Pontius
Pilate had not acquiesced, he would have had a major distur-
bance with which to contend.

Peter, Jesus' most enthusiastic follower, had denied Him in
public. His administrator, Judas, betrayed Him for a few pieces of
silver. The rest of His disciples were confused and in hiding. Only
John stood near the cross to receive from Jesus the assignment to
care for His mother, whose heart was pierced by the sword of perplexity, if not confusion. A search among His closest associates
would not have turned up a great deal of potential for church
planters or missionaries. Modern-day investigative journalists

would have had a field day exposing the flaws in the character of the charter members of Christianity.

Besides, Jerusalem already had a well-established religion. This religion was powerfully and irretrievably intertwined with the state, to the point that it was impossible to be a member of the Jewish nation without first belonging to the official religion. Moreover, the council of elders had powerful connections with the occupying Roman army, which had shown nothing but contempt for Jesus.

The disciples' most convincing argument to support their witness—Jesus' resurrection—had been successfully portrayed as a farce. The Jewish elders and the Roman soldiers had cunningly conspired to implant in the people's minds the notion that Jesus did not rise from the dead. Instead, they said, His disciples had stolen and hidden His body.

Finally, the group of disciples who received the Great Commission with specific instructions to begin in Jerusalem had no political, social or economic clout. Similarly, they were despised by the establishment as ignorant and unlearned in a city that prided itself in intellectualism. To add insult to injury, social prejudice was effectively used to discredit this band of Galileans. "Can anything good come out of Galilee?" was perhaps one of the most popular contemporary put-downs (see John 1:45,46).

The assignment to begin the Great Commission in Jerusalem, therefore, was as appealing and pathetic as being asked to go to Waco, Texas, to relaunch the Branch Davidian Church the week after David Koresh and his followers went up in flames. Humanly speaking, the disciples' chances of success were absolutely nonexistent.

However, Jesus clearly commanded them to begin in Jerusalem with the implication not to leave the city until they had succeeded there. If there was ever a difficult assignment, this was it.

From the Upper Room to Every Living Room

Within weeks of Jesus' departure, however, the disciples were accused by the religious experts in Jerusalem of having fulfilled the Great Commission in that city. Speaking on behalf of the council of elders, the high priest told them, "You [the disciples] have filled Jerusalem with [His] teaching" (Acts 5:28). There is only one way to "fill a city" and that is by doing it house by house. When their sworn enemies spontaneously concede like this, it is safe to assume that the disciples had succeeded in a big way.

How much time elapsed between Acts 1:8 and Acts 5:28? Just a few weeks! In a matter of weeks, the Church went from the Upper Room to every living room in Jerusalem.

Furthermore, the spiritual avalanche did not stop in the out-skirts of Jerusalem. It rumbled from one city to the next, fueled by religious persecution. It passed through the city of Samaria, where it faced and defeated the challenge of counterfeit religion, and multitudes rejoiced. It rolled into Antioch, overcoming the challenge of racism and cultural prejudice.

Actually, the church in Antioch was the result of an "honest mistake" made by some trigger-happy evangelists. They forgot that they were not supposed to speak the Word to non-Jews. As Acts 11:19-26 describes it, multitudes of Greeks and Gentiles heard the gospel, received it, and thus the first non-Jewish church began. Understandably, the apostles in Jerusalem were perplexed by this development. It is not that the Gentiles had not been converted before. For instance, Cornelius and his rela-tives and close friends had received the gospel (see Acts 10:24-48), but they represented a small group of God-fearing people with direct ties to the Jewish synagogue (see Acts 10:1,2). However, in the case of Antioch, we have multitudes of true pagans embracing Christianity with no Mosaic background whatsoever (see Acts 11:21,26). Fortunately, the apostles in Jerusalem sent Barnabas, also known as "son of consolation," to check out the situation. Barnabas, in addition to being bicultural (he was born in Cyprus), also had the gift of mercy. This enabled him to see "the grace of God" (Acts 11:23) beyond the blatant violations of Jewish rituals by the new believers. If someone biased, like James, had been sent instead, the outcome could have been disastrous. Watching them eat pork with unwashed hands on the Sabbath would have been enough for James to decree the end of the first Gentile church!

Barnabas proceeded to call an unemployed Jewish rabbi named Saul, who was somehow hiding in Tarsus, to come and help equip the Gentile believers in Antioch. What a perplexing assignment for a Pharisee of Pharisees! In spite of not having the full trust of the "denominational leaders" in Jerusalem (or maybe because of it!), Saul's efforts survived the test and Jesus' followers came to be known by the name "Christian" for the first time in Antioch.

Some time later, the Church in Antioch sent Barnabas and Saul (soon to be called Paul, see Acts 13:9) to take the gospel to cities in the remotest parts of the earth. One of those cities was Ephesus, in Asia Minor. Paul's first visit was a brief one (see Acts 18:19-21). On the second visit, Paul found a strange group of "disciples" who did not know who or what the Holy Spirit was, since they had only been baptized in the baptism of John. Paul baptized a total of 12 men and introduced them to the Holy Spirit. It appears that these 12 men, along with a cluster of God-fearing Jews from the local synagogue, became the charter members of the Church in Ephesus.

The parallel with the disciples in Jerusalem in Acts 1:8 is strikingly similar. A small band of believers facing one of the most thriving metropolises in Asia Minor: Ephesus. This was a city run by organized religion. The local cult of the goddess Artemis permeated every aspect of the city and its identity very much the way Mormonism and the Mormon Tabernacle define Salt Lake City, Utah. The political, economic and union environments were intertwined with this lucrative cult. Artemis's gatekeepers viewed any new religion with the same enthusiasm with which a hungry lion would welcome a lame gazelle. To make matters worse, the local synagogue that at first had welcomed Paul soon turned against him and his fledgling band of new converts, forcing him to move into a nonreligious building (see Acts 19:9). This was a major blow in a city where the temple building was as important, if not more so, as what went on inside the temple. So a quasicomical picture developed: the proponents of a new religion meeting in a rented hall facing Artemis, whose sumptuous shrine gave identity to the city. Humanly speaking, there was never a more uneven fight.

However, two years later the entire city of Ephesus had heard the gospel, and one of the most dramatic power encounters registered in the entire Bible had taken place, resulting in multitudes of converts.

> God did extraordinary miracles through Paul,...handkerchiefs and aprons that had touched him were taken to the sick, and their illnesses were cured and the evil spirits left them....Many of those who believed now came and openly confessed their evil deeds. A number who had practiced sorcery brought their scrolls together and burned them publicly. When they calculated the value of the scrolls, the total came to fifty thousand drachmas. In this way the word of the Lord spread widely and grew in power (Acts 19:11,12,18-20, NIV).

Like Jerusalem before, the spiritual explosion did not confine itself to the city. It systematically spread through all Asia Minor to the degree that in Acts 19:10 the Holy Spirit declared through Luke, His scribe, in unequivocal terms that "all who lived in Asia heard the word of the Lord, both Jews and Greeks." When Paul finally left Asia Minor, he was able to say to the Church in Rome (Rom. 15:23) that there was no reason for him to stay in "these regions." Powerful!

It happened again! A small, struggling church had reached an entire city, and from there it had conquered the region beyond. In a relatively short time, the gospel went from Tyranus's classroom to every living room in Asia Minor.

The Beginning of Prayer Evangelism

The statement made in Acts 19:10 clearly indicates that the Great Commission was indeed fulfilled in Ephesus and in Asia Minor. By this I mean that the Early Church publicly testified to everybody living there that Jesus is God, that He died for the sins of mankind, that He rose from the dead and was ready to come into their lives in a tangible way. All of this was validated by God through the signs that followed the preaching as first outlined in Mark 16:20, "Then the disciples went out and preached everywhere, and the Lord worked with them and confirmed his word by the signs that accompanied it" (NIV).

How did the Early Church manage to take the gospel from the confining environment of the Upper Room to cities all over Asia Minor?

The Bible does not spell out a specific method. However, right after Pentecost in the book of Acts, we have a description of the lifestyle of the Early Church. Acts 2:42 probably sums it up well,

"And they were continually devoting themselves to the apostles' teaching and to fellowship, to the breaking of bread and to prayer." The lifestyle consisted of four elements: (1) the study of the doctrine of the apostles; (2) fellowship; (3) the breaking of bread; and (4) prayer. This particular verse makes it very clear that the new believers did this "continually."

PRAYER IS THE KEY TO THE SUCCESSFUL FULFILLMENT OF THE GREAT COMMISSION.

It is interesting to note that only one of these four elements reaches beyond the group: prayer. Studying the doctrine, fellowshipping and breaking bread were ministries *to* the group. In home meetings all over Jerusalem, clusters of believers enjoyed each other in unity. They joyfully celebrated the Lord's Supper while they assimilated what the Holy Spirit taught through the apostles, all in an atmosphere of intense dialogue with God through prayer.

Can you imagine the beauty and the effectiveness of those prayers? They were directed by the sound teaching of the apostles, fueled by a desire to see the Lord's return as highlighted during the breaking of bread and empowered by the spiritual unity reflected in the fellowship they had with each other. Undoubtedly, those were very effective prayers! Could it be that prayer was the primary vehicle used to reach entire cities for Christ?

I suggest that prayer—this kind of prayer—is *the* key to the successful fulfillment of the Great Commission, then and now.

If this is so, where else in the sacred record can we go to gain further insight? Since Paul was the most effective church planter in the New Testament, and Timothy was one of his closest associates, I suggest we look at 1 Timothy 2:1-8. In this passage, Paul gives Timothy instructions regarding prayer and evangelism:

> First of all, then, I urge that entreaties and prayers, petitions and thanksgivings, be made on behalf of all men, for kings and all who are in authority, in order that we may lead a tranquil and quiet life in all godliness and dignity. This is good and acceptable in the sight of God our Savior, who desires all men to be saved and to come to the knowledge of the truth. For there is one God, and one mediator also between God and men, the man Christ Jesus, who gave Himself as a ransom for all, the testimony borne at the proper time....Therefore I want the men in every place to pray, lifting up holy hands, without wrath and dissension (1 Tim. 2:1-6,8).

To capture the full impact of this passage, it is necessary to clarify a point that has been distorted by our cultural bias. Paul was not writing to the senior pastor of a local church as we know it today. Nor was he outlining the format for a midweek prayer meeting. Quite the contrary. Paul was addressing Christians who did not own church buildings or have midweek prayer meetings the way we do. This passage has to do as much with public prayer meetings as with private ones. Rather than suggesting the order of service for a church meeting, Paul here presents a citywide prayer strategy since the Greek of 1 Tim. 2:8 literally says, "I want men to pray in every place"! I believe this passage embodies the essence of evangelism as practiced by the Early Church—the essence of what I call "prayer evangelism." Let's take a closer look.

"First of all, then, I urge that entreaties and prayers, petitions and thanksgivings, be made on behalf of all men" (v. 1). Paul is telling Timothy to organize the Church so that prayers are said everywhere on behalf of all men in particular cities. As you know, in this passage the word "men" is used in the generic sense. It means men and women. The first assignment, then, was to make sure that everybody in town was prayed for.

What does that mean in our city? In San Jose, California, where I live, it means that the Church in the city must pray for 810,000 people. That is the total population of the city at the time of this writing.

Special emphasis is next placed on praying "for kings and all who are in authority" (v. 2). Who is the modern equivalent of kings as far as our city is concerned? The mayor, the chief of police, the fire marshal, the president of the school board, the editor of the local newspaper—in essence, *all* the people who shape the life of the city in one way or another.

I see at least three basic reasons for this special emphasis on praying for "all in authority."

The first reason is because of their influence on the quality of life in the city. If a garbage collector makes a mistake and backs his truck into a container, the worst that can happen is that somebody may need to buy a new garbage can. But if the mayor, or the chief of police, makes a mistake, the entire city suffers. This was painfully illustrated in Los Angeles through the stream of unfortunate incidents connected to the police brutality associated with the infamous Rodney King case.

The second reason for this emphasis on praying for *all* in authority is because of their lack of real influence in some areas. No one knows better how limited human solutions are than do those who are in authority. Men and women in government know very well that many of the problems for which they are expected to provide solutions *have no solution*, humanly speaking. This is why, out of desperation, it is not uncommon for them to rely on practitioners of the occult for help and advice. We saw this in Panama with General Noriega, in Uganda with Idi Amin, and we also saw it in the White House during the Reagan years. In spite of the efficiency of the Secret Service, the protection of the FBI, the shrewdness of the CIA and the insight of the National Security Council, Nancy Reagan sought the advice of one such practitioner to "protect" her husband from harm. We continue to see it today on Wall Street as CEOs of leading investment companies, with graduate degrees from Harvard, subscribe to the tenets of the New Age to guide them in their decisions.

Why would someone commit intellectual suicide like this? Because people in authority *know* that it will take supernatural intervention to solve the problems they face. Man's limitations are painfully evident to those in the so-called positions of power. The higher the person is, the more evident this axiom becomes. The personality cult that swept them into office (in the case of politicians) and the all-powerful image they carefully cultivate (in the case of CEOs), combined with raw human pride, may prevent them from publicly acknowledging their limitations, but most will admit it in private when it is safe to do so.

This is why it is so important for the Church to be there, interceding for our leaders, connecting them to the genuine source of power: God. Weeds grow more easily where nothing has been planted. So do witchcraft and the New Age movement. Like Daniel, we must be there to tell them that "there is a God in heaven who reveals mysteries" (Dan. 2:28). This, in turn, will lead them to acknowledge, like Nebuchadnezzar did, that "Surely your God is a God of gods and a Lord of kings and a revealer of mysteries" (Dan. 2:47). In essence, we must pray for them because they are potentially open to prayer due to the realization of their inability to influence major events.

The third reason for the emphasis on praying for *all* in authority is because of the influence of demonic powers on them. Like ivy plants clinging to walls, demonic forces attach themselves to governments and those in positions of prominence in order to influence by proxy. All through the Bible we see this; for instance, the Egyptian pharaohs, the Canaanite kings, King Ahab and Jezebel in Israel, and Sergius Paulus, the proconsul of Paphos (see Acts 13:7). The world system is under the evil one (see 1 John 2:16) and evil structures operate alongside political ones. This is where the action is today as far as spiritual warfare in our cities is concerned. God's army must be present in that battlefield.

The Kind of Prayers the Church Should Offer

Moving along in Paul's instruction to Timothy regarding prayer and evangelism, the apostle says, "I urge that entreaties and prayers, petitions and thanksgivings, be made on behalf of all men...in order that we may lead a tranquil and quiet life in all godliness and dignity" (1 Tim. 2:1,2).

When we hear the expression "a tranquil and quiet life," we usually visualize a self-serving scenario. Practically speaking, we may take this to mean that city hall will approve the user's permit for our new youth facility, that the county planning commission will vote favorably on the expansion of our conference center, that the state board of education will leave us alone and not interfere with our Christian school curriculum. In essence, we take it to mean "leave us alone" so we may enjoy a quiet and tranquil life! However, this is not the main thrust of this passage.

Paul says that the outcome of the prayer thrust should be to live in *all* godliness and honesty. There is only one way for Christians to live in an environment characterized by *all* godliness and honesty: it is for many unbelievers to become Christians, and those who don't, to become aware of the existence of God *and begin to fear Him*. Then, and only then, all godliness and honesty will permeate the city where the Church exists.

This was the case in the Old Testament with kings such as Nebuchadnezzar (see Dan. 3:28,29; 4:34-37), Cyrus (see Ezra 1:1-4), and even Pharaoh (see Exod. 12:31,32). In the New Testament, the classic example is Cornelius, a Roman centurion whose soldiers—I am sure—did not openly engage in bribery and extortion as others did because of Cornelius's God-fearing character (see Acts 10:1,2).

The objective of Paul's instructions to Timothy is very simple and extremely clear: pray that everybody in your city, and especially those in authority, *will become Christians!* To this end, Jesus has already made provision by "[giving] Himself as a ransom for all" (1 Tim. 2:6). The will of God has been clearly stated: God wants all men to be saved (v. 4). What is it that is still lacking? That the Church begin to pray for *all* men (vv. 1,2).

What an awesome responsibility. This is like setting up a banquet table in a remote area of starving Ethiopia. Jesus has already provided the food. The Father has set the table with enough chairs for the entire population and placed a personalized welcome card on each plate. What is still lacking for the starving multitudes to enjoy it? That the Church, God's post office, deliver the invitations. What a tragedy for such a banquet to go unattended because of negligence on the part of the messengers.

The Relationship Between Prayer, Revival and Evangelism

The concept of praying for everybody to be saved sounds strange because we usually associate prayer with revival more than with evangelism. However, let us examine for a moment our idea of revival.

When we think of revival, what kind of thoughts come to mind? Intimacy with God, holiness, worship, praise and unhindered fellowship with other saints. Right? Do we realize that each one of those is better experienced in heaven? If this is what we

---

OFTEN OUR IDEA OF REVIVAL IS EXTREMELY SELF-SERVING AND, THUS, UNBIBLICAL. THE ULTIMATE EXPRESSION OF REVIVAL IS THE CONVERSION OF THE UNSAVED.

---

crave for, we are better off dropping dead right now and going to heaven immediately. Heaven is where worship, praise, holiness and intimacy with the Father will reach an absolutely unimaginable level. This is why revival must have as its focus the glory of God and, as its result, the evangelization of the lost. These two are closely connected to each other; for Jesus, in His High Priestly prayer, connected the glory of God with the salvation of the lost (see John 17:20-23).

Often our idea of revival is extremely self-serving, and thus, unbiblical. A revival that fails to bring the lost to Jesus is a self-serving revival, centered on man's needs and wants, and not on God's glory. Many times our cry for revival has the implicit hope that if revival comes, our pews will fill up, finances will abound, counseling will no longer be so demanding and the ministry in general will be more enjoyable. We tend to confine the "healing of the land" promised in 2 Chronicles 7:14 to the healing of the Church. But the healing of the land requires primarily the healing of the lost. They are the primary "virus carriers" that spread the disease called sin with its devastating consequences. The greater the number of them who come to Christ and live the Christian life in all godliness and dignity, the greater the scope of the healing of the land. The ultimate expression of revival *is* the conversion of the unsaved.

On this point, we are further hindered by cultural myopia and a distorted historical perspective. Our notions of revival are sometimes dictated by theological assumptions hatched in a context in which Church and state rule together.

First, we project onto the New Testament Church the image of the theocracy of God over Israel.

Second, we often perceive the Church as one in partnership with a somewhat "Christian" state. This first occurred in the fourth century under Emperor Constantine and eventually led to the union of Church and State during the Middle Ages. It also happened in England in the seventeenth century after the religious schism with the Catholic Church. In America, this is further compounded by the belief that America was, and still is, a Christian nation.

All of this, then, leads us to assume that if the Church is healed, the state will automatically be healed because of the influence of the Church on society. Nothing could have been further from the mind-set of the Early Church. Paul and Timothy operated in a world in which none of these assumptions was valid. The Church was definitely the underdog, so much so that in many cases it was forced to operate underground. Martyrdom was a real possibility for most Christians. The state and society were so corrupted that, in the eyes of the Church, the only way to change them was through radical mass conversions. In 1 Timothy 1:9,10, Paul provides us with a clear picture of the kind of people to be included in our prayers. "Realizing the fact that law is not made for a righteous man, but for those who are lawless and rebellious, for the ungodly and sinners, for the unholy and profane, for those who kill their fathers or mothers, for murderers and immoral men and homosexuals and kidnappers and liars and perjurers, and whatever else is contrary to sound teaching."

This is very much the environment in which the Church works in the Third World today. Like the Church in the first century, the Church in the Third World today *knows* that unless large numbers of their non-Christian neighbors are converted, there is no hope for godliness on this side of heaven. To them this is an absolute nonnegotiable. Whereas in the West, and especially in the United States, we still cling to the notion that revival will come if we have more presidential prayer breakfasts, constitutional amendments to allow prayer in schools and to ban abortions, if the Church gets involved in politics and if we go back to our Christian roots. There is some truth to this, but there is much more that is still missing. The so-called Christian roots are practically nonexistent today, and no amount of legislation will ensure a change of heart for the unconverted. The only way to do so is to lead them to Christ. Then, and only then, will *all* godliness and honesty permeate the land.

The Church has been entrusted with something that every politician on earth would give an arm and a leg to have: the power to see hearts changed. When the heart is changed through the redeeming power of Jesus Christ, personal value systems change. When the new values are reflected in daily life *and* in elections, the nation changes for the better. Let's not downgrade the fullness of the divine Pentecost recorded in Acts chapter 2 to the human attempt to obtain political influence expressed by the disciples in Acts 1:6.

How Should We Pray for the Lost?

We tend to interpret the command to pray for all men in a very narrow way. When it comes to "praying for kings and all who are in authority" (1 Tim. 2:2), we usually limit ourselves to repeating their names on a daily basis as part of our prayers. Some go further and print a map of the world where the names of presidents and prime ministers are listed over each nation, then they pray for them. All of this is definitely good, but it is not all that Paul had in mind. God already knows the prime minister of Mozambique or the president of Mauritania. God is not suffering from Alzheimer's disease so that we must remind Him of those names. To pray effectively for them, it is necessary to go beyond this first step. We should go to those in authority and ask what their prayer requests are. They already know that many of the problems they face require a miracle. Those who need a miracle will tend to hope for a miracle if they need it badly enough.

The openness of the lost to intercessory prayer on their behalf has been the greatest surprise I have encountered in our city-reaching ministry. I have yet to be turned down by *anyone* in authority to whom prayer has been offered. Recently, a group of pastors and I met with the vice governor of the most powerful province in Argentina. After the initial "chitchat," I told him, "Mr. Vice Governor, these pastors represent a network of prayer cells that cover the entire city. We wish to know what problems you are facing in the province that will require a miracle. We want to pray for you."

He immediately smiled, thanked me for the offer, and asked about the details of the prayer-cell network. I gave him the three-minute version of 1 Timothy 2:1-8. I told him how we, the Church, are told by God to uphold people like himself in prayer and how the power of God is available to those that seek His face.

He smiled again, and, turning to one of his assistants, said, "Fernandez, I am appointing you 'Secretary of Miracles.' Anytime the governor or I face an impossible situation—which is quite often—I will call you and you will contact the pastors." Then he turned to us and asked, "That's the way it works, right?" What was supposed to have been a 15-minute meeting extended to an hour and a half. At the end, he welcomed our suggestion of closing in prayer. We laid hands on him and prayed. When we were done, with tears brimming in his eyes, he hugged us and invited us to come back to "talk to the governor about this thing...prayer."

A pastor who is part of a city-reaching thrust in a Canadian city told me a similar story. He had gone with a group of pastors to meet with an extremely liberal alderperson who, in addition to being actively pro-abortion, was promoting the legalization of prostitution in the city. The pastors wanted to apprise her of their position on those issues. As soon as the pastors walked through the door, the alderperson told them by way of greeting, "I want you to know that I am a feminist!" With that kind of predisposition, no constructive dialogue was possible. The atmosphere was very tense, and the meeting did not prove to be productive.

As they were leaving, the leading pastor told the alderperson, "We would like to pray for you as we are instructed by God to do. What can we pray for?" There was an immediate change in the atmosphere. The alderperson was both flustered and pleasantly surprised. Recovering from the initial shock, she blurted out, "Pray that I will do a good job as a public official." Since that day, the pastors have prayed for her. Since then she has reversed her position on legalized prostitution and has softened her stand on abortion. In fact, she has taken some positions so close to the pro-family point of view that some of her liberal supporters have publicly criticized her. She asked for prayer to be able to do a good job, and that is exactly what she got!

Recently, my friend Poncho Murguia, a pastor in Ciudad Juarez in northern Mexico who is leading a city-reaching plan there, took me to city hall, where I was asked to address a task force working to reduce crime in the city. We sat across from a group of 20 specialists who had been selected and empowered by the local government to find a solution to the severe crime problem affecting Ciudad Juarez. They invited me because they had heard about a dramatic turnaround in Argentina's largest maximum security prison. Only two people on the task force were born-again Christians. As I addressed the panel, I contrasted the conditions before and after the breakthrough in Argentina. Then I went on to explain, using as many secular terms as I was able, that the reason for the breakthrough was the power of prayer. I held nothing back while clearly presenting the need for the intervention of God in extreme situations like the one they were facing.

When I was done, they gave me a very warm ovation, and one of the members of the task force made a motion that I pray for them right there. It was seconded and unanimously approved. The chairperson asked me, "Would you pray for us, Mr. Silvoso?" I was elated. Just to make sure we were all in agreement, I turned to a macho-looking Mexican man seated next to me (he looked as severe as Pancho Villa must have looked on a bad day) and asked him, "What do you think? Should I pray?"

He looked me straight in the eye and said, "Of course. We need it!" I went ahead and prayed for them, and as I did, I sensed their spiritual hunger. When the meeting was over, everybody came up to shake my hand and to invite me back soon.

People in authority are open to prayer. We must realize this.

They do not demand that those prayers be answered. All they ask for is that someone close to God *say* prayers. Unbelievers do not have the theological hang-ups we Christians have about prayer. It seems to us that if we pray for something and nothing happens, God will get a black eye. This is not the case with most non-Christians. They are grateful that in a moment of palpable need, someone will volunteer to talk to the Supreme Being about their problems.

Prayer is the most tangible trace of eternity in the human heart. What is it that everyone (including atheists) usually does when facing an impossible situation? They pray! Month after month I find in the "Drama in Real Life" section of the *Reader's Digest* a reference to prayer when the subject of the story has reached the bottom of the pit. Prayer is common to every religion on the face of the earth.

Life magazine, in its February 1994 issue, published a cover story on prayer. The article quotes Gallup Poll results indicating that 95 percent of Americans have had at least one prayer answered!

The account in 1 Kings 18 depicts Israel's darkest hour—when Ahab and Jezebel ruled with impunity and the prophets of Baal had the run of the nation. On behalf of God, Elijah confronted and successfully resolved the crisis through prayer. "You call on the name of your god, and I will call on the name of the Lord, and the God who answers by fire, He is God" (1 Kings 18:24). Elijah was able to bring resolution to an extremely complex crisis involving the political, religious and economic life of the nation through public prayer. The most interesting thing is that the people agreed with his approach: "And all the people answered and said, 'That is a good idea'" (1 Kings 18:24). Once the power of God was displayed and His fear had gripped the nation afresh, Elijah offered prayer for the most urgent need:

rain. The best way to pray intelligently for the unsaved, and espe-cially for those in authority, is to get to know them and to main-tain contact with them in order to pray for their felt needs.

Felt Needs Versus the Most Important Need

In order to pray effectively for the unsaved, we must become aware of the difference between the most important need a per-son has and what that person feels is his most important need—what is known as the "felt need." Usually these two are not one and the same in the mind of the unsaved. Man's most important need has already been determined by God: the salvation of his soul. However, the felt needs of the lost are defined by the lost themselves; it is what *they feel* is most important to them.

The lost are unable to clearly see their most important need because "the god of this world has blinded the minds of the unbelieving" to the gospel (2 Cor. 4:4). When we pray for their felt needs and God answers, their eyes are opened to the reali-ty and the power of God, and this in turn leads them to recog-nize their need for salvation. This is what Paul may have had in mind when he said that the Lord sent him "to open their eyes so that they may turn from darkness to light and from the dominion of Satan to God" (Acts 26:18). All through the book of Acts we see that opening the eyes of the unbelievers hap-pened in a context of "extraordinary miracles" (Acts 19:11), which undoubtedly were intended to meet the felt needs of those involved.

Unfortunately, nowadays when praying for the lost we usual-ly limit ourselves to asking God in private that they come to Jesus. Indeed, this is their most important need. However, we must go beyond this first step. We must discern what it is that *they* consider important and pray for that need to be met by God. When this happens, it acts as an eye-opener as far as the gospel is concerned.

This was Jesus' approach. His first miracle, turning water into wine, is still one of the most difficult to explain (see John 2:1-11). A great deal of theological heat has been generated by arguments about whether it was real wine or not, whether people could get drunk with it or whether it was "tipsy-free." Why would Jesus provide wine for a party where it had run out either because of poor planning or because the guests drank too much too fast? Simply put, because wine was the felt need of the hour, especially for the father of the bride whose reputation was at stake. At that particular moment, the father of the bride was not concerned about heaven or hell or the forgiveness of his sins. Most likely he was consumed with shame because all his friends and associates were there, and he had failed them. From Jesus' perspective, salvation was the number one need, but as far as the father of the bride was concerned, it was wine. "Give me wine or give me death" could well have been the man's motto.

What did Jesus do? He turned water into wine and thus met the felt need of the hour. As soon as the guests tasted the wine, they knew that something extraordinary had happened. Surely they must have asked, "Who did it?" In all likelihood, their eyes turned to Jesus. I am sure the father of the bride never forgot Jesus' favor, and perhaps that played a role in his salvation later on.

Another example of this is revealed in the story of Zaccheus in Luke 19:1-9. He was as ruthless as a mafia Don and as devastating as the head of the Medellin Drug Cartel, with the legal clout of the regional director of the IRS, all rolled into one. He was a thief who probably stole as much from the Romans, for whom he worked, as from the Jews among whom he lived.

Zaccheus's felt need, what he craved for the most, was respect. What was it that he deserved the least? Respect. The local establishment had done a superb job of shunning and despising him (v. 7).

When Jesus went to Jericho, Zaccheus wanted to see Him. The Bible makes it clear that, while looking for a place to see Jesus, he "ran on ahead" (v. 4), where most likely the least important people gathered. Even there, on account of his short stature, he was not able to find a good spot. This is how this man, who craved recognition, found himself climbing a tree and leaning on a branch, very much like an animal, in his desire to catch a glimpse of Jesus. For someone who coveted respect, this was the picture of ultimate humiliation. Never in his entire life had Zaccheus sensed his number one felt need more deeply and painfully than when he hung on that tree in full view of his contemporaries. The whole exercise was a painful reminder that he lacked more than physical stature. He had failed to measure up. His character was definitely flawed. On that day he *knew* he would never get the respect he so desperately lusted after.

Against this backdrop, what was Jesus' first official act upon entering Jericho? He showed Zaccheus respect. He told him, "Today I must stay at your house" (v. 5). This chagrined his contemporaries who grumbled, "He has gone to be the guest of a man who is a sinner" (v. 7). Did Zaccheus deserve to be honored? No, not at all. But Jesus was in the habit of meeting men's felt needs first in order to draw them to salvation. What was Zaccheus's response? He repented, gave half of his wealth to the poor and returned everything he had stolen at 400 percent interest because, in Jesus' words, "Today salvation has come to this house" (v. 9).

Another example of meeting felt needs is Paul's experience in

Philippi (see Acts 16:1-34). An earthquake had rocked the jail where he and Silas had been locked up after being tortured. The chains had fallen off the prisoners and the doors had swung open. The prisoners were free to escape. What was the jailer's number one felt need at that moment? Job security. He needed reassurance that the prisoners had not fled since, in some cases, he responded for them with his own life. What did Paul do? He met that particular need by telling the jailer, "We are all here" (v. 28). His felt need met, what is the jailer's reaction? "Sirs, what must I do to be saved?" (v. 30).

When Jesus stood in front of Lazarus's tomb, he highlighted the obvious for the sake of the unbelievers in the audience. He said, "I knew that Thou hearest Me always; but because of the people standing around I said it, that they may believe that Thou didst send Me" (John 11:42). In this passage, Jesus stated as clear as daylight the cause-and-effect relationship between answers to public prayers and belief on the part of the lost. This is why, when praying for unbelievers, it must be done with this kind of biblical expectation that the answer to those prayers will lead them to faith. Obviously, this is what Paul had in mind when he wrote to Timothy (see 1 Tim. 2:1-8).

Meeting the felt needs of the lost opens their eyes to the reality of God and allows them to make a vital connection between His power and His love for them (see Mark 1:40,41; Acts 4:9-12). Most unsaved people believe in the power of God. The universe itself is clear testimony of God's power. What most of them do not believe is that God loves them. When God's power, shown through an answer to prayer, is released on their behalf, they are finally able to make that connection. As Paul explained to King Agrippa, once their eyes are open, they have a choice to turn from darkness to life and from the dominion of Satan to God (see Acts 26:18).

Acceptance Versus Approval

The main factor that keeps us from praying consistently for the felt needs of the lost is our inability to distinguish between acceptance and approval. We are afraid that if we pray for a cure to be found for AIDS—which afflicts and is spread largely by homosexuals and IV drug users—somehow we will be condoning a highly objectionable lifestyle. Likewise, we are afraid that if we pray for a corrupt politician, we will be compromising the pristine nature of the gospel. So we choose not to pray. Through our verbal and nonverbal communication, we demonstrate judgment and condemnation, rather than love and acceptance. Though Christ died, the ultimate sacrifice for us when we were still sinners, we, His followers, refuse to extend grace to those in the same condition. What a contrast!

I know of no church that criticizes its pastor for not taking care of the needs of the lost sheep (salvation) but know of too many churches that have fired their pastors for not taking care of the 99 sheep that are safely tucked into the fold. Nothing could be more opposed to Jesus' teaching about the role of the pastor. In Luke 15:1-7, He emphasizes how the good shepherd leaves the saved sheep to go after the lost one. Our selfish preoccupation with our cosmetic needs at the expense of the eternal life of the lost is the ultimate expression of the religious spirit that controls many Christians today.

Jesus loved sinners. He came to earth not because this was a holy place, but because it was populated *exclusively* by sinners. Because of this, He, the holy one, modeled a sinner-friendly lifestyle that conveyed full acceptance without bestowing approval of their deeds. Jesus stayed in their homes. He ate at their tables. He attended their parties. Not once did He compromise His holiness because He was able to accept the sinner without approving of his lifestyle in an atmosphere overflowing with compassion. There was no need for Him to belabor the point, because sinners already knew that He disapproved of their lifestyle. For those sinners to see that Jesus was willing to fellowship with them in spite of their lifestyle made Jesus more intriguing and more attractive to them. At one point, Jesus had His feet washed by the tears and dried with the hair of a repentant prostitute (see Luke 7:36-50). No one feels more attracted to a Savior than someone who fully knows how truly lost he or she is.

A pastor friend of mine was visited by a homosexual who was dying of AIDS. Without disclosing his illness, the homosexual invited the pastor to have lunch, and they went out to a restaurant. Halfway through their meal, the homosexual paused, looked the pastor in the eye and blurted out, "I am dying of AIDS," while tensely waiting for the pastor's reaction. With tear-filled eyes, the pastor reached across the table and touched the homosexual's arm while saying, "I am sorry. I am truly sorry."

Later, the homosexual received Jesus. He explained his decision to the pastor: "Do you want to know why I decided to receive Jesus? When I told you I was dying of AIDS, I was watching your body language. I wondered if you would quickly lean back, away from my face, or if you would surreptitiously move your glass and your plate toward you. I was not listening to your words, but I was watching the language of your body. Instead of rejecting me, you reached out and touched me. Your eyes filled with tears. You empathized with me. You accepted me. Then and there, I decided that your God is the God I want to meet when I die."

We must shake off the religious spirit that prevents us from lovingly accepting the sinners for what they are: sinners. This religious spirit causes us to despise and reject them on the false assumption that we are better than they are. Pound per pound of flesh, we are no better; we are simply better equipped. Take Jesus away from us and what do you have left? A bunch of lost sinners. As Christians, we have created in our churches a hierarchical order of sins. Adultery is not permitted, and pastors lose their pulpit if they go for it. Pride, however, is tolerated and in many cases encouraged, especially if it is coated with self-righteousness. By feeling good for the sins we do not commit, we fail to see the crucial need we have for the grace of God on account of the sins that we *do* commit.

We are like two travelers stranded at an airport. One missed the plane by just one minute. He got there just as the plane was taxiing away. The other one was an hour late. Even though both missed the plane, the one who missed it by one minute gives the other one a terrible time because he was 59 minutes later than him! What difference does it make? By one minute or by one hour, both missed it and both were left behind.

Likewise, we have all fallen short of the glory of God. Some by a little; but to God, it's a lot. That's why it is by grace, and grace alone, that we have been admitted into the Church. And it is only by His grace that we will remain in it. Spiritual pride is the greatest obstacle to genuinely and lovingly accepting sinners. We must accept the lost and graciously minister to their felt needs so that their eyes will be opened to the reality of the power and the love of God. Like Jesus, we must accept them as they are so we can show them the way to change.

The Club of the One-Hundredth Sheep

Why would God answer prayers on behalf of people who are living in sin, cut off from the glory of God and following the prince of the power of the air? Because of all of the above. Such desperate conditions trigger His grace. Prayers for the felt needs of the lost have a higher priority than the prayers for the needs of the saved. The reason is simple: The needs of believers are cos-

---

WHEN CHRISTIANS BEGIN TO PRAY
FOR THE FELT NEEDS OF THE LOST,
GOD SURPRISES THEM WITH ALMOST
IMMEDIATE ANSWERS TO PRAYER. IN FACT,
PRAYER FOR THE NEEDS OF THAT ONE-
HUNDREDTH SHEEP IS THE SPIRITUAL
EQUIVALENT OF DIALING 911.

---

metic needs. This is not to say that the needs of believers are not important to God. They are. But unbelievers have a more vital, essential need. Their eternal destiny hangs in the balance. To believers, a crisis is a temporary problem affecting their comfort level this side of heaven. To unbelievers, it is either heaven or hell.

The Bible tells us that the shepherd leaves the 99 sheep alone, safely tucked away in the fold, in order to go after the lost one (see Luke 15:1-7). He actually makes the one-hundredth sheep the focus of His care and attention. Some people have the idea that God only looks at sinners through the stained glass windows of our church buildings, or that He will not hear their voices until they have joined the church choir. Nothing could be further from the truth. God's heartbeat is for the lost. He loves them to the point of having given the very best for them: His Son. His eyes are constantly searching for the lost.

Nowhere is this more evident than in the area of prayer. Time and again, when I ask in my seminars how many have come to the Lord because someone prayed for them, almost everybody raises a hand. When I further ask how many of those prayers had to do with felt needs, the same number of hands go up. This is why as soon as a city is saturated with prayer cells, and Christians begin to pray for the felt needs of the lost, God surprises them with almost immediate answers to prayer. In fact, prayer for the felt needs of that one-hundredth sheep is the spiritual equivalent of dialing 911.

Ruth and I used to go horseback riding in a ranch run by an Argentine gaucho by the name of Alvarez. Mr. Alvarez heard the gospel and began to attend church, but he was not a believer. He was still hovering over the threshold that separates the lost from the saved. Missiologists use a measuring tool called the Modified Engel's Scale to track people's spiritual journey. It begins at -10 and ends at +10. Zero marks the threshold dividing life before and after accepting Christ. For instance, the Ayatollah Khomeini would register -10 and the apostle Paul a +10, and so on. Mr. Alvarez would register one day at -1 on the Modified Engel's Scale, another day he would be at 0, but before he could get to a +1 he would make a U-turn toward -1. We used to pray that God would "shove" him into the Kingdom. God answered that prayer through another person's prayer: Mr. Alvarez's.

One Sunday he went to church and listened to a sermon based on James 5. The preacher emphasized the need to pray for the sick and to anoint them with oil. How much of the message Mr. Alvarez understood is unknown. However, the morning after hearing that sermon, he woke up to find that his most valuable bull was dead. That was a major tragedy. For a cowboy to lose his prize bull is like an admiral having his flagship sink. It is a disaster of catastrophic proportions. If there was a day when Mr. Alvarez knew what his felt need was, it was that day. As he stared at the dead bull, he remembered the teaching he had heard the night before. He went to the kitchen and found a can of olive oil. He then walked outside and anointed the lifeless animal and prayed, *and the bull stood up and walked!*

When Mr. Alvarez told me about it, I had the same skeptical look that you probably have right now. I wondered if it really happened. I knew he was an honorable man who would not make up such a story, but I wondered if the bull was really dead. And that is when I made the mistake of asking him if that could have been the case. Mr. Alvarez took off his glasses and looked me straight in the eye with such an intensity that I felt the dermis of my soul getting an instant tan. With a booming voice he said, "Young man, I have been a cowboy for over half a century. I know cows and bulls inside out. If I tell you it was dead, it was dead! Understood?"

Why would God raise a bull from the dead? For the same reason Jesus would do something as unusual as turning water into wine. It was a felt need so real that, once met, it could not fail to open the eyes of the lost to the reality of God's power and love.

Mr. Alvarez finally became a Christian. With his conversion came the transfer from the One-Hundredth Club to the ninety-ninth. Never again did he have an experience as dramatic as that one. In fact, once I remember seeing him take aspirin for a headache. Taking aspirin for such a minor ailment after seeing a bull raised from the dead seems like a contradiction. Nevertheless, it is not a contradiction when you understand that those felt needs have a low priority in the club to which Mr. Alvarez was transferred shortly after his conversion.

The How and the Where

Where are we to pray? Everywhere. Not just at an annual concert of prayer, but everywhere. As Paul told Timothy, "I want the men in every place to pray, lifting up holy hands, without wrath and dissension" (1 Tim. 2:8).

There is only one way to pray everywhere as far as a city is concerned and that is by opening prayer cells throughout that city. This is what the pastors in Resistencia did. They opened more than 600 lighthouses all over the city. Not a single neighborhood was left without a prayer house.

How are we to pray? Lifting up holy hands. This has to do with personal and collective holiness. This is a key point. Prayer evangelism as presented in this passage is not a program but a lifestyle, such as the one described in Acts 2:42-47:

> And they were continually devoting themselves to the apostles' teaching and to fellowship, to the breaking of bread and to prayer. And everyone kept feeling a sense of awe; and many wonders and signs were taking place through the apostles. And all those who had believed were together, and had all things in common; and they began selling their property and possessions, and were sharing them with all, as anyone might have need. And day by day continuing with one mind in the temple, and breaking bread from house to house, they were taking their meals together with gladness and sincerity of heart, praising God, and having favor with all the people. And the Lord was adding to their number day by day those who were being saved.

It is not enough to develop a plan to cover every neighborhood in the city. First and foremost, holiness must permeate the Church. The Church must rediscover the beauty and the effectiveness of prayer that characterized the Early Church. When the original group of pastors in Resistencia celebrated the Lord's Supper together, they dealt with sins, such as individual and denominational pride, that had accumulated over a long time. After taking the Lord's Supper, there was a clear display of holiness in each one of them. Now their hands were capable of piercing the spiritual darkness enveloping Resistencia because they had become *holy hands*.

How else are we to pray? Without wrath and dissension. The word "dissension" in the *King James Version* is "doubting" (1 Tim. 2:8). This indicates the two conditions necessary for effectual prayer: freedom from irritation toward our fellow man (no wrath) and confidence toward God (no doubting). Kenneth Wuest says the word "doubting" means "disputatious reasoning, skeptical questions or criticisms...whether of God's character and dealings, or of the character and behavior of those for whom prayer is offered."[1] To effectively implement this, we must agree to walk in the light, as He is light, and to confess our sins to God and to one another so that the blood of Jesus will cleanse us (the Church) from all unrighteousness (see 1 John 1:7). This is the kind of unity described by Jesus in John 17:23 that causes the world to believe that the Father indeed sent Him.

All the congregations in the city must realize that, biblically speaking, there is only *one* Church in the city. It is a Church that meets in many congregations, but it is still one Church. Although many undershepherds are watching over those congregations, only one Chief Shepherd watches over the Church (see Heb. 13:20).

In Calgary, Alberta, Canada, my friend Phil Nordin, a charismatic pastor, decided to teach this truth to his people in an objective way. Phil invited several congregations in town to send a representative each Sunday to share from the pulpit the prayer requests of that particular congregation. After that, Phil and his elders would lead in prayer for the sister congregation. Prior to this new prayer initiative, Phil's church and a local Baptist church had been at odds with each other for a number of years. The root of this problem preceded Phil's tenure, but it was very real nonetheless. The animosity was so strong that it was part of the public domain. It was a classic example of the dissension referred to by Paul in 1 Timothy 2:1-8.

Eventually, Phil invited the Baptist pastor to send a representative on a chosen Sunday. To his relief, the pastor readily agreed. However, 10 days before the appointed time, he called to ask for a postponement, saying, "I'm afraid I won't be able to make it."

Phil said to him, "You don't understand, brother. You don't have to come. Just send us a representative."

The Baptist pastor replied, "It is you who does not understand. I need to go personally, and I plan to take my elders with me."

I happened to be preaching at Phil's church on the day the invited pastor and his leaders came. At the appointed time, they walked up to the podium and the pastor said, "I have come here to repent on two counts, personally and corporately, for all the bad things I and the church I represent have said about you. We have never mentioned you by name from our pulpit, but everybody knew we meant you. Would you forgive me? Would you forgive us?"

Deeply moved, Phil stood up, extended forgiveness and also requested forgiveness for his church's share of the problem. When both pastors embraced, I'm sure angels sang for joy at the sight of such a dramatic display of God's grace. Not a single eye was dry in the audience. What a dramatic validation of the deep spiritual truth that there is only one Church that can exist without wrath or dissension!

Praying for Your "Jerusalem"

Can you picture your city from God's perspective? Try to imagine it as God sees it. A city enveloped in thick spiritual darkness. This darkness is made mainly out of man's sins, which act as a shield that prevents people from seeing the light of the gospel. Now imagine the Church in the city repenting of its share of sins and coming together as one body. Picture the Holy Spirit expressing the fullness of Christ in that Church. Now watch the sum of the believers piercing that shield of darkness by lifting up holy hands in which they carry the names and the needs of *all* the inhabitants of the city. Satan cannot stop them because his only active weapon is sin, and they have clothed themselves in holiness. Day and night the names of each one of the inhabitants is presented before God. What a turnaround for the Church! Satan's perimeter has been compromised and God's saints are marching on, raiding Satan's most cherished possessions: the souls of men.

How possible is this? Let us choose what could well be the darkest spiritual place in America: the San Francisco Bay Area. This is where the Church of Satan was founded; where witches and warlocks have legal status; where homosexuals and lesbians heavily influence government; where selfishness rules. Humanly speaking, the San Francisco Bay Area—home to six million people—seems to be beyond hope.

But is it hopeless? Not at all! There are already 4,400 Bible-believing congregations in the San Francisco Bay Area. You may say, "But what is that compared to 6,000,000 people?" Well, if each one of the 4,400 congregations were to plant 14 prayer cells—something that is entirely within the realm of possibility—and each one of those prayer cells were to intercede for 100 neighbors—which is the average number of people who live in one city block—then the Church in the Bay Area would be praying for 6,000,000 people by name *daily!*

The Church in the Bay Area is already strategically positioned to strike at the enemy. What is lacking for this to happen?

First, the Church must awaken to the fact that this is not an option, but a command. It is the explicit will of God that the Church pray for all men to be saved.

Second, the Church must repent of sin and do away with the wrath it has accumulated.

Third, the Church must deal with the issue of disunity by addressing the dissension that has kept Christians separated, causing the 4,400 congregations to act more as independently owned POW camps than as divisions of the same army responding to the directives of the same commander in chief. As on the day of Pentecost, they must come together in one accord (see Acts 1:14; 2:1).

Passion for the Lost

The three preceding considerations address the mechanics of how to pray for the lost in our city. However, in order to be able to do it effectively and persistently, we must have a passion for the lost. I am not talking about having a keen interest in the salvation of sinners. No! I am talking about an all-consuming *passion* for the lost ones. I am not talking about subscribing to a program to evangelize people. No! I am talking about a lifestyle through which we devote every ounce of our energy to winning the lost. If you lack this kind of passion, do not be discouraged. This is not something with which we are born, nor something that can be learned. It can neither be bought nor taught. It has to be imparted by the Holy Spirit. To receive this, we need to go to God in full repentance to plead for an impartation of His heartbeat for the lost.

In 2 Peter 3:9, we read that God is patient toward us (the believers), not willing that any (of the unbelievers) should perish, but that all should come to repentance. This passage, along with 1 Timothy 2:4-6, states in unequivocal terms that God's will is for all men to be saved. Of course, this does not necessarily mean that all men *will* be saved. That issue is a very complex one, but for the purpose of knowing how to pray according to the will of God, it should suffice that God's will is known: He wishes all men to be saved and none to perish. This is His will, and we must frame our prayers accordingly.

The day I became a Christian I was totally overwhelmed by the love of God. I could not fully grasp the fact that all my sins had been forgiven once and for all. The joy of the Lord was so tangible that the night I met Jesus I sat on my bed and tried not to fall asleep for fear that in the morning the joy would be gone. However, the next day the joy was still there, and it grew as the days went by. I shared Christ with everyone in my family and each one of my friends. In school, I stood up in class and told them about Jesus. When my teachers penalized me for it, I counted it a blessing. They needed to hear the gospel, and I was in a position to tell them. So I shared with them, "In season and out of season" (2 Tim. 4:2).

I was terribly afraid that one of my friends, family members or classmates would die and go to hell! I knew that God wanted all of them to be saved, and I wanted to please the One who had saved me. When one of my friends fell fatally ill, I barged into the room where he was confined, and I led him to Christ just hours before he died.

When I would see funeral processions go by, my heart ached at the possibility that the stranger whose body was on its way to the cemetery may already be suffering in hell. I never doubted for a moment that God wished all men to be saved and none to perish.

Unfortunately, after a while I became "theologically educated." I was introduced to speculative thinking that provided "reasons" for me not to share the gospel with the lost and still be comfortable. I became very articulate at explaining why the salvation of the lost was none of my business. After all, God had already predestined each and every one of those who eventually would be saved, and, consequently, He had predestined others to hell. In my theological labyrinth I even found a turn that led me to a comfortable place where I mused on the incorrectness of praying for the salvation of the lost. I thought salvation was an issue that belonged exclusively to God. I told myself, "Do not be presumptuous to the point of daring to tell God whom He should save." Soon my regular prayer vigils were replaced by "more productive activities."

Finally, the day came when I was able to go to a funeral or watch a funeral procession on its way to the cemetery without feeling any pang in my soul. When I would run across biblical passages such as 2 Peter 3:9 or 1 Timothy 2:3,4 that directly challenged my complacency by stating that God "desires all men to be saved," I quickly brushed them off. I would say to myself, "For now I see in a mirror dimly...now I know in part, but then I shall know fully....Don't let those verses bother you."

I had built pseudo-intellectual walls that blinded me to the biblical truth of God's love and passion for the lost. I had insulated those walls so as not to hear the cry of the perishing. All the paintings I hung on those walls depicted the beauty of my salvation. None of them showed the stark tragedy of sinners' eternal separation and torment.

Occasionally, I would revel in the intellectual fabric of my egotistical convictions. However, my heart was dry. Where a

wellspring of joy used to be, now parched soil was quickly turning to dust. My soul, once so lush and alive, was becoming deso-
late. Deep down, my misery began to spiral up to the point that
I was unable to ignore it any longer. I began to reminisce about
the freshness of my now lost first love when only one thing was

---

IF YOU WANT TO REACH YOUR CITY FOR CHRIST, YOU MUST CATCH GOD'S HEARTBEAT FOR THE LOST.

---

certain: God's presence. Everything else was a question mark, but
I didn't care. God was with me and that was enough. He was all
I needed. What a contrast to where I found myself now. Now I
had an answer for every question, or so I thought, but God's presence was nowhere to be found.

At this time in my life, 2 Peter 3:9 hit me like a two-by-four
right between my eyes. The expressions "not wishing for any to
perish...all to come to repentance" struck me time and again
until I fell on my knees and cried out to God for a baptism of
compassion for the lost. As I repented of my spiritual complacency, God's grace washed away the apathy. As I sang, "Cause me
to come, to thy river, O Lord, cause me to drink, of your river, O
Lord, cause me to live, by your river, O Lord," God's love flooded my soul and restored the joy of my salvation.

Catching God's Heartbeat

If you want to reach your city for Christ, you must catch God's heartbeat for the lost. The best way I know to illustrate this is by sharing with you one of my childhood experiences.

When I was growing up in Argentina, "siesta" time was mandatory. Every human being *had* to take a nap. For us children, this was cruel and unusual punishment. Nap time was when the whole town belonged to us. Every grownup was lying down, and we kids had the unrestricted run of the place.

My friends and I successfully conspired to sneak out of our bedrooms as soon as we heard the "all clear" signal marked by the rhythmic snoring of the adults. However, one day my father, a strict disciplinarian, finally caught me. In no uncertain terms he commanded, "From now on you are to nap in my room, on my bed, next to me. Understood?"

"Yes, sir!" I replied.

From that day on I was subjected to a two-hour daily torture; that's how long nap time lasted. In order to kill time I made up mental games. I imagined that cracks in the ceiling were rivers, spots were cities, moldings were mountains. So I constructed my imaginary maps of the world. When I saw two flies, I named one Jose and the other Maria. I would imagine that they went on dates. When a third, smaller fly appeared, I said, "They got married and had a baby!" Anything to kill time!

After a while, my father's breathing would become rhythmic, clearly signaling that he was in sleepland. However, the moment I saw him horizontal and with his eyes closed, I was driven to slowly and carefully crawl toward him. Once I was next to him, I would put my head on his chest and listen to his heartbeat. What I did not know at the time is that because both my mom and dad had lost one of their parents in childhood, I was controlled by a subconscious fear of losing one of them. Seeing my father with his eyes closed always triggered that fear. As I leaned my ear on his chest, his heartbeat reassured me emotionally. I even put lyrics to his heartbeat. "I love you, son. I won't die." Over and over. Oh, how good it felt!

Right now I want to invite you to lean your ear on God's chest and listen to His heartbeat right now. Listen carefully and you will hear two sounds: none...all. None to perish. All to come to repentance. Continue to listen until His heartbeat becomes your heartbeat, until you see all of your unsaved relatives, friends, neighbors and coworkers in the monitor of your soul. As their names and faces come up, listen to God say, "None to perish...all to come to repentance." Listen long enough until your man-made intellectual fortress of self-serving theological excuses crumble. Stay put until God's love for the lost floods your heart, rises to your mind and completely renews it.

Yes, catch God's heartbeat! Now move out of the circle of your relatives, friends and neighbors. Let God show you your city, each and every one of its inhabitants. Listen to God's heartbeat for your city: "None to perish...all to come to repentance." Let the rhythm and the melody of His heartbeat completely envelop you, totally flood you, absolutley overwhelm you until you find yourself swimming in the ocean of His love for the lost—until your soul cries out with everything within it, "Lord, give me this city or I'll die!"

Note
1. Kenneth S. Wuest, *Commentary on the Pastoral Epistles* (Grand Rapids, MI: William B. Eerdman's Publishing Co., 1983), p. 45.

3

The Battleground Is the Heavenly Places

PRINCIPLE: In order to take the gospel to every creature, the Church is called to engage the forces of evil. The battleground is the heavenly places. This is where the battle for our cities is won or lost.

PICTURE FOR A MOMENT THE BEST COMMANDO IN THE WORLD. THE top experts have trained him in tactics, strategy, martial arts and survival. The equipment he carries is state of the art. In his possession are some of the most sophisticated miniature electronic devices available. Nothing but the very best makes up his arsenal of weapons and equipment. His mind has been enriched beyond measure by the assimilation of the most critical information needed to carry out his mission. He is the closest thing to a human supercomputer to ever walk this earth. Thousands of hours and millions of dollars have gone into making him the most effective fighter in the world.

Watch him now on his last day in town in a Third World country. Tomorrow he will travel to the war zone, but today he is relaxed, enjoying a drink in a busy sidewalk cafe. It is hard not to be relaxed while sitting in the shade of lazily swaying palm trees, caressed by the balmy breeze blowing from the nearby ocean. Surrounded as he is by friendly faces, it is even harder for him to believe there is a war going on right now. Everything is enjoyable around him, and he is determined to relish every moment of it.

Traffic is heavy at this time of the day, and many vehicles crowd the street. A motorcycle peels off from the colorful caravan of cars whose ages span from early Model T Fords to the latest Cadillacs. The driver of the motorcycle slows down as he draws near to the sidewalk cafe where the commando is enjoying himself. All of a sudden a gun goes off and the commando goes down, a bullet through his head. A young guerrilla fighter, dressed in rags and educated with little more than elementary-level schooling, has disposed forever of the best human fighting machine in the world. Thousands of hours' worth of training and millions of dollars worth of equipment lie wasted in a pool of blood caused by a 5¢ bullet. He is dead—not on account of what he knew, but what he did *not* know.

The principle: In active warfare, the most critical information is not what you know, but what you *don't* know. Especially if your enemy knows that you don't know it. The corollary of this principle is that it is fatal to step into a war zone unawares. The worst mistake in war is to not know where the battleground is located.

In order to reach our cities for Christ, the Church must engage and defeat the occupying army of demons under Satan's command who are blinding the lost to the light of the gospel (see 2 Cor. 4:4; 10:4,5; Eph. 6:12). This means warfare, spiritual warfare. Revelation 12:11 paints a picture of how victory will be won: "And they overcame him because of the blood of the Lamb and because of the word of their testimony, and they did not love their life even to death." Where is the battleground where the Church must engage Satan and his demons?

Costly Ignorance

If we are planning to reach our city for Christ, we must know at all times where the battleground is. Often, Christians become

---

THE CHURCH TODAY IS DANGEROUSLY IGNORANT OF THE SCHEMES OF THE DEVIL. SOME PEOPLE MAKE IT A POINT OF PRIDE NOT TO KNOW MUCH ABOUT THE DEVIL AND HIS DEVICES, AND HAUGHTILY DECLARE THAT THEY WILL FOCUS ON JESUS AND FORGET THE DEVIL.

---

war casualties when they least expect it, and in places where they sincerely believe they are out of danger. This is why so many Christians have been seriously wounded in the safest of all places, such as in church, at home, or while fellowshipping with other believers. To them, the battlefield was somewhere else, most likely on the mission field, thousands of miles away. Or, they think, perhaps the closest battlefield would be in the so-called inner city, usually among the ethnic ghettos, where pimps, drug dealers and gangs struggle for survival. In those awful places, yes! Closer to home? Never! What a dangerous miscalculation!

Our real enemy is Satan. He uses the flesh and the world to seduce us, but he is the source of that seduction (see Eph. 2:1-3). He is the master of deception (see John 8:44). He is the inventor of spiritual guerrilla warfare (see 2 Cor. 2:10,11). Lacking real authority to defeat us, he has compensated by perfecting the art of subversion and trickery (see 2 Tim. 2:25,26). He has more than made up for his limitations by developing deceptive schemes of all sorts (see Eph. 6:11). The success of those schemes always depends on one thing: the ignorance of the saints, which he actively promotes (see 2 Cor. 2:11; 11:3).

Generally speaking, the Church today is dangerously igno-rant of the schemes of the devil. In fact, some people make it a point of pride *not* to know much about the devil and his devices. They haughtily declare that they will focus exclusively on Jesus and forget the devil. In contrast, the apostle Paul boldly stated, "For we are not ignorant of his [Satan's] schemes" (2 Cor. 2:11). Paul, the man entrusted with the richest spiritual revelations concerning the Trinity and the redemptive work of Christ, also made it a point to know what Satan was up to. Some people seem to have rewritten James 4:7 to say, "*Ignore* the devil and he will flee from you," instead of "*Resist* the devil and he will flee from you."

"The Heavenlies" Here and Now

Nowhere is this ignorance more damaging than in the reality and the location of the spiritual battleground: "the heavenly places," or as the Greek literally says, "in the heavenlies" (Eph. 3:10). The average church member in the Western world has no idea what this expression really means. It is used five times by the apostle Paul in his epistle to the Ephesians. Therefore, it must be an important, foundational component of God's revelation concerning spiritual warfare. Yet, somehow we seem to have no clue what it really means. Because of our ignorance on this important point, we are vulnerable to the enemy's deceptive schemes against us. The devil knows this and uses it to neutralize—and in many cases, eliminate—our effectiveness in Christ, in spite of everything else we may know about Christ!

What are "the heavenlies"? When believers in Ephesus read or heard the term "the heavenlies" in Paul's epistle, they evidently understood what the apostle meant. There was no need for them to pause to do a word study, nor to engage the services of a local scholar at the nearby synagogue to decipher the meaning of this expression. Today, however, we are at a great disadvantage. The passage of time, along with the dramatic cultural and religious differences between us and the world of Paul and his contemporaries, have conspired to cloud our understanding of the subject.

To put into perspective the difficulty the average Christian in the Western world has in grasping this concept, imagine that you have lived in Mexico City all your life. You are familiar with smog and everything associated with it, such as itchy eyes, irritated nose and smog alerts. Now picture yourself in the village of Thule in the northernmost part of Greenland, above the Arctic Circle, trying to explain to a native what smog is all about. How would you do it? There is nothing in that remote, unpopulated part of the world capable of providing a suitable frame of reference to understand it. Nor is there anything in the mind of the native that may enable him to relate to this new concept. You show him a picture of downtown Mexico City on a bad day, with a brownish cloud all over the city, and you say to him, "This is what smog looks like."

To this he may reply, "How long does it stay there? One minute? Five minutes?"

"No! It stays there forever," you say.

Now he is perplexed as he compares the brownish cloud with the pristine air all around him, and he asks, "How long do people breathe it? They could do it for more than a few minutes, right?" When you tell him that people breathe it day and night, 24 hours a day, he cannot believe it.

We all understand that it is nearly impossible to explain something new to someone who has no frame of reference in which to fit the new concept. This is what usually happens to us in the Western world with the notion of "the heavenlies." For example, the average Westerner has serious difficulty accepting the fact that demons and angels are active and present in *our* world. It is even harder to believe that any interaction can take place between the natural and the supernatural realms. Even though he admits he doesn't fully understand what Jesus meant when he said, "Whatever you shall bind on earth shall be bound in heaven" (Matt. 18:18), he has already concluded that it cannot mean what the text literally says. For Christians in the West, Paul's teaching that we, the Church, are seated with Christ "in the heavenly places" (Eph. 2:6) and that "the manifold wisdom of God might now be made known through the church to the rulers and authorities in the heavenly places" (Eph. 3:10) is closer to a figure of speech or to a poetic style than to plain gospel truth.

However, when Christians in Ephesus read in Paul's epistle the term "in the heavenlies," they knew it referred to the spiritual realm where angels, demons and even we—the Church—operate. When they heard the admonition that our struggle is not against flesh and blood, but against principalities and powers, they knew it was a direct reference to spiritual powers that existed and operated *in the same sphere* in which the Church did. Otherwise, the command to stand firm against those forces of wickedness "in the heavenlies" would have been meaningless. "The heavenlies" is a concept totally familiar to the Early Church. Because that is where the warfare takes place (see Eph. 6:12), we had better become thoroughly acquainted with it ourselves. Otherwise, everything we know may become invalidated because of what we don't know regarding this cosmic battleground on which we are expected to face and defeat the master of deception: Satan (see Rev. 12:11).

It is understandable why Western Christians have difficulty with the expression "in the heavenlies." When we think of heaven, we either think of a faraway realm where God sits enthroned, or we think of the believer's future eternal home with God in heaven. This is exactly the opposite picture from what the apostle Paul is teaching in Ephesians. Though the literal translation of these words is indeed "in the heavenlies," the best functional translation would probably be "in the spirit realm."[1]

Commentators have wrestled for centuries to more fully understand Paul's view of "the heavenlies." I do not profess to be a biblical scholar; I am a Christian practitioner. Thus, I humbly offer an explanation that I believe is biblical and has also been confirmed by years of experience with the spirit world.

The Darkness of the Enlightenment

Another reason we have difficulty understanding "the heavenlies" as the spirit realm is the impact the Enlightenment of the eighteenth century has had on Western culture. This devastating secular movement removed every reference to the supernatural from the "scientific" lexicon. The axiom seemed to be, "If you can't prove its existence scientifically, it doesn't exist." The Church in the West was not immune to the onslaught of the Enlightenment, and some of it was incorporated into its theological presuppositions. This, in turn, was carried to the four corners of the earth by the Western missionary movement of the eighteenth through the twentieth centuries.

In this context, it is interesting to note that the greatest growth of Christianity in the Third World has occurred where the cultural and theological dominance of the Church in the West has been replaced by the indigenous Church's own cultural and theological initiatives and worldview. It is equally interesting that the Church in the West has remained suspicious of these indigenous movements, and in many cases has rejected the genuineness of the mass conversions on suspicion of religious syncretism.

However, if we track on a world map the "hot spots" where the Church is growing rapidly today, we will find that in each one of those areas, such as Korea, China, Guatemala, Nigeria or Argentina, the national churches have an understanding of the heavenlies, or the spirit realm, quite different than the one historically held by the Church in the West.

The GI Bill Fallout

Another reason for our difficulties in understanding the spirit world can be connected to the indirect impact of the GI Bill on the Church in the United States. The GI Bill was an act of Congress that made federal money available for college education to those who had served in the U.S. Armed Forces. Theological and religious institutions were included as options. The traditional evangelical seminaries and Bible schools had already embraced a theology that excluded several of the more controversial power gifts. Along with this, was the view that casting out demons belonged more to the Apostolic Age or to pioneer missionary ministry among spirit worshipers. In countries with a strong Church, demons were not usually in evidence. Thus the influence of the Enlightenment was already in evidence in their theological presuppositions.

With the advent of government-financed "Christian" education under the GI Bill, most Christian theological institutions felt they must "upgrade" their curriculum by bringing in more courses in the social sciences. As a result, the secularizing influences originating out of the Enlightenment made even greater inroads into these Christian training institutions. It became even harder to understand the biblical worldview of the spirit realm. Thus, thousands of graduates entered our churches and mission fields basically ignorant of the activity of the spirit world on earth and "in the heavenlies."

Satan gained a decisive advantage in his struggle against the Church because of the Church's growing ignorance of the spirit world. Besides, how long can a hungry fox and a mother hen and her chicks live together? Like the commando described at the beginning of this chapter, the Church, especially in the West, has been partially neutralized. In spite of enjoying powerful means of communication, sophisticated teaching tools, political freedom, financial backing and the largest pool of talent ever assembled, it has failed to reach the world for Christ. Worse yet, in many countries the Church is losing ground, with more churches being closed than those being planted. Like the U.S. Pacific fleet anchored at Pearl Harbor on December 7, 1941, the Church in the West today presents too easy a target for Satan. We do not believe we are at war. We do not know where the battleground is located, and, in spite of the might of our weapons, they are neither loaded nor aimed at the right target. We are unaware of how vulnerable we are. We are better fitted for a parade than for an amphibious landing!

Ephesians: A Road Map of the Heavenlies

We need to expose and destroy Satan's scheme with the truth of God's Word. A good way to start is by taking a close look at the book of Ephesians.

I have chosen Ephesians for three major reasons.

One, it is *the handbook* on spiritual warfare of the New Testament. It contains more power words connected to warfare in "the heavenlies" than any other book in the Bible. That is probably because it was written to a church where the new believers needed special help in combating and penetrating the world of evil supernaturalism that dominated Hellenistic and Ephesian society.

Second, I have chosen Ephesians because it is a favorite of both traditional evangelicals and charismatics. Because unity is essential for effective evangelism, a solid middle ground must be found on which Christians can walk and work together. Traditional evangelicals consider Ephesians the finest grain of wood from which to carve out the doctrine of the Church because the epistle dwells heavily on the nature and the function of the Church. It is also a favorite with Pentecostals and charismatics, especially chapter 6, which includes extensive teaching regarding God's armor, and also direct references to spiritual warfare.

Finally, this epistle was addressed to a church *that succeeded in reaching an entire city for Christ.* It was an accomplishment that took place in the context of open, tangible, dramatic spiritual warfare under the watchful eye of Paul, the theologian, assuring us that no violation of essential doctrine would take place (see Acts 19:11-20; Eph. 6:10-20). Much of the contemporary talk about city taking, territorial spirits, spiritual warfare and so on, is based on Paul's teachings in this epistle.

God's Dilemma

In chapter 2 of Ephesians, Paul describes a sinister character whom he calls "the prince of the power of the air" (Eph. 2:2). Before Christ's death and resurrection, this princely being had a jurisdiction, or authority to govern, in the heavenly places. He is called a "prince"—which describes his rank—"of the power of the air"—which explains his area of domain.

Paul's teachings in Ephesians about the believer's and the Church's warfare with Satan, and "the powers" (or demons') hierarchy, is complex and confusing for those of us who live in a totally different sociocultural-spiritual context. I will attempt to simplify the subject by using word pictures with diagrams; their weakness is that they are too literal. They attempt to describe invisible actions and beings using human word pictures and diagrams. Their strength is that they can help us visualize the invisible so we can understand what has occurred and is occurring "in the heavenlies."

The Cosmic Grave

The center of Satan's jurisdiction appears to be what I call a "cosmic grave," in which every human being ever born (with the exception of Jesus Christ) has been entombed.

All who live outside of Christ are dead and entombed. Instead of dirt, Satan uses sins and trespasses to bury his captives, who are described as "children of wrath" (Eph. 2:3). They are all dead in their "trespasses and sins" (Eph. 2:1 [see Diagram 1]).

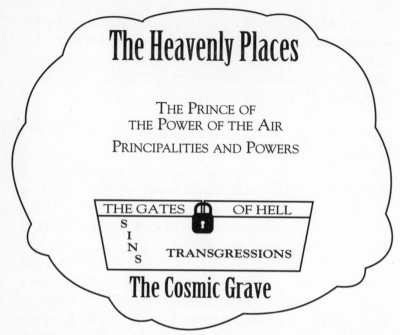

The Heavenly Places

THE PRINCE OF
THE POWER OF THE AIR

PRINCIPALITIES AND POWERS

THE GATES   OF HELL

S
I
N
S   TRANSGRESSIONS

The Cosmic Grave

"*And you were dead in your trespasses and sins, in which you formerly walked according to the course of this world, according to the prince of the power of the air, of the spirit that is now working in the sons of disobedience*" (Eph. 2:1, 2).

DIAGRAM 1

Drawing from other passages in the Bible, it is safe to assume that "the gates of hell" (Matt. 16:18, *KJV*), which I reinterpret to fit my word picture, kept a tight lid on this cosmic grave, and that prior to Jesus' resurrection, the padlock of death kept those gates secured (see Heb. 2:14,15; Rev. 1:18). The whole picture is the epitome of despair—scores of people eternally buried, rotting in their own sins and trespasses, and programmed to follow the course of an evil master.

However, God loves that lost world (see John 3:16). The specific focus of His love is on the masses of humanity suffering in that cosmic grave under the dictatorship of the "prince of the power of the air." In fact, God loves them so much that He is willing to pay the highest price—the life, the death, the blood of His Son (see John 3:16,17; 1 John 4:9).

God's interest in lost sinners presents Him with a twofold dilemma.

First, how can He, a holy God, bring to Himself sinners—children of wrath and disobedience—who are programmed to follow this evil prince?

Second, how can He rescue them from a cosmic grave that is *legally* under someone else's jurisdiction?

God has the power to do it, but His power never violates the holiness of His character. Prior to Jesus' death, if God would have intervened directly, Satan could have accused God of trespassing because the kingdom of the earth and its glory had been given to him, "And the devil said to Him, 'I will give You all this domain and its glory; for it has been handed over to me, and I give it to whomever I wish'" (Luke 4:6).

Cosmic Checkmate

The answer to this dilemma is found in what unfolds alongside each mention of "the heavenlies" in the rest of the epistle of Ephesians. Five times the term "heavenly places" is used in Ephesians. The first time it has to do with the Father (see Eph. 1:3), the second time with Jesus (see Eph. 1:20,21), the third with the Church (see Eph. 2:6), the fourth with the principalities and powers (see Eph. 3:10), and the last time with the struggle between the Church and those principalities and powers (see Eph. 6:10-12).

If we imagine the conflict between God and the devil for the salvation of man in terms of a chess game, each one of the five references to "the heavenly places" mentioned represents a move by God that eventually leads to cosmic checkmate. Checkmate is from a Persian word meaning "to trap a ruler so that he cannot escape." It is used in the game of chess to trap the opponent king and thus win the game.

First Move:

God seeded the heavenly places with all kinds of spiritual blessings for the benefit of the captives in anticipation of their liberation (see Diagram 2).

"Blessed be the God and Father of our Lord Jesus Christ, who has blessed us with every spiritual blessing in the heavenly places in Christ" (Eph. 1:3).

DIAGRAM 2

God seeded the formerly dark heavenlies with the bright lights and spiritual blessings He prepared "before the foundation of the world" (Eph. 1:4) for those who would believe in Christ. We could say that, like seeds buried in the ground under the winter snow, God's blessings for the Church-to-be were scattered all over the heavenly places "before the foundation of the world" in anticipation of the rising of the "Sun" of Justice, who would thaw the ground and cause those seeds to sprout. Unknown to Satan, his kingdom had already been invaded in the eternal, sovereign plan of God.

Second Move:

God applied a one-two punch by sending Jesus first to the lowest parts of Satan's kingdom (see Eph. 4:9) and then raising Jesus to the highest place in the heavenly places (see Eph. 4:8; 1:18-22 [see Diagram 3]).

Speaking figuratively, the first punch deposited Jesus' feet at the bottom of the grave and confined the prince of the power of the air, along with his principalities and powers, under the feet of Jesus (see Eph. 1:22; 1 Pet. 3:22). The second punch placed Jesus in the highest possible place in the heavenly places—at the right hand of God—and established Him as head of the Church (see Eph. 1:18-22). Also, on the way out of the grave, Jesus took with Him the keys of Hades and death, thus eliminating the effectiveness of the padlock that formerly secured the gates of hell as shown in Diagram 1 (see Eph. 4:8; Heb. 2:14,15; Rev. 1:18).

What do we see as a result of God's one-two punch? Figuratively speaking, Jesus' feet are in the lowest part of the heavenly places and His head in the highest. His head and His feet are in position, so to speak. What is still missing? His body. This leads us to the third move described in Ephesians 2:6-10.

"What does it mean except that He also had descended into the lower parts of the earth? I pray that the eyes of your heart may be enlightened, so that you may know what is the hope of His calling, what are the riches of the glory of His inheritance in the saints, and what is the surpassing greatness of His power toward us who believe. These are in accordance with the working of the strength of His might which He brought about in Christ, when He raised Him from the dead, and seated Him at His right hand in the heavenly places, far above all rule and authority and power and dominion, and every name that is named, not only in this age, but also in the one to come. And He put all things in subjection under His feet, and gave Him as head over all things to the church" (Eph. 4:9; 1:18-22).

DIAGRAM 3

Third Move:

Figuratively speaking, God now proceeded to effect the largest transfer of "building material" in the entire history of the universe. He did it by moving human beings (sinners) from Satan's grave into the heavenly places, where He seated them (as saints) there with Jesus (see Eph. 2:6). The now vulnerable and unsecured gates of hell could not prevail against God's command (see

"And He put all things in subjection under His feet, and gave Him as head over all things to the church, which is His body, the fulness of Him who fills all in all....And raised us up with Him, and seated us with Him in the heavenly places, in Christ Jesus" (Eph. 1:22,23; 2:6).

DIAGRAM 4

Matt. 16:18). From among those whom He transferred, Paul later tells us that He appointed some to be apostles, some to be prophets, others to be evangelists and still others pastor-teachers (see Eph. 4:11). He did this for the purpose of building up the Body of Christ until it has reached the full measure of Christ (see Eph. 4:11-16). Filling the "all in all" mentioned in Ephesians 1:23 reflects the fullness of Christ in the Church as it occupies the heavenlies, thus displacing the prince of the power of the air and his underlings from their control in the heavenlies. They are now confined in subjection under Jesus' feet (see Eph. 1:22). This is a powerful metaphor of Christ's absolute lordship over all things visible and invisible (see Diagram 4).

Now the picture is complete, showing Jesus' feet at the lowest part of what used to be Satan's domain, His head at the highest part, and His body—the Church—in between those two.

Fourth Move:

God established the Church in the heavenly places as both an example and a witness to the principalities and powers. God did this "in order that the manifold wisdom of God might now be made known through the church to the rulers and the authorities in the heavenly places" (Eph. 3:10 [see Diagram 5]).

The Church is an example to the principalities and powers. An example of what? Of God's grace, a major theme of Ephesians (see Eph. 1:2,6,7; 2:5,7,8; 3:2,7,8; 4:7,29; 6:24). Grace is something Satan cannot relate to because he is absolutely outside of its scope. When Jesus was hanging on the cross, Satan was relying on the letter of the law for a technical victory. He knew he could not touch Jesus Himself on account of His sinlessness, but he was counting on being able to continue to keep mankind inside his cosmic grave on account of its sinfulness. To this effect, he was using the "act of the decrees"—the law of God that mankind had violated—as his claim of authority over his cap-

"In order that the manifold wisdom of God might now be made known through the church to the rulers and the authorities in the heavenly places" (Eph. 3:10).

DIAGRAM 5

---

tives (see Col. 2:15). He was counting on the fact that God's law declared that the soul that sins must also die (see Ezek. 18:4).

However, Satan overlooked a mystery that was hidden in Christ, a mystery called "grace" that came to light when Jesus' body was pierced. Grace allows God to grant unmerited favor without violating His holiness on account of Christ's expiatory sacrifice. When Christ's body was lanced and His blood shed, a new dispensation began: the dispensation of grace. In absolute perplexity, Satan watched Jesus open a new way of access for man to the Father, not on the basis of man's own righteousness, but on the righteousness of Christ imputed to them. Now God has put men and women, saved by grace, on display in the heavenly places as an example of that grace to Satan and his underlings.

God's strategy consisted of sending Jesus on a rescue mission to set the captives free and then to turn them into well-trained soldiers to fight their former master for the souls of those still held captive. The Church, made up of the redeemed now turned spiritual commandos, is built on the rock of Jesus Christ, the one who redeemed them, the Son of the living God. Against this combination "the gates of hell shall not prevail" (Matt. 16:18, KJV).

Finally, according to Ephesians 3:10, the Church has an active role of making known to the rulers and authorities in the heavenlies the manifold wisdom of God. The manifold wisdom of God is what we have just discovered—God's plan of salvation through the grace of Christ. The Church makes it known both by its example and also through the word of its testimony spoken into the spirit world, declaring to the powers their defeat by Christ and our authority in His name to claim lost souls for the kingdom of God.[2]

Fifth Move:

Ephesians 6:12 says, "For our struggle is not against flesh and blood, but against the rulers, against the authorities, against the powers of this dark world and against the spiritual forces of evil in the heavenly realms" (NIV).

In four moves God has deprived Satan of his rightful control of the heavenlies. By making Christ the "fullness of all in all" in the Church as it occupies the heavenly places, God has displaced Satan and his hosts and confined them under the feet of Jesus.

The Church has now been placed as *potentially* in control of the heavenly places once ruled by the prince of the power of the air.

But the Church must engage and defeat the enemy to retake the heavenlies in the name of her Lord, so that the eyes of those still being held captive by Satan will be opened. Though Satan and his evil powers have already been defeated by Christ, they have not yet been abolished (e.g., cast into the lake of fire). They are allowed to hold mankind captive until God's liberating army, the Church, invades Satan's kingdom, rescuing men and women from bondage. This is the warfare so vividly described by Paul in Ephesians 6:10-20. Even though the focus of Ephesians 6:10-18 is usually interpreted as more defensive than offensive, this warfare is both *defensive* and *offensive* as we will soon see.

We are to stand firm against the schemes of our enemy (see Eph. 6:10-14a) because Satan attacks the Church now seated with Christ in the heavenlies (see Eph. 2:6). How does he do it? To answer this question, we must understand that in this picture of the Church in the heavenlies there are two constants and one variable (see Diagram 6).

The first constant is Jesus' position of authority over Satan and his demons. They are under His feet, and He is far above them and every name of this age and of the age to come. This can never change. In fact, the expression "far above" used in Ephesians 1:21 in the Greek implies that Jesus is so high in the heavenlies that it is absolutely impossible for his enemies to bridge that gap.

The other constant is Jesus' position of authority at the right hand of God in the highest point of the heavenly places. Nothing can ever alter that. He is there waiting until all His enemies are finally placed as a footstool under His feet. Paul declares elsewhere that He is also there to intercede for the Church (see Acts 2:34,35; 1 Cor. 15:25-28; Heb. 1:13; 10:13).

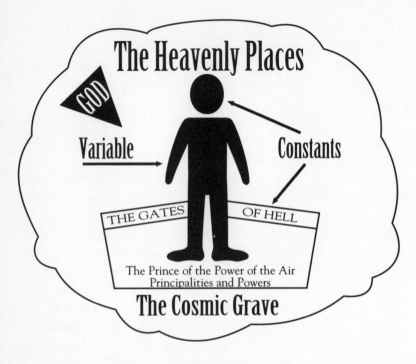

The Heavenly Places

GOD

Variable

Constants

THE GATES   OF HELL

The Prince of the Power of the Air
Principalities and Powers

The Cosmic Grave

DIAGRAM 6

The only variable is the position of the Church vis-à-vis the demonic forces, as it confronts Satan and his "forces of wickedness in the heavenly places" (Eph. 6:12).

Satan cannot challenge Jesus' authority over him and thus he must remain under His feet. Likewise, he cannot question God's decision to place Jesus in the highest place, interceding for the Church. So what option is left open to him? To challenge the position of the Church in the heavenly places, since the Church has been set up as an example and a witness to him and his hosts (see Eph. 3:10). This is where Satan concentrates his attack—on the only variable element in the equation. Why would Jesus constantly intercede before God for the Church unless such intercession is directly related to the Church's struggle against Satan? God the Father does not need Jesus to remind Him of what His shed blood accomplished. Jesus' intercession has to do with the warfare between the Church and Satan.

Satan's Counterattack

The battle lines have been drawn. What is Satan's strategy? Since he was dispossessed of authority by Jesus and confined under His feet by God, he needs a place to stand over, a jurisdiction over which he can exercise authority. He cannot go to Jesus for this, since Jesus stripped him of his weapons and made a public spectacle of his army, "Having canceled out the certificate of debt consisting of decrees against us and which was hostile to us; and He has taken it out of the way, having nailed it to the cross. When He had disarmed the rulers and authorities, He made a public display of them, having triumphed over them through Him" (Col. 2:14,15).

Satan's only option is to try to deceive the Church, God's agent on earth, into yielding to him what has been entrusted to her care by God, much like what he did to Eve, and then Adam, in the garden. This is why the Church is exhorted to put on the full armor of God and "to stand firm against the schemes of the devil" (Eph. 6:11). Satan has no power; this is why he must resort to deception in order to obtain that which he has no right to. The Church, which is the target of this scheme, is never told by Satan the whole truth regarding the proposed transaction. This is Satan's usual approach. For instance, when Eve ate the forbidden fruit, she thought she was doing something innocuous, when in reality she was initiating a process that would eventually transfer the dominion of the earth to her Master's enemy. This is why

Satan has chosen another seemingly innocuous weapon to use against the Church.

What is Satan's weapon? Anger. The anger that Paul refers to in Ephesians 4:26 is not Satan's anger, but that of Christians, primarily directed at each other. In Ephesians 4:26,27, Paul warns

---

BY INSERTING THE OLD DISKETTE
WHERE THE NEW ONE SHOULD BE,
SATAN IS ABLE TO USE GOD'S HARDWARE
TO PRINT HIS PROGRAM ON GOD'S PAPER.
WHAT A CLEVER SCHEME!

---

believers not to let the sun go down on their anger and thus "give the devil an opportunity."

Paul does not say not to get angry. He says when you are angry, do not sleep on it. Deal with it immediately. Apply grace and so eliminate the source of your anger. Anger, like the desire that drove Eve to eat the forbidden fruit, is a normal emotion. Because anger touches us so much and so often, we fail to see— like Eve in the garden—that what appears like a minor problem can, in reality, be a major scheme of Satan that has terrible and eternal consequences.

The word "opportunity" is used here as a place or region. It is the Greek word *topos* from which we get our English word "topography." It can also be translated "office," suggesting an area of jurisdiction. A jurisdiction is a sphere of influence entrusted to someone. What Paul is saying is, "Do not fail to forgive those that hurt you lest you create an area of jurisdiction for the devil to have authority over." This is the jurisdiction that Satan so desperately needs in order to do war against the Church. In the context of Ephesians, that jurisdiction is located in the heavenlies.

As soon as such a jurisdiction is created, Satan and his demons are able to invade the heavenly places from where they had been previously displaced. They are able to do this because Christians, through unresolved anger, deny the validity of the example described in Ephesians 3:9,10 by depriving each other of grace. Instead of forgiving, they choose to make the offender pay for the offense. When Christians fail to forgive their offenders, in reality, they are withholding grace from them. Since Christians are set in the heavenlies as a testimony and an example of God's grace to the rulers and authorities, when they deny grace to each other they invalidate their testimony. They are no longer an example. The new life is not in evidence, but the old self is. They behave like the children of wrath and disobedience they once were when Satan ruled unimpeded over them. In essence, Christians have reverted to the old pattern used by Satan to control their behavior inside the cosmic grave. By inserting the old diskette where the new one should be, Satan is able to use God's hardware to print his program on God's paper. What a clever scheme (see Diagram 7)!

When we connect the unresolved anger mentioned in Ephesians 4:27 with the resulting grieving of the Holy Spirit described in Ephesians 4:30, we immediately see a highly destructive combination. These two elements allow the devil and his forces of wickedness to move into jurisdictions in the heavenly places created by our disobedience. Because Satan cannot challenge Jesus' authority, he then challenges the Church in the realm of delegated authority. In essence, it is a repeat of what he did in the Garden of Eden.

Basically, these are the only two moves available to the devil

The Heavenly Places

GOD

Principalities and Powers

Principalities and Powers

Principalities and Powers

THE GATES   OF HELL

The Prince of the Power of the Air
Principalities and Powers

The Cosmic Grave

"And do not give the devil an opportunity" (Eph. 4:27).

DIAGRAM 7

to orchestrate a counterattack: Christians, angry at each other, no longer walk in the light and, therefore, fellowship is broken. This, in turn, prevents the blood of Jesus from cleansing them from all unrighteousness (see 1 John 1:7). Because of those sins, the Holy Spirit is grieved and the fullness of Christ in the Church as it sits in the heavenly places becomes compromised.

It is reasonable to assume that as the fullness of Christ—expressed by the Church—decreases, the influence of the prince of the power of the air increases in the heavenly places. That is why, when Satan has the upper hand in a city, we always find a

Church that is deeply divided with members, congregations and denominations angry at each other.

Consequently, it is futile to try to win a city for Christ without first resolving the anger expressed in divisions among Christians in that city. Paul stated this in 1 Timothy 2:8 when he listed the need to eliminate wrath and dissension as a prerequisite to reach all men through prayer evangelism. Jesus stated clearly in John 17:21 that the unity of the Church is essential for the world to believe. The battleground is the heavenly places. That is where we must stand firm against the schemes of the devil. If we have already succumbed to his scheme, we must void the jurisdiction we created for him to have authority and immediately retake the lost ground.

The Trigger

What is it that causes so much anger among Christians? Without doubt, it is most often something that is said. The trigger that fires this kind of anger, as described in Ephesians 4:26,27, is what Paul calls "unwholesome words" in Ephesians 4:29: "Let no unwholesome word proceed from your mouth, but only such a word as is good for edification according to the need of the moment, that it may give grace to those who hear." This trigger—unwholesome words—is so subtle and so well disguised that it amounts to a state-of-the-art scheme. In many ways, we have come to believe that words are of little consequence. We may say "talk is cheap," but every major relational tragedy is set in motion by unwholesome words. Those words, like a tsunami taking place undetected in the deepest part of the ocean, trigger a chain of events that eventually destroy the effectiveness of our stand against Satan (see Diagram 8).

What is the definition for unwholesome words? According to this verse, it is that which tears down rather than builds up—

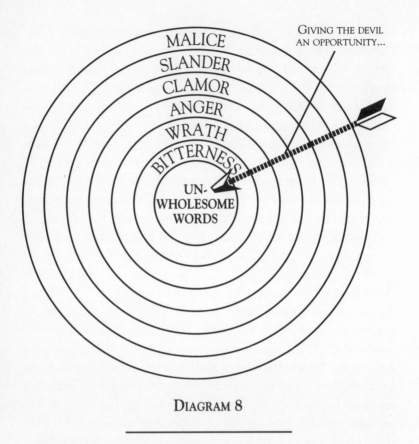

DIAGRAM 8

---

truth without grace. It is telling the truth devoid of "edification according to the need of the moment" (Eph. 4:29). To do so is more cruel than choosing not to meet the need at hand. It is definitely far worse than that. It is making sure that the need is highlighted by the raw edge of truth and then made more painfully evident by withholding the grace needed to meet such need. The object is clear: to tear down. In so doing, we become Exhibit A for the accuser of the brethren (see Rev. 12:10).

We are more easily offended by the truth than by lies. If someone says something false about us, it hurts us, but somehow we are able to sleep in peace because we know, deep down, that there is no substance to it. However, when someone says something critical that we know is true—partially or totally true—it makes us angry and takes away our sleep. We feel judged and condemned because somebody has voiced something that may still be true, but was spoken without grace. It may be something with which we desperately need to deal, a weak point where we need to change, something we have continually tried to suppress in light of our inability to correct it. But telling the naked truth without grace is tantamount to passing judgment.

Truth without grace is devastating. For instance, if you remove God's grace from my life, all that is left is a wretched sinner. I do not want to face that kind of naked truth. Likewise, truth without grace can be enslaving. For instance, in Matthew 18:18 we are told in a context of broken relationships, "Whatever you shall bind on earth shall be bound in heaven; and whatever you loose on earth shall be loosed in heaven." The context refers to two people who have had a disagreement. Jesus instructs the one who seems to be in the right to seek the other party out for the purpose of effecting reconciliation. If he is not successful he is instructed to take two witnesses and repeat the procedure. If that fails, he should engage the church. If the offending party does not hear the church's admonition, he should be considered a Gentile and a tax collector.

Matthew 18:15-20 is a favorite passage to deal with broken relationships in the church. Unfortunately, it seems that every time people choose to follow the procedures outlined in Matthew 18, rather than fixing the relationship, they make it worse. Why? I believe because we fail to incorporate grace to the truth under discussion.

When someone has done a wrong to us we go to that person with a certain degree of anger and confront him with the truth.

When that person refuses to repent on our terms, we take two witnesses, who usually are close friends of ours, not so much to effect reconciliation but to document the offender's refusal to repent. When he does not respond the way we demand it, we then take it to the church—a church that the other party no longer attends.

The church usually writes a letter to the offending person, outlining his disobedience and gives him a certain time to repent. When he does not repent, the church now considers the offending Christian a Gentile and a tax collector. And some churches have used these two terms—"Gentile" and "tax collector"—as synonyms for unbelievers so they can justify themselves in pursuing a lawsuit in secular court.

Why is it that in following "biblical procedure" we usually make the problem worse? I believe it is because we fail to discern the intent of the procedure outlined in Matthew 18:15-20. We are given the option to bind or to release, and we usually choose to bind. Please, notice the context. In the parable of the lost sheep in Matthew 18:10-14, we have Jesus' clear admonition that God does not want any one of those sheep to perish. Following the passage dealing with the discipline issue, we have the parable of two debtors (Matt. 18:21-35). Notice that the king became very angry with the party that was right, because of the party's failure to release the offending party.

I believe a better way to deal with the issue is that once we have exhausted all the avenues for reconciliation, we release the offender rather than bind him. As Stephen did in Acts 7 and as Jesus did while hanging on the cross, we should pray for God not to count the offender's sin against him. By doing this, we are sending grace to the offender and to the devil. Satan hates nothing more than grace, because grace neutralizes his most effective weapon: sin. Where sin abounds, grace overflows. Every time somebody offends us we should forgive that person unilaterally, because in so doing we take the truth of that offense and wrap it in grace. It is amazing how grace changes evil deeds into monuments of goodness. Jesus did this when He took man's evil deeds at calvary and changed them into God's gateway of grace.

But what about the terms "Gentile" and "tax collector"? What about them? A Gentile is someone who is outside of God's covenant with God's people. And a tax collector is a member of God's people who is working for the enemy. These two categories are worthy of pity. I believe that what Jesus is saying is to be merciful to them. Have pity on them, because they are working for the enemy. Release them. Do not bind them. Do not ignore the truth of their misdeeds, but rather use that truth to bind them and make them pay, as the slave did in the parable of the two debtors. Add grace to that truth and turn it into a blessing. By adding grace to Saul of Tarsus, Stephen changed him into Paul of Antioch. Truth plus grace is a powerful combination.

Truth always has two sides. The greater the truth, the farther apart those sides are. When it comes to the truth itself, Jesus, no single person on earth can claim a corner on its understanding. However, so many times self-appointed proponents and guardians of that truth claim the right to its *full* understanding. This is tantamount to their considering themselves greater than the truth itself and their positioning themselves over the truth to "instruct" others that, in their estimation, lack the "complete" understanding that they ascribe to themselves. Ridiculous! No wonder the Bible warns us that "knowledge puffs up" (1 Cor. 8:1, *NIV*).

This is so serious that in Ephesians 4:3 Paul exhorts us—primarily the ministers—"to preserve the unity of the Spirit in the bond of peace." He doesn't say in the bond of common doctrine or denominational allegiances or truth as we understand it. He says peace. This is because when brethren who differ on important issues are at peace with each other, they are then able to grow *together* in the understanding of the truth. Not for the sake of proving their particular point of view, but for the sake of what truth spoken in a context of grace does: it sets people free.

Offensive and Defensive Warfare

The spiritual warfare in the heavenly places to which we are called is both defensive and offensive. One of the arguments sep-arating evangelicals from charismatics is the "stand firm" approach of the former in contrast to the "retake" approach of the latter. Evangelicals emphasize that the thrust in Ephesians is to maintain the ground already conquered. Therefore, they object to the militancy of charismatics who, in the evangelicals' minds, are chasing too many devils in too many places. Charismatics counter this criticism with a record of victories and spiritual advances hard to deny. They spell out a constant and consistent stream of testimonies that seem to validate their emphasis on taking or retaking ground formerly possessed by the enemy. I see no contradiction in these positions.

When the Church moves into an area for the first time, it must attack rather than defend. The target area is under Satan's domain, and he must be evicted. The only way to evict an entrenched enemy is by moving in and taking over his foxholes. This is what the Early Church did in Jerusalem (see Acts 2—6), in Samaria (Simon the magician, see Acts 8), in Ephesus (see Acts 19) and eventually in every new region it entered. Moreover, in Ephesians 6, Paul associates the preaching of the gospel with intercession (see Eph. 6:15,19,20) and the struggle against principalities (see Eph. 6:12,18,19).[3] It always takes a power encounter of some sort to establish the Church for the first time, because the Church has to displace the existing satanic structure. This validates the charismatics' perspective.

However, once the ground has been taken, the Church must immediately switch to a defensive mode and turn the conquering army into a defending army. This is the setting in which Paul's epistle to the Ephesians was written. Failure to do so may result in the position being overrun by the recently evicted enemy. "Standing firm" is a must (see Eph. 6:14). Otherwise, a back door as big as the front door will develop, causing the Church to lose the sprouting seeds to the birds of the sky (Satan and his demons) as described in the parable of the sower in Mark 4:3-20. All of this gives credence to the evangelicals' perspective.

When the Church fails to defend its conquered position, Satan conducts a counterattack and retakes the ground. This was the case with the Church in Galatia. Paul rebuked them and asked them, "You foolish Galatians, who has bewitched you?" (Gal. 3:1). The term "bewitch" is a direct reference to satanic activity. In a case like this, an offensive move is required inside the Church to repel Satan's attack. This, in turn, validates the charismatics' approach. No wonder Paul used the term "struggle" to describe the relationship between the Church and the forces of wickedness.

When I shared these insights on the heavenly places with Cindy Jacobs, a dear friend and worldwide intercessory prayer leader, she asked me a question that helped me refine the offensive/defensive/offensive thrust better. As I explained how the people transferred out of Satan's cosmic grave are inducted into the Church, which in turn evicts Satan and his forces of wickedness, forcing them to be confined under the feet of Jesus, I overemphasized the defensive posture to which the Church is then called.

I remember Cindy saying, "But, Ed, where is the place for the intercessors? My intercessors?" She is the president and founder of Generals of Intercession, and she spoke like a general whose division was about to be mothballed. "Intercessors are very active in the Church today," she continued, "and they usually conduct offensive missions that are absolutely necessary. Where do they fit if all the Church must do is defend?"

Cindy had a point, and an important one. Offensive operations must be conducted inside the perimeter of the Church, if and when that perimeter has been infiltrated by the enemy (see Col. 4:12; compare Phil. 4:2,3; Eph. 6:19,20).

Charismatics and evangelicals are really both looking at two different sides of the same coin. In order to see the whole of the coin, both perspectives are needed. That is why Paul says in Ephesians 6:10, "Finally, my brethren, be strong in the Lord, and in the power of his might" (KJV). The word "and" here is a key word. It indicates that to be strong in the Lord and to be strong in the strength of His might are two different, though complementary, things. The first one could be interpreted as describing primarily a defensive mode. We take refuge in the Lord. We hide under His mighty hand. We take our position in Christ. We abide in Him. The second aspect, although present within the first one, is more forceful and is used when confronting the enemy. It is the power of His might working through us that enables us to defeat the forces of wickedness entrenched in the heavenly places over a city or region.[4]

Traditionally, evangelicals have dwelt on "being strong in the Lord," while charismatics have specialized in "the power of His might." It is not either-or. It is both. Historically, both groups have often faced each other in severe anger. Both groups fail to see how weak they are in the areas where traditionally they have been thought to be strong.

In 1985, I hosted in Argentina one of the most brilliant evangelical Bible teachers of our time. His local congregation numbered in the thousands, and more than 100 radio stations carried his program daily. His books had blessed countless thousands. As

he toured the country and saw literally thousands of new converts all over, he repeatedly reminded me of the need for more
Bible teaching. I had no problem with that. However, he also
began to impeach the genuineness of some of the ministries to
which I introduced him. He questioned them because he did not
see the kind of Bible exposition he considered essential for those
ministries to be authentic. When I pointed out to him that many
of those ministries have been around for quite some time and
that thousands of believers attested to their solidity, he went into
a tirade about the absolute necessity of more—much more—
expository Bible teaching.

When I pointed to the rich prayer life of those believers,
which no doubt surpassed his own prayer life, he dismissed it as
an exercise in emotionalism. "Bible teaching," he repeated.
"There must be more Bible teaching!"

Now, I'm a Multnomah School of the Bible guy ordained at
Peninsula Bible Church in Palo Alto, California, by the late Ray
Stedman, one of the finest Bible expositors trained at Dallas
Theological Seminary. I am a man of the Book, and I believe in
Bible teaching. Sensing that my guest was abusing truth, I decid-
ed to try to sober him up a little bit. I asked him, "Is Bible teach-
ing the answer?"

"Yes," he replied.

"Are you a Bible teacher?" I asked.

"Yes," he said.

"Are you a good Bible teacher, and if so, is your congregation
well taught?" I inquired.

"Absolutely," he declared.

"Well," I said, "how about inviting John Wimber to do a healing seminar at your church?"

"Never!" he said.

"Why not?" I asked.

"He'll mess up everything and everyone!"

I said, "If Bible teaching is the answer, if you are a good Bible teacher, and your people have been well taught for years, how can John Wimber mess them up in just one weekend?"

He had no reply.

The area where he thought he was the strongest was really the weakest.

On the other hand, charismatics usually see themselves as experts in regard to the person and the gifts of the Holy Spirit. If there is one area where they have considered themselves strong, it is in matters pertaining to the Holy Spirit. However, this is not always so.

A charismatic leader was invited to speak at a conservative church. In the course of her ministry there, she spoke in tongues into the microphone to the dismay of the pastor who invited her. She went on to utter prophetic words (something the church was not used to) and tried to do something charismatic to bring into evidence the Holy Spirit's presence. Needless to say, it was not a positive experience. When I asked her why she did this, she replied, "I was so full of the Holy Spirit that I could not contain myself." Really? I do not think so. Quite the contrary. I believe that this "expert" on the Holy Spirit was so insecure about it that she went into all those displays to prove to herself that He was there. Like the conservative Bible expositor, she revealed a weakness right at the center of her perceived strength. The only way to maximize the strengths and cancel out the weaknesses is by together "speaking the truth in love" (see Eph. 4:16).

On the other hand, evangelicals and charismatics are strong in areas where traditionally they view each other as weak. For instance, charismatics, whom many evangelicals would consider inferior in the area of Bible exposition, know a lot more about what the Bible teaches about angels, miracles, the gifts of the

Spirit and Body life. At the same time, evangelicals, whom many charismatics would perceive as weaker in the area of practical faith, score higher when it comes to having faith in the most difficult circumstance: when God chooses to remain silent or to say no in a context of crisis. Obviously, we are all members of the same Body and no particular member can boast. We are interdependent.

It Works!

In Ciudad Juarez, Mexico, in May of 1993, more than 100 pastors and leaders publicly repented for the division caused in the Church by their anger at each other. They all knelt down and said a prayer of repentance. Then they asked forgiveness of the Church for having taught her the wrong way. Finally, they embraced each other. As they did so, the power and the presence of God became very tangible. Emotional, spiritual and even physical healing took place right then and there. The blood of Jesus was finally flowing unimpeded, and all unrighteousness—and its consequences—was being washed away.

The balance of power was altered in the heavenlies. Since then, city hall has begun to open up to the Church. A new, positive atmosphere is in evidence all over the area, so much so that across the river in the Texas city of El Paso, pastors noticed what was occurring and yearned for such a move of God in their city. Four of them decided to get together and do the same. They repented and began to pray together. Then, on November 29, 1993, those four pastors invited other pastors to the civic center for a service of reconciliation. I was invited to minister. When I asked how many people we should expect, I was told between 50 and 200. When the doors opened, nearly 2,000 Christians representing many congregations—both Hispanic and Anglo—flooded the place.

As pastors publicly repented and their congregations agreed, lives were changed on the spot. The joy of the Spirit was in evidence. Pastors immediately noticed a wider door through which to reach the lost. The next day, Anglo and Hispanic pastors gathered to discuss how to lay down the foundation for "Plan El Paso," a plan to share the gospel with every person in their city. What had happened? Satan and his demons lost their jurisdiction, and the fullness of Christ in the Church sent them back under the feet of Jesus.

This was dramatically illustrated in Argentina when, on November 15, 1993, we called the Church in La Plata to hold a prayer meeting in the main plaza, but the authorities had decided not to grant us the proper permit. There was ample room for our frustation to turn into anger with its devastating consequences.

City Hall never said no, but it never said yes either. This ambiguous stance allowed the ruling authorities—closely connected to the Free Masons and to the most reactionary elements within the Catholic Church—a broad range of options. If we went ahead with our plans, they could jail us for conducting a meeting without a permit, or if we challenged them on constitutional grounds, they could claim that they never denied us the permit.

If you conduct a meeting in a public place in Argentina without a permit, you are liable to be arrested and your equipment, sound system, vehicles and so on can be confiscated. In close cooperation with the pastors in La Plata and under the leadership of Sergio Scataglini, a dear friend and fellow missionary, we chose a path that allowed us to be wise as serpents while remaining harmless as doves.

We waited until enough people had gathered to make a mass arrest impossible. Then, the young people began to sing and that allowed us to spot the undercover agents. (You can always tell the undercover agents apart because, even though they can mimic the songs, they can never imitate the joy of the Lord.) These undercover agents were there to surreptitiously identify the leaders in order to arrest them and, thus, bring the meeting to an abrupt end. Under Sergio's leadership, we ran a five-ring circus with action on several fronts so that no one could be identified as "the" leader. Finally, when enough people had gathered, the sound truck was quickly moved into place and before you could count to 10, an "impromptu" prayer meeting was underway.

A pastor from England came to the podium and asked forgiveness of the Argentines for England's massacre of teenage soldiers during the Falkland War. An American asked forgiveness for U.S. Secretary of State Al Haig's duplicity during the early peace negotiations. This touched a deep nerve in the Argentines present, because close to 2,000 teenage draftees lost their lives during the meaningless Falkland War. An Argentine pastor came forward to extend forgiveness, while asking the same for the fact that Argentina started the war. It was a most moving moment. There was hardly a dry eye in the crowd of almost 3,000 people. None of this was planned. The Spirit was truly in command.

After this, the heavens opened up and prayer after prayer went up on behalf of the Catholic Church—which has opposed us so fiercely—on behalf of the Pope and the Cardinals, the Bishops and the Archbishop. At that moment, a group of born-again Catholics came to the front of the podium and the whole crowd exploded in praise and worship. People reached out to them, embracing them, kissing them. It was a most memorable and healing moment!

Immediately after that, as I stood on the platform, somebody tugged my leg and asked me to lean down. A well-educated man shook my hand while saying, "I am a public official and I am ashamed of what we have done by denying the permit for this marvelous act. I am an atheist, but I want to publicly repent on behalf of the government for this terrible deed. Would you forgive me and those I represent?"

Can you feel the full impact of what this man said? "I am an atheist, but I want to publicly repent on behalf of those I represent...." An atheist repenting? Only God can do it! When I reported this to the public assembly, another spontaneous neverending clamor of praises to God swept the heavenly places.

On one side of the crowd stood the massive doors of the Catholic Cathedral, locked, projecting a sense of rejection. On the other side stood City Hall, brightly lit on the outside but uninvitingly dark on the inside. Officials and functionaries had retired early, afraid that we might face them with their own misdeeds. Ungodly men, both secular and religious, had tried to encircle the Plaza with enmity and mistrust, but God's people built an altar right in the middle of it and what the devil had intended for evil, God turned around for good!

What a service of reconciliation! First with the English and the Americans. Then with the Catholics and the city officials. What went on in that Plaza was a modern-day replay of Acts 2, where the Church had "favor with all the people" (Acts 2:47).

Following this, Cindy Jacobs prayed for the sick. Many people were miraculously healed, several of them unbelievers. Then, an invitation was given and many more came to the Lord. As we continued to minister to the needs of the people, a second wave of onlookers drew near. Being an evangelist, I could not resist the temptation, so I gave another invitation for them to receive the Lord. Scores of people with their hands upraised moved toward the platform from every corner of the Plaza. It was an incredible sight! By dealing first with the jurisdictions in the heavenlies, we were able to gain the upper hand over Satan.

The importance of the heavenly places cannot be overemphasized. Anytime you choose to sleep on your anger, you are inviting evil forces to move into the space entrusted to you in the heavenly places. These evil forces have a deadly agenda: to kill, to steal and to destroy, and you could be their first victim, and the trigger could be as close as your tongue!

> But no one can tame the tongue; it is a restless evil and full of deadly poison. With it we bless our Lord and Father; and with it we curse men, who have been made in the likeness of God; from the same mouth come both blessing and cursing. My brethren, these things ought not to be this way. Does a fountain send out from the same opening both fresh and bitter water? Can a fig tree, my brethren, produce olives, or a vine produce figs? Neither can salt water produce fresh (Jas. 3:8-12).

The Inheritance

If you received a phone call advising you that you had inherited a fortune, what would you do? First, you would claim it so the inheritance would become legally yours. Then you would deposit it in a safe place so no one could steal it from you. Finally, you would begin to use it wisely so it would multiply itself.

In Ephesians 1:18, Paul prays for the eyes of our understanding to be opened in order to comprehend "the riches of the glory of His inheritance in the saints." In essence, God's inheritance is to be found *in* the saints. Each saint represents a partial portion of His inheritance. This means that when I meet a Christian, I am introduced to a portion of God's estate. Unfortunately, the opposite is also true: Anytime I allow something to come between me and another Christian, to the point that fellowship is broken, I abuse something that is very dear to God.

If you were told you have been bequeathed a fortune, one of the first questions you would ask is, "How much? How big is the gift?" The lawyer or trustee would be in a position to tell you to how much you were entitled.

Likewise, it is perfectly possible for us to know the size of this divine inheritance. Notice how Ephesians 3:16 makes reference

---

THE MOST DANGEROUS SETTING FOR AN EXTREMIST IS TO REMAIN BY HIMSELF, ESPE-CIALLY IF HE HAS A RADIO PROGRAM, A WORD PROCESSOR AND A CONTRACT FOR A BOOK. IN THE ISOLATION OF HIS STUDY, HE CAN CONCOCT ALL KINDS OF SCENAR-IOS AND COME UP WITH CREATIVE JUSTIFI-CATION FOR HIS EXTREME POSITIONS.

---

to the "riches of His glory"—the same expression used in Ephesians 1:18 to introduce the subject of God's inheritance. This is the context for Ephesians 3:18, where we are told how big that inheritance is. It is as big as all the saints. It requires "all the saints" to be able to comprehend something that has height, depth, width and length. What is it? Even though the passage does not spell it out, it is safe to assume that it is the "fullness of Christ in the Church" referred to in Ephesians 1:23 and again in Ephesians 3:19.

The Interplay Between Extremes
It takes all of the saints to see the fullness of Christ in the Church. It also takes the whole Church to take the whole gospel to the whole city. When I visit a city for the first time, I try to

find out who are the local leaders standing at opposite extremes. That provides me with an instant reading on the breadth of the gap that needs to be bridged. Contrary to popular belief, it is not impossible, not even difficult, to have those two extremes working together. The reason: When two extremes are brought together, they cancel each other out!

The most dangerous setting for an extremist is to remain by himself, especially if he has a radio program, a word processor and a contract for a book. In the isolation of his study, he can concoct all kinds of scenarios and come up with creative justification for his extreme positions. However, take him to a Pastors' Prayer Summit where he has to share quarters, meals and meetings with other pastors, and things are bound to change quickly. Now he is no longer telling his word processor what his opponents are like. Instead, he is looking at them. He is no longer carrying on a one-way conversation as he records his radio program. When he talks, he has to listen for the reply that comes from across the room before he can continue. He can no longer make summary judgments dictated by his own biases and presuppositions. All of this is bound to make an impact. Fellowship among Christians in a geographical area reflects the sum of God's inheritance in that region. This is why Satan targets that fellowship for destruction.

During a Pastors' Prayer Summit I attended, I was aware of two key leaders who had opposed each other publicly on many issues. On the first day, one of them was seated at my table, and we were carrying on a conversation when the other one stopped by to ask me a question. No greetings were exchanged between them. The tension was so thick you could have cut it with a knife. However, that afternoon during the prayer time they found themselves praying out loud in the same room. Later on, when each one shared his vision for revival, they heard each other describe the same goal from two different directions. During the sharing time that followed, somebody made reference to spiritual leaders in the community and named *both* of them. Finally, at the end of the day, the Lord's Table was set up. Joe Aldrich, the president of Multnomah School of the Bible and the facilitator for the Prayer Summit, challenged us to go to the table in pairs and take the Lord's Supper together. To everyone's delight, these two leaders walked toward each other, knelt down, prayed for each other, and with tears streaming down their cheeks partook of the Lord's Supper—*together*!

Put the two extremes together, and they cancel each other out. What's more, they build a superb support for the middle ground on account of the wide span they represent.

Back to Kindergarten

Paul also reminds the leaders (apostles, prophets, evangelists and pastor-teachers) of some basic things. In fact, they are so basic that they sound like prekindergarten level. He tells them, "There is one body and one Spirit,...one hope,...one Lord, one faith, one baptism, one God and Father" (Eph. 4:4-6). Why would Paul state the obvious so emphatically? I see at least two reasons.

The first one has to do with the difference in perspective between leaders. An apostle's focus is in laying down a foundation for the Church in a region. A prophet is often focused on denouncing sin and exposing it. So right after the apostle is done laying down the foundation, and even before the concrete is dry, the prophet is bound to find something wrong with it and will want to deal with it. Even if it means tearing up the foundation!

To an evangelist, hustle and bustle are tools of his trade. His idea of a meeting is closer to a bus depot at rush hour than the orderly and dignified Sunday School class a teacher loves to conduct. To an evangelist, noise is welcome at all times, especially the noise of people going forward to receive Christ. To a teacher, the only noise allowed, and the one that he somehow enjoys, is the noise of three-ring binders snapping open and shut while changing notepaper. Put these two together, and you have potential problems. That is why Paul reminds them that there is only *one* body and that all of them equally belong in it.

The second reason such an exhortation is given to leaders is because, simply put, every division in the Church is always caused by a leader, never by a follower. In fact, many separatist leaders take great joy and pride in causing divisions. They see it as part of God's will. What they fail to realize is that they play right into the hands of the enemy for whom they are creating jurisdictions in the heavenly places.

"You": Singular or Plural?

Much of what I just said is difficult to grasp in the West. A major contributing factor to this difficulty is the limitation of the English language. For instance, in English, the pronoun "you" can be either singular or plural. There is no way to know by simply reading "you" (when it stands by itself without a qualifier) if it means "you alone" or "all of you." This, coupled with Western individualism, can lead to a personalized, individualized interpretation of the Scriptures. When we read "you" in Ephesians, our mind automatically computes "I." However, the original intent was "all of you" or "us." This is how we come up with some interpretations that seem to contradict what Paul is saying in this epistle.

Take, for instance, the expression "to be strengthened with power through His Spirit in the inner man" (Eph. 3:16). The popular interpretation of the inner man is best reflected by the idea of each one of us having a personal "inner man." That is why, in order to graphically illustrate this, we draw a human heart with a balloon shape inside it and we call that balloon shape the inner man—*my* inner man. Nevertheless, this passage seems to suggest a *collective* inner man—one made up of all the members of the Church as they come together. In the West, we concentrate on keeping our individual inner man in good shape, and we see no direct relationship between my health and the health of the Church overall.

However, in Paul's conception of the collective inner man, if one of the individual contributors pops, the whole balloon bursts. This is why we must emphasize that there is only one Church in our city. If one of the congregations does poorly, the *whole* Church does poorly. The greatest expression of the unity of the Church is the one that encompasses all its members. This does not mean there are no individual responsibilities and personal spheres of influence in the Church. Quite the contrary. Paul touches on the individual's inner strength and personal responsibility, especially in his epistles to Titus and Timothy.

But the issue that should not be overlooked is the one pertaining to the difference between personal and collective spheres of responsibility and authority in the Church. For instance, a single person has jurisdiction over his life, but not the life of his neighbor. A husband or father has jurisdiction over his marriage and family, but not the family next door. The same applies to a local congregation and to its God-given sphere of influence, which encompasses all its members. However, it takes a healthy, whole Church to be able to reach the entire city, because the key to doing so is the control of the heavenlies. When the Church walks in unity, expressing the fullness of Christ, the forces of evil are displaced from the heavenlies and confined under the feet of Jesus. Now the Church is in control of the battleground.

According to Jesus, this unity is what causes the world to believe. It is no coincidence that the expression "and the Lord added to their number daily those who were being saved" (Acts 2:47, NIV) appears in the context of the highest level of unity ever achieved in the Church. In that context, the fullness of Christ was at its highest, and Satan's stronghold on the lost at its lowest.

The theme of spiritual unity in Ephesians moves from the general to the particular, beginning in chapter 2 with ethnic unity (Jews and Gentiles). It moves on to unity in the Church among all the saints in chapter 3, to unity among the different ministries in chapter 4, to unity in marriage in chapter 5, climaxing with unity in the family and the workplace in chapter 6.

Paul does not introduce the subject of spiritual warfare until this solid foundation of unity has been laid. This is a *very* important point. Then, and only then, the Church is ready to engage the enemy. To do otherwise is dangerous. Maybe you have heard people say, "Since I learned about spiritual warfare, my problems have multiplied and things are worse than before. I do not want to hear anymore about spiritual warfare!" This person is suing for peace at any cost. It could well be the case of someone who jumped too quickly into Ephesians 6 without doing the homework pertaining to unity detailed in the preceding five chapters. Before moving forward, we must protect the rear and the sides of our army. To confront the "forces of wickedness in the heavenlies" over our city with a divided Church is to allow the enemy to introduce a "fifth column" inside the Church. Unity is essential!

Finally, every challenge the Church faces today is, in essence, a spiritual problem that has a natural manifestation. This is why it is so essential to understand the reality of the heavenly places, because that is where those challenges must be met and overcome. People are not responding to the gospel because the god of this world has blinded them. This is not natural blindness but spiritual blindness. In order to facilitate their "turning of darkness to light," we must first open their eyes; but we cannot open their eyes unless we take authority over the forces of evil that are keeping those eyes closed. And we cannot exercise the necessary spiritual authority unless we first void the jurisdictions created by our sins (usually unresolved anger) for those demons to have a claim against us.

Likewise, the most pressing problems we face today are spiritual in nature. Abortion, homosexuality, violence and bigotry are spiritual problems with a human shell. Let us meet the enemy—the real enemy, Satan—in the heavenlies and let's defeat him by using the divinely powerful weapons available to us. Every time we face our challenges in the natural (e.g., abortion, homosexuality, secular humanism), we are bound to respond in anger. In so doing, we compound the problem by giving the devil a jurisdiction on which to stand. The battle must be won in the heavenlies!

Summary

1. The battleground is the heavenly places.
2. Whoever controls the heavenly places, wins.
3. The Church must take its position in Christ in the heavenlies and defend against Satan's counterattack.
4. Satan's counterattack is aimed at fragmenting the unity of the Church through unresolved anger and wrath directed at each other. This creates jurisdictions in the heavenly places for Satan to exercise authority conceded to him by the Church. If unity is compromised, the credibility of the Church and the effectiveness of its message are diminished.
5. Voiding those jurisdictions is the first step toward bringing the Church to full strength for the purpose of reaching the city for Christ.

Notes

1. See Ephesians 1:3,20; 2:6; 3:10: 6:12; and see W. Bauer, W. F. Arndt, W. F. Gingrich, and F. W. Danker, *A Greek-English Lexicon of the New Testament and Other Early Christian Literature* (Chicago, IL: University of Chicago Press, 1979), p. 306, column a, 2a.

2. Even though the Greek construction is passive here just as it is in Philipians 4:6, spoken testimony is also denoted by the same Greek verb in Ephesians 6:19. If we compare Ephesians 6:17 mentioning "the sword of the Spirit" in the struggle with the powers and Matthew 4:4,7,10; James 4:7; 1 Peter 5:8,9, we can safely conclude that our witness must be active rather than passive. This is further illustrated by how the Spirit instructs a man to communicate a specific message to angels in Revelation 1:16; 2:1,8,12,18; 3:1,7,14.

3. See also Romans 15:30; Colossians 2:1; 4:12, as well as Matthew 4:4,7,10; James 4:7; 1 Peter 5:8,9.

4. "So that you can take your stand" (Eph. 6:11, *NIV*); see also Luke 10:19; Acts 26:18; 1 Corinthians 4:20; Ephesians 1:19-23; 2:6.

4

Strongholds: What They Are and How to Pull Them Down

PRINCIPLE: *Spiritual strongholds are Satan's secret weapon. It is through the surreptitious use of strongholds that Satan controls the behavior of the Church. They must be identified and destroyed in order to regain control of the heavenlies.*

THE WITNESS STAND IS AN IMPORTANT PART OF THE JUDICIAL process. When someone is called to testify in a case, the court clerk swears him in. With a hand on the Bible, the witness promises "to tell the truth, the whole truth, and nothing but the truth, so help me God." He is then led through his testimony by the lawyer for the party that called him as a witness. This is the easy part. The hard part comes when the lawyer for the other party cross-examines him. It is hard because the objective of the cross-examination is two-fold: to find inconsistencies in the witness's testimony, and to discredit the witness. The latter is usually done by attacking his character. If either one of these objectives is accomplished during the cross-examination, his testimony then becomes useless.

Picture for a moment a key witness in a case involving the possibility of capital punishment; if the defendant is found guilty, he may be sent to the electric chair. This particular witness is testifying for the defense, and his testimony is crucial to save the accused. As he approaches the witness stand, a sense of immediacy grabs everyone in the courtroom. Everything hangs on the balance of what he is about to say. This is where the defendant makes or breaks it.

The witness gives an excellent testimony. He says the right words and brings the right facts to bear on his story, ably lead by the defense counsel. But now the district attorney begins the cross-examination.

In a booming voice he declares, "Mr. Witness, I will not try to punch holes in your story. However, I believe that you are a liar, and I will prove it." Then he goes on to ask three simple questions: "Are you rich? Do you have clothes on? Is your eyesight normal?" To these questions, the witness answers with an emphatic yes. With a slight smile of satisfaction, the district attorney now moves in for the kill. He asks the witness the color of the tie worn by the defendant, who sits a few feet from the witness stand. No answer comes forth. The witness is totally blind, in spite of what he just said. Next the district attorney provides the court with Exhibit A, consisting of pictures that show the witness panhandling. This is accompanied by an affidavit signed by the director of the local rescue mission stating that the witness is currently living off the mission's charity. Finally, the DA asks the witness to stand up, and, to everybody's amazement, he is stark naked. His credibility has been destroyed. It doesn't matter if what he testified is true; no one will believe it.

Is it possible for someone to be blind and not know it? To be miserably poor and believe otherwise? To think in all honesty that he is dressed and to walk around naked? Yes, it is entirely possible. It happens every day. Where? In our churches. In fact, the problem is so serious that the Lord Jesus Himself sent a letter to a particular church, confronting it with this severe form of spiritual schizophrenia. Recorded in Revelation 3:14-22, the letter says:

> "And to the angel of the church in Laodicea write: The Amen, the faithful and true Witness, the Beginning of the creation of God, says this: 'I know your deeds, that you are neither cold nor hot; I would that you were cold or hot. So because you are lukewarm, and neither hot nor cold, I will spit you out of My mouth. Because you say, "I am rich, and have become wealthy, and have need of nothing," and you do not know that you are wretched and miserable and poor and blind and naked, I advise you to buy from Me gold refined by fire, that you may become rich, and white garments, that you may clothe yourself, and that the shame of your nakedness may not be revealed; and eyesalve to anoint your eyes, that you may see. Those whom I love, I reprove and discipline; be zealous therefore, and repent. Behold, I stand at the door and knock; if anyone hears My voice and opens the door, I will come in to him, and will dine with him, and he with Me. He who overcomes, I will grant to him to sit down with Me on My throne, as I also overcame and sat down with My Father on His throne. He who has an ear, let him hear what the Spirit says to the churches.'"

The situation was so serious that Jesus told them, "You think you have gathered in My name, but I have been left out" (see Rev. 3:20). Can you imagine Jesus shut out of His own Church?

In Revelation 12:11, we are told that our victory over Satan consists of three elements: the blood of Jesus, our testimony and our willingness to die. One element is constant, the remaining two being variable. The blood of the lamb is the constant because it represents a perfect sacrifice. However, our testimony and our willingness to die for Jesus, if necessary, are vulnerable to change. This is where Satan—the accuser, the spiritual district attorney—aims his attack.

Satan's Arsenal

To be able to understand how a person, or a church, can behave as the one just discussed, we need to take inventory of Satan's arsenal to find out what his weapons are and how he uses them against the saints.

Satan has three main weapons. The most obvious is sin. Satan is known as the tempter (see Matt. 4:3), and this is because of the expertise with which he uses this particular weapon. Sin is an active weapon. Like a guided missile, it seeks you. When it hits you, you know it immediately, because the wages of sin is death (see Rom. 6:23).

The second weapon is a passive one. Like a trap, it is surreptitiously set up for you to fall into. It is called "accusations." Satan is described in the Bible as the accuser of the brethren (see Job 1:6-12; Zech. 3:1; Rev. 12:10). This is what he does, day and night, before the throne of God. If he has the courage to do that before God (who knows all the facts inside out), imagine what he is capable of doing to you and me, mere mortals. Even though we are forgiven, he reminds us of every sin we have committed, and then, for effect, he adds every other sin we could have committed. We are called by God by name, but Satan shouts at us that we have been forsaken, that we are not good enough for the ministry. Even though we are protected by the One who has said, "Never will I leave you; never will I forsake you" (Heb. 13:5, NIV), he uses the problems and challenges we face every day as a ramrod to blind us to the solidity of that promise. "God has left you," he screams in our ear. "You are too bad."

Satan uses accusations to generate anxiety strong enough so we will come out from under the mighty hand of God (see 1 Pet. 5:6). This is why Peter admonishes us, "Casting all your anxiety upon Him, because He cares for you" (1 Pet. 5:7). Satan's objective is to paralyze us, very much like an animal that has fallen into a trap (see 2 Tim. 2:26; 1 Pet. 5:8,9). Likewise, we know when this weapon has been used against us successfully, because we lose our freedom of movement in Christ. Creeping anxiety takes over. Fear replaces faith, and despair overtakes hope (see 2 Tim. 1:7).

The Church in general is very much aware of these two weapons. Adequate Bible teaching helps to deal with their effect on us and how to defend against them. The fact that the consequences suffered by the victims are visible—death and spiritual paralysis—acts as a motivator for people to seek help. However, Satan's third weapon is the most dangerous. This particular weapon is virtually unknown to the average Christian. It is neither active nor passive, but dormant. Like an underwater mine, it can be planted and left undetected, waiting for the ideal moment to be activated. Because it is dormant, it is easy for the devil to conceal it from us. We usually find out about it when we survey the destruction it has wreaked on us. This devastating weapon is called "spiritual strongholds" (see 2 Cor. 10:4,5). It allows Satan to control Christians and make them do things that bring great damage to themselves and to others. He uses it to impeach our testimony, much like the DA in the opening story. It exposes a severe inconsistency between who we say we are and what we believe. Spiritual strongholds represent a state-of-the-art manifestation of deceit. This is consistent with Satan's treacherous character because he is also called the deceiver (see John 8:44; Rev. 12:9).

Strongholds—The Secret Storage Area

The classic passage dealing with spiritual strongholds is 2 Corinthians 10:3-5:

> For though we walk in the flesh, we do not war according to the flesh, for the weapons of our warfare are not of the flesh, but divinely powerful for the destruction of fortresses [or strongholds]. We are destroying speculations and every lofty thing raised up against the knowledge of God, and we are taking every thought captive to the obedience of Christ.

Like the average Christian today, I had no idea what strongholds were all about until recently. I never heard a teaching on it when I was being trained for the ministry in my home church. Nor did any of my professors in Bible school or seminary ever discuss the subject. However, when I began to identify some strongholds and to assess their devastating effect on the Church, I understood why. The efficiency of strongholds depends on their concealment. Like the underwater mine, once discovered, it can be disarmed, and it loses its effectiveness.

Like spies sent on a mission to find a new weapon whose existence and whereabouts have been kept absolutely secret, we are at a definite disadvantage. We are searching for something, but we don't know what it looks like. It is similar to the story I heard of somebody who went around opening and shutting his hands in an obvious attempt to catch something that remained elusive. When someone asked what he was doing, he said, "I am trying to catch a chiripitiflautico." His questioner was perplexed. He had never heard of a chiripitiflautico before. So he asked, "What does it look like?" To this the prospective catcher replied, "I don't know. I haven't caught one yet!"

Let us determine first where strongholds are located. If we can discover that, then it will be easier to define what a stronghold is. I know this approach works because I was forced to use it in finding a "misplaced" car. Ruth and I had flown to Los Angeles to visit Peter and Doris Wagner. Our good friends David and Kristen Wendorff waited for us at the airport and lent us their car for the drive to Pasadena, where the Wagners live.

The Wendorffs were leaving town for the day and would meet us the next day. I did not pay much attention to the car. I just drove it, and when we got to Fuller Seminary, I parked it on the street. However, I made the mistake of not reading the posted sign, which prohibited cars from being parked there from 4:00 to 6:00 P.M. When we came out of our meeting with the Wagners, the car was nowhere to be found. It had been towed away by the Pasadena Police Department. Determining what had happened was the easy part. Recovering the car proved to be the real challenge.

Peter told me, "I'll go with you to the police station. My son-in-law works there. What kind of car was it?" Then and there I realized the immensity of my problem. Except for the color of the car, black, I knew nothing about it. I had no idea what make,

model or year the car was, much less the license number. Not
even Peter's connections at the police department could help me.
The desk sergeant said to me, "How do you expect us to find a car
that you, the driver, have no idea what it looks like?" Obviously,
he had a point.

Then a thought occurred to me. If we could locate the lot
where the car was impounded, we could then find out the specifics

---

A SPIRITUAL STRONGHOLD IS A MIND-SET
IMPREGNATED WITH HOPELESSNESS THAT
CAUSES US TO ACCEPT AS UNCHANGE-
ABLE, SITUATIONS THAT WE KNOW ARE
CONTRARY TO THE WILL OF GOD.

---

about the car and then file a proper report. I sweet-talked somebody into telling me where the car was (the sweet-talk was necessary because by then we had begun to look very suspicious). Peter
drove me in his car. What followed was comical. Here was "Mr.
Church Growth"—Peter Wagner—and his disciple looking like
second-rate burglars casing a car lot! But it worked. I recognized
the car among the dozens that were there. We explained our
plight to the attendant, and he allowed us to get inside and copy
down all of the information, which eventually allowed us to file a
report, leading to the recovery of the vehicle.

Let us apply the same approach to help us find where strongholds are located. Once we find that out, we will then gather the
data that will enable us to describe them.

If I say "coffee, bacon and eggs," what do you think? Breakfast,
right? If I say, "Speculations, knowledge and thoughts," what are

you bound to say sooner or later? The mind, because that is where those three things take place. We use our mind to speculate. Knowledge is stored there and thoughts are generated by it. We found the lot! I believe it is safe to say that strongholds, as described in 2 Corinthians 10:3-5, are located in the mind.

What do they look like? Again, based on the passage at hand, I have developed the following definition: A spiritual stronghold is a mind-set impregnated with hopelessness that causes us to accept as unchangeable, situations that we know are contrary to the will of God.

The presence of a spiritual stronghold must be suspected when a Christian finds himself powerless to change a situation that he clearly knows goes against the will of God. For instance, the Bible teaches us in precise terms that we are to forgive our enemies.[1] We have no problem ascertaining what the will of God is on the subject. Forgiving our enemies is a must for us! However, time and again we are in a bind, unable to forgive a particular person. We find ourselves totally incapable of doing something that God requires of us.

Another example involves our spouses. The Bible tells us that he who finds a wife or a husband "finds a good thing" (Prov. 18:22); it is so good, in fact, that we are told to cease being two individuals and, by cleaving to each other, to become one flesh (see Matt. 19:4-6). The Bible states that a spouse is a gift from God. However, some people have so much trouble with their spouses that they wonder, *If this is the best God can do, I wonder what the devil has in mind?*

This is a typical stronghold. The will of God is clearly spelled out, but reality tells us a different story. In fact, it blatantly contradicts the stated will of God, and we find ourselves powerless to change reality as we perceive it. This, in turn, leads to hopelessness.

As you can imagine, these conflicting perceptions are extreme-ly difficult to live with. So how do we cope with them? By allow-ing a "lofty thing" to go up in our minds. A partition is raised to separate our minds into two compartments. On one side is the knowledge of God; on the other side is human speculation. A speculation is a conclusion based on an assumption that cannot be proven. The partition—what Paul calls a "lofty thing raised up against the knowledge of God" in 2 Corinthians 10:5—is meant to block the knowledge of God in the presence of which it is impossible to successfully speculate. It is as frustrating as trying to focus the left eye on one object and the right eye on another.

The Visible Expression of a Stronghold

This fragmentation results in us developing what James describes as a "double mind." According to James, the consequence of a double mind is instability "in all his ways" (Jas. 1:8). This insta-bility is what prevents us from dealing satisfactorily with those things we know run contrary to God's will. When we are con-victed about it, we bail out by using rationalizations and specula-tions to avoid acting on it. We say something like, "I know what the Bible says, but there is a definite difference of opinion among scholars about what this passage really means. After all, we are removed by almost 2,000 years from the original writers." Or we engage a merry-go-round of counselors, hoping to have our ratio-nalizations validated by one of them. And so we go on and on, speculating.

For instance, when we go to church and hear the Word of God, we honestly believe it. We even say a loud "amen" to it. If we are preaching, we pound the pulpit as we declare what the will of God is regarding a specific issue. Our explanation is sup-ported by Bible references. We state it in an unmistakably authoritative mode because we are quoting the Word of God.

However, later on, as we walk to our cars in the church parking lot, we are also walking out of compartment A in our minds and going into compartment B. Insurmountable problems are ready to challenge us again. As we survey them, we immediately begin to speculate how to deal with them, using our own resources, quickly forgetting what we have just heard. How can we honestly believe one thing one moment and something different the next? Because we have a double mind (see Jas. 1:8).

Can you imagine the devastating effect of this on pastors and leaders? How can they believe God for a miracle for their cities if they find themselves unable to enjoy their marriages or forgive someone who has hurt them or to believe God for a breakthrough in their local congregation. Every time the Holy Spirit reminds them of the vision that caused them to become ministers, the devil activates the stronghold and a deafening loudspeaker blasts out: "Don't you dare believe it! Look at the pool of misery you are in." This is why it is futile to attempt to reach a city for Christ without first identifying and destroying the strongholds in the minds of the leaders (see Jas. 1:6-8).

The difference between a stronghold as presented in 2 Corinthians 10:3-5 and a satanic scheme (see 2 Cor. 2:11) is that, in the case of the former, the person knows what the will of God is but finds it impossible to do it. This, in turn, produces an atmosphere of hopelessness where faith is disabled. Whereas, a scheme is a surreptitious operation of the devil that allows him to harm the unsuspecting believer without being detected. I believe that Satan uses sin, anxiety and strongholds to produce his deadly schemes, but he uses strongholds openly primarily to create the kind of instability described by James (see Jas. 1:6-8; 3:13—4:4) that eventually prevent the Church from effectively using the divinely powerful weapons (see 2 Cor. 10:4). When Christians know what the will of God is and do otherwise because of a stronghold, Satan is able to blackmail them. Like the DA of our opening illustration, Satan impeaches the character of the witness because he cannot challenge the blood of Jesus that is being testified about.

What Does a Stronghold Look Like?

Here are five characteristics of a spiritual stronghold:

1. *Strongholds are located in the mind.* I already dealt with this previously. However, as a corollary, let us be reminded of the Church at Laodicea (Rev. 3:14-20), whose members honestly believed themselves to be rich, wealthy and self-sufficient, only to be exposed as poor, wretched, miserable and blind. This is further illustrated by Paul in Romans 8:6,7: "For the mind set on the flesh is death, but the mind set on the Spirit is life and peace, because the mind set on the flesh is hostile toward God; for it does not subject itself to the law of God, for it is not even able to do so."

2. *Strongholds are often made up of good thoughts.* This characteristic of a stronghold greatly contributes to its ability to go undetected. We seldom suspect our good thoughts. However, Satan uses this very cleverly. Our own good thoughts create a blockage for the excellent thoughts of God to come in. Such a case in point is Peter in Matthew 16:21-23. What was the strongest word Jesus ever used to rebuke a human being? It is the word "Satan," when Jesus called Peter by that name (Matt. 16:23). Never before and never after did Jesus use that term again to refer to another human being. This is even more perplexing when we consider that Peter was one of Jesus' key disciples. Actually, he was the leader of the group. Why would Jesus denounce Peter so harshly? Was he suggesting that Jesus should lie, steal money or commit fornication? Not at all. Peter had just given Jesus well-meaning, compassionate advice. When Jesus

predicted that He would suffer and die, Peter said, "God forbid it, Lord! This shall never happen to You" (Matt. 16:22). To which Jesus replied, "Get behind Me, Satan!" Why did Jesus identify Peter with Satan? Because he was setting his mind on man's interests rather than God's (see Matt. 16:23).

In other words, Jesus was saying, "You are looking at this from man's point of view rather than God's." By calling Peter "Satan," Jesus identified man's perspective with Satan's. Being the Son of

---

THE MOST DANGEROUS PIECE OF EQUIP-
MENT A CHRISTIAN CARRIES IS THE MIND
BECAUSE OF ITS ABILITY TO PRODUCE
THOUGHTS. THE EVIL THOUGHTS OUR
MINDS PRODUCE ARE MORE EASILY SPOT-
TED AND IDENTIFIED. IT IS THE GOOD
THOUGHTS THAT OUR MINDS ARE CAPABLE
OF THAT OFTEN LEAD TO DISASTER.

God, He was able to see through the wall of speculation present in Peter's mind, and He called it as He saw it. This is why I say that strongholds are often made up of good thoughts. The enemy of the best is not the worst. This is very easy to spot and easy to prevent from happening. The enemy of best is *good* because good and best can be easily confused. Satan knows this, and he uses it to his advantage. This is why we are exhorted to take "every thought captive to the obedience of Christ" (2 Cor. 10:5), not just the evil thoughts, but all of them—the good ones included. The Church of Laodicea was not cold (evil) but lukewarm (good), and this prevented it from realizing that it was not hot (excellent).

To understand this more fully, we must look deeper into the context of the Matthew 16 passage. One of the tragedies of modern-day Bible translations is man's well-meaning additions to the original text by way of subtitles, paragraph headings and so on. I can live with chapter and verse divisions because they help locate a specific passage, but many chapter divisions are located in the wrong place. Many times, a new chapter or section begins with the words "likewise," "therefore" or "moreover," which clearly refer the reader to the preceding chapter or section. Matthew 16:23 is a classic example of the confusion created by man's addition to the Word of God. "But He turned and said to Peter, 'Get behind Me, Satan! You are a stumbling block to Me; for you are not setting your mind on God's interests, but man's.'" Most Bibles have a dividing subtitle between verse 23 and verse 24: "Then Jesus said to His disciples, 'If anyone wishes to come after Me, let him deny himself, and take up his cross, and follow Me.'" This subtitle divider leads the reader to believe that verse 23 was the end of Jesus' explanation and that verse 24, with its reference to self-denial and picking up the cross, is a different subject—in essence, a call to discipleship.

However, Jesus begins in Matthew 16:24 with what amounts to a paraphrase of 2 Corinthians 10:5. Denial of self is what "taking every thought captive to the obedience of Jesus Christ" is all about. Taking up the cross implies dying to ourselves, and this spells death for our speculations as well. Following Jesus means leaving behind our own understanding and submitting to His guidance.

The most dangerous piece of equipment a Christian carries is the mind because of its ability to produce thoughts. I am not so concerned with the evil thoughts our minds produce. Those are more easily spotted and identified. It is the good thoughts that our minds are capable of that often lead to disaster.

Let's take the case of church splits. When neutral parties analyze a church split, they never find a group of good people being opposed by a group of evil people. Usually, the arguments on both sides of the split are quite reasonable. In fact, they both sound good. And that is the problem! They are good rather than excellent. Only God can provide the excellent thoughts. Church splits often take place because people, relying on their own understanding, choose not to deny themselves. Both parties provide "good reasons" for their point of view that blocks God's best.

Something similar occurs during the process that eventually leads to divorce. Well-meaning, compassionate advisers counsel divorce on the basis of some very good reasons. They say, "It is better for the children, because they won't continue to be exposed to a bad example" or "It will give you a fresh start, and you certainly need one. You will definitely learn from this mistake, and next time you will do better." These good thoughts cloud the reality that God hates divorce and that He has already provided us with divinely powerful weapons to deal with its cause. This, in turn, keeps us from using those weapons and we thus settle for a good solution rather than God's best. Instead of denying ourselves, standing on God's promises and fighting for our marriage, we choose divorce for "good reasons." As good as they are, they are short of excellent.

In no way am I suggesting that divorce is an unforgivable sin, nor do I wish to add insult to injury to those trying to recover from its severe consequences. God is a God of love and mercy, and He is always able to restore. The point I am making is a narrower one. As long as we entertain only good options, we will never experience God's best. In Matthew 5:3, Jesus said, "Blessed are the poor in spirit, for theirs is the kingdom of heaven." Who are the poor in spirit? Those who do not rely on their own wisdom. Those who need to be led. Our self-sufficiency is the material of which the "lofty thing raised up against the knowledge of God" is made (2 Cor. 10:5).

3. *Strongholds often develop in the shadow of our strengths.* In military science, a stronghold is always built somewhere that is

---

WE ARE CONSTANTLY AWARE OF OUR WEAKNESSES, THUS MAKING IT MORE DIFFICULT FOR SATAN TO USE THE ELEMENT OF SURPRISE. BUT WHERE WE PERCEIVE OURSELVES AS STRONG, WE TEND TO RELAX ON THAT PARTICULAR POINT.

---

already strong. Rather than constructing a fort at the bottom of a floodplain, military engineers build it on top of a hill or at the entrance of a bay—both of which are already strong points. Likewise, Satan often targets our natural strengths in order to position his strongholds.

There is a very simple reason for this. We are constantly aware of our weaknesses and, therefore, we keep a close watch on them, thus making it more difficult for Satan to use the element of surprise. But not so with our strong points. Where we perceive ourselves as strong, we tend to relax on that particular point (see 1 Cor. 10:12,13). For instance, when it comes to my spiritual weaknesses, I pray about them every day. I do "spiritual Jazzercize" in the presence of the Lord every morning, pleading for help and mercy. The consequences of my past mistakes are too painfully in view for me not to do so. However, when it comes to my natural strengths, I am not so watchful. Overconfidence is always one step away, and this allows Satan to move into that area with great freedom.

Let me give you an example. Think of the worst thing that ever happened to you. Got it? Why was it so bad? Most likely because it was totally unexpected. Right? Why was it so unexpected? Because you never thought that it could happen to you like that. And why is this so? Because you knew you were strong in that particular area. In essence, something unexpected happened to you along the lines of your strength.

Basically, what happened is that a natural strength was pushed beyond its limits and, thus, turned into a weakness. This often happens in Christian circles such as seminaries. What is the natural strength of a seminary? Teaching, right? However, by exaggerating that particular strength, a seminary may cause harm along the lines of that strength. For instance, the two least likely things to be found on seminary campuses are a strong prayer emphasis and an aggressive evangelism program. Why is this so? Is it because the faculty decided against it? No, usually it is because they taught too much of a good thing, such as the sovereignty and the omniscience of God. These two, when taken to an extreme, preempt the need for evangelism and for making our needs known to God.

The areas of our lives where we feel most confident are the areas in which we are most likely to develop overconfidence. Proverbs 3:5 says, "Trust in the Lord with all your heart, and do not lean on your own understanding." But confidence in self preempts the need to depend on God for guidance. We are not on the lookout for God's direction because we feel we can handle it. In essence, we have no early radar warning system to alert us to impending disaster.

I suggest that you take inventory of your perceived strengths.

Watch them. Make a list of avenues available to the enemy through your flesh to undermine those strengths. You need to do this constantly! For instance, in the areas where I am weak, which are also the areas where I have failed before, I have the road memorized. I know the way in, and I also know the way out. Unfortunately, I have been there plenty of times. I can lecture on how Christians are enticed and lured away in those particular areas. The moment one of my regular temptations heads my way, I immediately recognize it.

However, in other aspects of my life, where I have historically been strong, I do not have the same frame of reference to recognize the work of the enemy. I have no early warning system. I'd better watch out. This is why so many times in the counseling room we hear heartbreaking stories of a man or a woman who has failed where they expected it the least. "I never thought I would go for something like that," we hear them lament, while they struggle not to drown in a sea of remorse. "I have always been strong in that area. What happened to me?" What happened is Satan crept in and hid in the shadow of their strength. The moment they blinked twice, he built a stronghold.

This is painfully illustrated by Abram's mistake regarding his nephew Lot. God told Abram, "Go forth from your country, and from your relatives and from your father's house, to the land which I will show you" (Gen. 12:1). If you look at this verse carefully, you will see that the last two specifications are repetitive. God told Abram to leave his relatives and to leave behind his father's house. The members of his father's house *were* relatives. Why would God be repetitive? I believe it is for emphatic purposes. If Abram left behind his relatives and everyone who was a member of his father's house, that would leave only him and Sarai.

However, in Genesis 12:4 we read, "So Abram went forth as

the Lord had spoken to him." So far so good, but then it contin-ues, "and Lot went with him." No divine sanction. This addition is there to reflect Abram's choice. Since Lot was part of Abram's father's house, he should have been left behind.

Why do you think Abram took him? I do not believe Abram disobeyed God purposely. Being an old man with no children of his own, he was probably fond of children and very loving. This was definitely his strength. Because he did not watch out, that strength was abused. It was used to cause him to disobey God. I imagine Abram never suspected that he had disobeyed God. However, let us look at what happened.

Lot prospered alongside Abram, and the resulting conflict between their employees provided God an opportunity to steer Lot away from Abram. In Genesis chapter 13, we see Lot moving his tents toward Sodom, a city described as "wicked exceedingly and sinners against the Lord" (Gen. 13:13). This shows us why God was repetitive in his instructions to Abram (see Gen. 12:1). God knew that Lot's heart was in the wrong place.

Then, in Genesis 14, God passes judgment against Sodom and Gomorrah and their honorary citizen, Lot. Four kings declared war against the kings of Sodom and Gomorrah and three other cities. The four kings executed the judgment of God. By the time they were done, Sodom and Gomorrah had ceased to exist as cities. In Genesis 14:11, we are told, "They took all of the goods of Sodom and Gomorrah and all of their food supply, and depart-ed." Lot and his people were also taken captive.

A fugitive then advises Abram of the situation, and what does Abram do? Out of a tender heart, wishing to do his best, he reverses the consequences of God's judgment. First, he rescues Lot, and then, when the king of Sodom asks him to return just the people and not the recovered goods (see Gen. 14:21), Abram refuses and in so doing, he allows the wickedness to be reestablished in those sinful cities. Later, in Genesis chapters 18 and 19, we see how dearly everyone, including Lot, paid for this.

Can anybody find fault with Abram's actions from a *human* perspective? No, of course not. Who could blame a loving, caring uncle for going to the rescue of his nephew? However, from God's perspective, Abram's good was used to interfere with His best.

This is why Hebrews 4:12 presents the need to separate the soul fom the spirit through the two-edged sword, which is the Word of God. The soul reflects our own thoughts; the spirit, God's. When these two are mixed we fail to discern the intentions of our heart. "For the word of God is living and active and sharper than any two-edged sword, and piercing as far as the division of soul and spirit, of both joints and marrow, and able to judge the thoughts and intentions of the heart" (Heb. 4:12).

4. *Strongholds are often activated by painful trauma.* Time and again I have sat across from people in the counseling room who have told me something like this, "I will never forgive again. Never!" And then I later find out that the person has been gifted by God with the gift of mercy. Or someone will tell me, "I will never give money to the Church, ever!" and I will discover he has the gift of giving. Why would someone who is equipped by God with mercy choose not to forgive, which is the mainstay of that gift? And why would someone with the gift of giving become selfish and self-centered?

This basically happens because of abuse along the lines of God-given strengths. The ensuing trauma has built a pain reservoir deep enough to last a lifetime. That pain acts like a trigger. Anytime God provides an opportunity to exercise these gifts, the devil neutralizes it by activating that pain.

This could well be the case with Peter when Jesus appeared for the third time to him and the others after His resurrection (see John 21). Peter was always the first one to speak up, to ask questions, to volunteer information. However, this time, Peter did not say much. When Jesus questioned him about his love for Him, Peter answered Jesus in the affirmative but held back any comments regarding the shepherding of Jesus' sheep. The born leader was shying away from leadership. Why, if Peter was a born leader? On many occasions in the Gospels, Jesus had distinguished him as such. However, when Jesus told Peter he was going to betray Him, he argued back with a haughty display of self-assurance. He seemed to be saying, "I know I am strong and loyal. Therefore, I know I will never let you down." Unfortunately, he left out of the equation the third player: Satan. Satan knows when overconfidence is in place and how to take advantage of it (see 1 Cor. 10:12). Peter seemed to have been reluctant to exercise his God-given gift because of pain—pain caused by the traumatic events of the past.

5. *Strongholds create a double mind that results in spiritual and emotional instability.* In the third chapter of his epistle, James warns us, "Teachers...shall incur a stricter judgment" (Jas. 3:1). In an era when we have elevated the office of teacher to the pinnacle of prestige in the Church, this warning is hard to understand. Unless, of course, we put it in the context of James's teaching on strongholds.

In chapter 1 of his epistle, James states that the double-minded man is unstable in all his ways (see Jas. 1:8). Such a person is capable of subscribing to two different—even opposing—views on account of the "two-diskette" capability of his mental computer. He then chooses to remain double-minded on account of selfish ambition (see Jas. 3:14). Selfish ambition refers to a personal agenda that is so dear to him that he is willing to sacrifice everything else, even God's agenda, to carry it out. He has made a decision not to surrender certain thoughts to the obedience of Christ.

When such a person is entrusted with teaching, the potential

for the devil to infiltrate and influence the Church rises expo-
nentially. He is like a radio receptor with two different bands,
and a trusting, listening audience. One band picks up the wisdom
from below (see Jas. 3:15), which is earthly, natural and demonic. The other one tunes in to the wisdom from above, which is

---

STRONGHOLDS MUST BE DESTROYED. THEY
ARE NOT TO BE REMODELED. THEY ARE
NOT TO BE REPAINTED OR COVERED WITH
WALLPAPER. THEY ARE TO BE *DESTROYED*.

---

from God. He is thus sending out mixed signals, and because of
that, his audience is misled. This, in turn, results in him receiving a harsher judgment because he knew better.

As you can imagine, someone who one day expounds on God's
wisdom, and the next day acts on wisdom that is earthly, natural
and demonic, will certainly develop some problems leading to
emotional and spiritual instability, in addition to harming those
entrusted to his care.

Quarrels also become part of the picture, as warned by James
in 4:1. Quite often, teachers with a personal agenda (which is a
polite way of describing selfish ambition) start, promote and
engage in strife among the brethren without realizing the magnitude of the evil they perpetrate. They may believe they are being
persecuted. They see themselves as the victims rather than the
victimizer. Can you imagine the devastating effect of such a person on a ministerial alliance that is striving to reach a city for
Christ? Never is a person in the wrong more dangerous than

when he honestly believes he is right, especially if the person is in a position of authority or influence.

What to Do with Strongholds

According to 2 Corinthians 10:5, strongholds must be destroyed. They are not to be remodeled. They are not to be repainted or covered with wallpaper. They are to be *destroyed*. Studying James 4:7-10, I see four steps to accomplish this:

1. *"Submit...to God" (Jas. 4:7)*. This entails a truth encounter. Jesus Christ is the truth, and this truth has been revealed to us through the living Word of God. Determine by the Word of God what is God's will. Choose to believe it, and confess it with your mouth in opposition to the circumstances that contradict the Word of God. "Not as I will, but as you will" (Matt. 26:39, *NIV*) should be your prayer. Bring down the partition that has allowed you to store two opposing views in your mind. Call truth "truth" in spite of your feelings, if necessary. Invite Jesus to come in. This is what Jesus Himself indicated to the Church of Laodicea, which was controlled by a stronghold so severe that it lost touch with reality (see Rev. 3:14-21). If it was good for them, it should be good for you also! I am not saying you should receive Him as your Savior anew. I am suggesting you invite Him into the compartment in your mind where your rationalizations and speculations reign.

A well-educated lady attended one of our seminars where she was exposed to this teaching. Her son had been away from the Lord and was doing drugs. She had tried to reason with him but to no avail. She disciplined him, but it made no impact on his attitude and behavior. After much pain and many tears, she gave up. Even though she knew that her son was a gift from God to her and her husband, she was unable to reconcile this with the fact that now her son was walking with the devil. She "reasoned" herself out of pain by telling herself, "He is old enough to drive a car and old enough to buy alcohol. Now it is his problem, not mine."

At the seminar, she made a decision to reenter the battle-ground. She chose God's Word and God's promises over Satan's lies. She took a decisive stand in the heavenlies, interceding for her son and claiming him for God. As soon as she began doing this, the old pain, uncertainty and perplexity came back like a flood. However, she stood her ground by faith in the Word of God. A few weeks later, her son began to respond to the gospel. Today, he is in full-time Christian service.

2. *"Resist the devil" (Jas. 4:7).* The most effective way to resist the devil is by dying to the old self. When you take your position in Christ (see 2 Cor. 5:17; Gal. 2:20), you place yourself com-pletely outside of Satan's reach. Being in Christ also takes care of your speculations. In Christ, everything is certain and proven. Renew your mind by memorizing Scripture. Nothing stops the devil like a statement prefaced by "It is written" (Matt. 4:4,7,10). If you meet the conditions set forth in the Scriptures—"Resist the devil"—God has promised that "he [the devil] will flee from you" (Jas. 4:7).

A distressed mother came forward for prayer at one of our sem-inars. She told the old, familiar story of a rebellious daughter who had turned her back on her family, the Church and the Lord. She was involved in all kinds of sin. She requested that we have intercessory prayer for her daughter. Less than a week later, the woman called to report that her daughter had come back to the Lord. However, it was through an unexpected avenue. As the mother began to submit to God, she was instantly convicted of sin in her own life. The Lord showed her that she had provided an entrance for the devil through her pent-up anger. She fully repented before God. She submitted to God and began to resist the devil in the area of her life where she had yielded to Satan, while aggressively claiming her daughter "in the heavenlies." Two days later, her daughter, who had not been home for months, called to ask permission to come for a visit.

When the daughter came, the mother asked forgiveness for her poor Christian example. This touched the daughter, who also repented. Today, both of them are walking with the Lord. As this mother died to her old self, Satan lost his grip on her, and, through her, the grip he had on her daughter. When she decided to resist the devil, Satan had no choice but to flee because he had no claim on her.

3. *"Draw near to God"* (Jas. 4:8). The need to go back to God exists because we have drifted away from Him through our speculations. The sum of our speculations reflects the full measure of the distance we have walked away from God. Once Satan's hold on us has been broken, there is an immediate need to go back to God.

I remember the case of a woman afflicted with what is commonly called "multiple personality disorder." She had been treated by pastors, counselors and psychologists. There had been some improvement, but it never went past a certain point. As I counseled with her, I discerned a stronghold in her mind. Because of the painful trauma suffered as a child at the hands of her father, she was unable to take God at His word. Intellectually, she knew that God is love, but her own speculations voided the effectiveness of that truth. Every time she hit a certain point in her recovery, she stopped and turned around for fear of rejection on the part of God. We taught her to "cast all her anxiety on God *because He cares.*" The stronghold was destroyed by faith in the Word of God, as she forced herself to cross the barrier of fear of rejection. Ever since she crossed that threshold, she has been on the road to steady recovery.

4. *"And He will draw near to you"* (Jas. 4:8). The most com-

mon fear after realizing the depth and the gravity of our disobedience, is the fear of rejection by the One whom we have offended. That is why God promises that when we draw near to Him,
He will draw near to us. Notice the contrast between the devil
fleeing from us (see Jas. 4:7) and God drawing near to us (see Jas.
4:8). How reassuring! When the woman I discussed previously
reached out to God, not only was she able to pull down a major
stronghold, she also opened up the way for God to draw near to
her with blessings and unprecedented joy. No fear of rejection is
possible in God's warm embrace.

The Final Blow

James 4:8 says, "Cleanse your hands, you sinners; and purify your
hearts, you double-minded." Cleansing our hands refers to the
outward manifestation of the stronghold, while purifying our
hearts refers to the inward dimension. The first part, that which
is visible, is easier to deal with. A person living in adultery will
find it easier to break up the adulterous relationship than to rid
himself of the immoral drive responsible for the sin. This is why
this particular verse says "cleanse your hands,...*and* purify your
hearts." The first phrase describes the symptom; the latter
describes the root cause.

A heroin addict who has been in a detoxification program for
30 days will walk out with no physical addiction because his body
has been deprived of drugs for a month. However, the first thing
he is likely to do upon recovering his freedom is to inject himself.
Why? Because even though his hands are cleansed, his heart has
not yet been purified. He remains psychologically addicted. He
continues to have a double mind, and a powerful battery of speculations is always on standby to prevent him from doing what
God says he should. A stronghold has been totally destroyed only
when a double-minded person becomes single-minded.

James has a straightforward prescription for this: "Be miserable and mourn and weep; let your laughter be turned into mourning, and your joy to gloom" (Jas. 4:9). As you see the ugliness of your own sin, you will be drawn to His holiness. There is no better frame for God's grace than the gap between your sinfulness and God's holiness. Where? In the presence of the Lord. For how long? Until He exalts you. He will decide when you have been purified. You must wait and listen for His voice. In the meantime, "Do not speak against one another" (Jas. 4:11). This means that you should not justify yourself by blaming others. It's *your* heart, after all. You have no control over others, but you have full control over your response to their deeds.

The ultimate objective of this exercise is to eliminate double-mindedness. In Psalm 51, David says, "Against Thee, Thee only, I have sinned, and done what is evil in Thy sight, so that Thou art justified when Thou dost speak, and blameless when Thou dost judge" (Ps. 51:4). What David is saying is: "God, You are in control. I am guilty, and You are righteous. There is only one opinion that counts, and that is Yours, oh Lord. I will not speculate but rather accept Your word."

When we sin, our tendency is to justify ourselves and to minimize the evil done. We plead guilty, but always with a request to say something on our behalf. As long as we do that, we perpetuate the existence of a double mind. We will not be free from sin until we are able to see sin the way God sees it. We must see it through His eyes.

This is why the command in James 4:9 is to be miserable, to mourn, to weep, to turn our laughter into mourning. The best way I have been able to implement this is by going into His presence, alone, and letting Him show me my sin as He sees it, and also through the eyes of those people my sin has hurt, because the presence of the latter will cause me to be defensive and less than fully transparent. It has to be done in His presence with no wit-nesses! I must remain there until all my self-serving arguments collapse and I fully repent. Now I have only one mind: God's mind. Now my hands will remain clean because, by purifying my heart, I have eliminated the root cause: double-mindedness.

Personal Application

Perhaps God has convicted you of double-mindedness. Now you are able to see the stronghold in your life, and you want to tear it down. Let me encourage you not to give up. Persistence is the opposite of instability. I suggest that you determine what the will of God is and begin to hammer away at your wall of arguments. If your children are not walking with the Lord, con-fess God's promises regarding your children. If pastors in your city are divided, proclaim God's view on the matter. If your marriage is on the rocks, confess God's Word regarding mar-riage. Use God's words like a sledgehammer, and hit those situ-ations repeatedly (see Matt: 4:4,7,10; Eph. 6:17). Never give up. Do it, day in and day out. Memorize pertinent Scripture and quote it out loud!

Ray Trembath, a pastor friend of mine in the San Francisco Bay Area, told a story that illustrates this point. He told how a friend of his who was remodeling his home hired a contractor to demolish a cement wall. He watched as the contractor hit the wall with a sledgehammer. One blow, 2 blows, 3 blows, nothing happened. Then 10 and 15 blows, and still nothing happened. He continued—30, 35 blows, and still nothing. Finally, on the 36th blow, the wall developed a horizontal crack. On the next one, a spiderweb pattern of cracks appeared. On the 38th blow, the wall cracked all over. At that point, the contractor put the sledgehammer down and picked up a small hammer and a chisel, and, little by little, he brought down the wall.

This is also how a stronghold must be destroyed. That formidable stronghold you are looking at may seem to be made of solid granite. However, the Word of God is powerful (see Matt. 4:4,7,10; Eph. 6:17). The gospel is the power of God (see 1 Cor. 1:18). Choose God's Word over the circumstances. Confess the Word of God. Every time you do it, you are applying a sledgehammer blow to that granite wall. Keep doing it. Sooner or later, the first crack will appear. After that, it is only a matter of time before the whole thing crumbles.

"For the weapons of our warfare are not of the flesh, but divinely powerful for the destruction of fortresses" (2 Cor. 10:4). Before we attempt to bring down Satan's stronghold over our city, we must destroy all the personal strongholds, or fortresses, he has placed in our own lives. Everything opposed to the will of God *must* come down. We must be set free, totally free, in Christ. Without that kind of freedom, our attacks on the forces of evil will never amount to anything more than a riot inside a POW camp. However, if the Son truly sets us free, we will soon be conducting an amphibious landing to secure God's perimeter in our city (see John 8:36). Prayer evangelism as described in 1 Timothy 2:1-8 requires "holy hands." Are you already destroying strongholds in the innermost part of your soul? Go for it!

Note
1. See Matthew 5:43-48; 6:12; Mark 11:25; Romans 12:14,17,19,20.

5

Praying with Authority

PRINCIPLE: *The believer is a deputy of the Court of Calvary assigned to enforce the judgment awarded to Jesus: the salvation of the lost. The believer is to use this delegated authority mainly in prayer.*

GENERAL JONATHAN WAINWRIGHT WAS THE ONLY U.S. GENERAL captured by the enemy during World War II. He was left in charge of Corregidor, Philippines, by his superior, General Douglas MacArthur, when he was forced to flee to Australia to organize the Allied forces' massive counterpunch that eventually defeated Japan. MacArthur's orders to Wainwright were very clear: Never surrender. Fight to the end.

Wainwright tried very hard to stick to the letter of that order. However, the massive, systematic, merciless destruction he saw around him finally forced him—against his convictions—to surrender. He, and what was left of his ragtag army, were shipped off to prisoners-of-war (POW) camps all over Asia. Thousands died while in transit. Wainwright himself ended up in a POW camp in Mongolia. The Japanese guarded him as a precious prize. After all, he was the only U.S. general they would ever capture.

During those terrible years of captivity, Wainwright labored under tremendous guilt. As he saw his body deteriorate and had come to depend on a cane to move around, he also saw his soul experience even greater deterioration. He felt like a total failure for having surrendered Corregidor.

In due time, Douglas MacArthur led his troops to total victory. The Rising Sun became the Setting Sun as MacArthur and his troops evicted the Japanese from island after island all over the Pacific. He eventually occupied Japan and took up residence in Tokyo. The once-formidable Japanese empire finally surrendered to the "fugitive from Corregidor." When this happened, POW camps were liberated all over Asia. Because Wainwright was held in Mongolia, far away from Tokyo, his camp commandant was able to keep the truth from him for a while. Consequently, Wainwright continued to behave like a POW.

Can you picture the Japanese commandant watching Wainwright *after* Japan's surrender? He knew they would soon switch places, and the commandant must have trembled at the possibility of facing a captive who would become his captor. Every time he saw him, the Japanese commandant must have felt tremendous uneasiness. A fully armed, properly fed commandant, with more than adequate military force at his disposal, was afraid of the weak, emaciated, dysentery-plagued remains of a ragtag army and its limping general. Why? Because the commandant's power over them was based on a lie. I can picture him wondering, *Has he found out the truth yet? If he has, what will happen to me?*

The only thing that enabled the Japanese commandant to keep up this fraud was Wainwright's ignorance of the truth. Wainwright had been liberated, but he did not know it. Neither was he aware that, like every allied POW all over Asia, he had been ordered by his commander in chief to take charge of the camp. Because Wainwright did not know the truth, he continued to submit to the commands of his captor, even though his captor no longer had power over him.

Pharaoh's Greatest Fear

Something similar happened more than 3,000 years ago in Egypt. At that time, the Egyptian kings, also called "pharaohs," were among the most powerful monarchs on earth. The story opens in Exodus chapter 1 with an unnamed pharaoh, who had at his disposal one of the best fighting machines of his time. Warring chariots enhanced the already awesome power of his infantry and cavalry. His army had defeated every foe within thousands of miles and now was guarding the Egyptian empire.

Pharaoh's power was absolute. He had no Congress to deal with because none existed. While he did have a council of advisers, he was not obligated to obey their advice. He was a "divine ruler." He belonged to the realm of the so-called gods. His word was law. He never had to worry about the Supreme Court overruling him. He himself was the Supreme Court, the supreme politician, the supreme commander—all three rolled into one—not only of Egypt but of the surrounding countries.

However, the pharaoh in our story did have a nagging fear—a consuming fear that must have kept him awake at night. He was afraid of something so devastating that not even his mighty army could help him. The immense wealth of Egypt was incapable of buying a solution. His political savvy was not enough to deal with it.

Eventually he revealed his fear to his subordinates. Most likely it happened in the seclusion and privacy of a council of war. There, among his generals and advisers—in what would be the modern equivalence of the National Security Council—he finally blurted it out, "Behold, the people of the sons of Israel are more and mightier than we. Come, let us deal wisely with them, lest they multiply and in the event of war, they also join themselves to those who hate us, and fight against us, and depart from the land" (Exod. 1:9,10).

What kind of people were the Israelites that Pharaoh was so afraid of them? Did they have an army mightier than his? Did they possess overwhelming economic power? Were they allies of powerful enemies? Did they have something more effective than the mighty chariots in Pharaoh's army? No. None of these.

The people Pharaoh was afraid of were shepherds. The most powerful weapon in their arsenal was the staff they used to lead their flocks. Humanly speaking, they were totally powerless, but, like that Japanese commandant in Mongolia, Pharaoh was afraid not so much of the people but of the truth that, if discovered, would empower them. Listen to him outline his strategy: "Let us deal wisely with them." This is not the language of a despot who is in total control but rather the machinations of a schemer who knows he lacks real power. What he fears most is what every outmanned, outpowered general also fears: war. "Lest they multiply and in the event of war, they also join themselves to those who hate us, and fight against us" (Exod. 1:10). He knows that if war breaks out, he will lose. War must be avoided at all cost!

What is the core of his fear? It is not so much that he will be killed or that his country will be invaded, but rather that "they depart from the land [of captivity]" (Exod. 1:10).

From a military and political perspective, this line of reasoning does not make sense to us, but it did make sense to Pharaoh. Why? Because he knew his stronghold on the Israelites was based on a lie, and no one fears the truth more than liars. They know that truth cannot be shot down or dynamited. Truth sets the captives free (see John 8:32).

Satan's Greatest Fear

Satan's greatest fear today is *identical* to Pharaoh's. His uncontrollable fear is that the Church of the Lord Jesus Christ will realize that it is mightier than him! He is literally scared that every believer will fully understand the practical implications of the biblical truth that "greater is He who is in you than he who is in

---

ALL OVER THE THIRD WORLD, WHERE THE CHURCH IS ON FIRE, WE FIND AN EVER-EXPANDING NUMBER OF TESTIMONIES OF DRAMATIC ANGELIC INTERVENTION ON BEHALF OF THE CHURCH.

---

the world" (1 John 4:4). He's afraid the Church will discover a war is going on and will join it. And, entering that war, the Church will ally itself with those who hate Satan. And who are, besides God Himself, those superior forces that Satan fears so much? Angels! A host of angels so formidable that it cannot be numbered (see Deut. 33:2; Rev. 5:11). Jehovah is the Lord of hosts—hosts of angels twice the size of Satan's demonic army.

The reality of angels cannot be denied. The book of Acts contains 20 references to angels. On almost every occasion, when the Church was in danger or in confusion, angels were dispatched to the battlefield to help. This is not something that ceased with the completion of the biblical canon. All over the Third World, where the Church is on fire, we find an ever-expanding number of testimonies of dramatic angelic intervention on behalf of the Church.

Like Pharaoh's fear, the core of Satan's fear is that the Church "will depart from the land." What land? The land of captivity in which it is being held. Why? Because his entire empire, all over the world, will crumble even faster than the communist empire, once the Church begins to tell the truth. Satan's prisoners will leave the dungeons as they hear of their spiritual emancipation. His strongholds over our cities will be rapidly overtaken as angels are sent to assist a praying Church (see Heb. 1:14). To this end, the Church must learn how to pray with authority. Not as begging for crumbs from a cunning POW commandant but rather as an advancing army that knows it's destined for victory.

The picture presented by Paul in 1 Timothy 2:1-8 is one of scores of prayer cells all over a city at war with the one keeping the people captive. Those prayer cells are not to be relief agencies operating by the mercy of the occupying army; they are to be spiritual beachheads forcing the occupying army to retreat and setting the captives free. To do this effectively, the Church must understand and learn to use the authority delegated to it as it prays for all people in the city. The normal state of affairs between the Church and Satan is war, all-out war. Praying with authority entails stating the truth (see Matt. 4:4,7,10; Eph. 6:17), demanding that the usurper leave (see Matt. 4:10; Jas. 4:7) and radioing for help to evict him (see Rom. 15:30; Eph. 6:18; Col. 4:12), if necessary. Angels will quickly oblige (see Acts 27:22ff).

Angels are itching to be dispatched by God, not so much to comfort POW's in Satan's camp, but to aid them as they fulfill the Great Commission all over the world (see Acts 12:5; Heb. 1:14).

All through the Old and New Testaments we see examples of Satan enslaving God's people by hiding the truth from them— "dealing wisely with them," as Pharaoh said. Throughout the Bible, we also see deliverance come when God's people discovered the truth by accessing God's power through prayer. It happened in Egypt with Moses (see Exod. 3:14); in Babylonia when Daniel entreated God (see Dan. 2:18ff; 6:10; 9:1—10:20); in Persia when Nehemiah decided to rebuild the wall (see Neh. 1:5-11); in Acts when Peter was delivered from jail the night before his scheduled execution (see Acts 12:5ff); and again when Paul and his companions were spared after a dramatic shipwreck (see Acts 27:22ff). In all these cases, truth was revealed in answer to prayer, and angels were dispatched to ensure that God's answer to those prayers reached the intercessors.

How can we make sure that Satan's greatest fear *does* come to pass? The first step is to realize that we, the Church, are being held captive by this supernatural Pharaoh. In order to break free from his POW camp, we need to learn how it is that we ended up there. And for that, we need to go to the Bible to see how Pharaoh did it more than 3,000 years ago.

Satan's Three-Point Plan

Pharaoh knew that he did not have power, so he resorted to deceit. He came up with a three-point plan: to deceive, to dominate and, eventually, to destroy God's people.

1. He deceived them. The Israelites were never slaves of Pharaoh, but he convinced them otherwise. To do so, he had to "deal wisely" with them, which is a delicate way of saying he cheated them. Why was he able to succeed? The clue is found in Exodus 1:6: "And Joseph died, and all his brothers and all that generation." Those who had firsthand information of their real status had died. It seems that as those facts were relayed from one generation to the next, somehow truth was compromised. Uncertainties gave room to doubts that in turn gave rise to conflicting interpretations. That was all Pharaoh needed. He never wielded a weapon; he simply hid the truth from them. He became the master over two million Jews. Ignorance is a mighty weapon.

Satan is using the same weapon against the Church today. Paul, Peter, John and those who had "seen, heard and touched" the truth with their own eyes, ears and hands, had died (see 1 John 1:1). As the sacred record was passed from one generation to the next, we have become increasingly unsure of which promises are for today and which ones were meant only for an earlier time (the Apostolic Age). We have even devised what appears to be respectable ways to explain our spiritual misery, our moral feebleness and our supernatural anemia. We are so afraid of embarrassing God with prayers He might not answer that we have ceased to pray for miracles.

My good friend Omar Cabrera pastors what C. Peter Wagner has defined as a "centrifugal church"—a church where the pastors gravitate toward the people rather than the other way around. Omar's congregation, which numbers close to 85,000 members, meets in several campuses all over Argentina on account of its size. The mainstay of this church is prayer, especially prayer for the felt needs of the lost. Omar always opens the service with a prayer for the sick. Many are healed, although more are not. A visiting theologian from the United States once observed this phenomenon and later accosted Omar with questions. "Why is it," he asked, "that not everybody is healed when you pray? What happens to those prayers that go unanswered?"

Omar, in that unique style of his, replied, "That is a very important question, sir. So much so, that I myself asked God the same thing. Would you like to know what He told me when I inquired why some prayers went unanswered?"

Somewhat perplexed, the visitor replied, "By all means."

OUR PRAYERS SEEM TO BE WRITTEN BY LAWYERS WHO QUALIFY EVERY SENTENCE TO PROVIDE GOD WITH A WAY OUT IN CASE NO ANSWER COMES.

Omar said, "God told me that it is none of my business. My business is to pray for them. His business is to decide what to do with those prayers!"

Some people have a theology of powerlessness—a theology designed to explain why God will not do what He has said in His Word that He *will* do, no matter what. When a brand-new believer walks up to us with stars in his eyes, saying, "Look, look what I found in the Bible. I was worried about my unsaved relatives, and I asked God to reassure me. He led me to the passage in Acts where Paul tells the Philippian jailer, 'Believe in the Lord Jesus and you and your household shall be saved.' I knew then and I know now that this promise is for me, that my entire family will come to the Lord. What do you think?"

Well, what do we think? We clear our throats, try to look authoritative, and say something like, "Let me explain to you what this passage really means." By the time we are done explaining what we think it means, it no longer means what God said it means.

Our prayers seem to be written by lawyers who qualify every sentence to provide God with a way out in case no answer comes. Our elders' meetings are often devoid of the spiritual power so prevalent in the Early Church. It seems that implementing their decisions always hinges on three things: resources, effort and risk management. There is no difference between this and what goes on every day in secular board meetings.

Some of our seminaries are staffed with professors who teach about miracles but have never seen one. We learn about revivals, but we never experience one. We study about prayer, but it seldom radically changes things around us. We hear about a victorious Christ before whom every knee must bow, and at the same time we watch the enemy move boldly all over the place. No wonder, then, that a theology of powerlessness has become so prevalent. We have idealized defeat and canonized failure to the point that it sounds more spiritual to speak of those than of victory.

I remember an incident at a congregation in my hometown that displayed a theology of powerlessness. At their annual assembly, the presiding elder announced with a self-effacing tone, "We have good news to share. Last year our congregation numbered 86. This year the Lord has chosen to purify us, and we are now down to a healthier 54. Narrow is the way that leads to salvation. Praise God for this mighty deed." How much worse can it get?

What has happened? We have turned the battlefield we were supposed to occupy victoriously into a massive POW camp. We have become content with surviving rather than overcoming. We have believed the lie that we are not to engage the enemy. We have looked at the impotence of the staff in our hand in comparison to the might of the enemy's oncoming chariots, and we have concluded that we are not meant to fight. "The world belongs to the evil one," we say, "so let us not fight." After all, we await new heavens and a new earth. In so doing, like the Israelites of old, we fail to realize that, unless we depart from the land of captivity, the chosen people will never move into the Promised Land. Unless we raid the enemy's camp and set the captives free, those captives will never make it to heaven. In essence, we have been deceived.

2. *He dominated them.* Deception *always* breeds domination. "So they [the Egyptians] appointed taskmasters over them to afflict them with hard labor....to labor rigorously;...they made their lives bitter with hard labor" (Exod. 1:11,13,14). Like an extremely efficient POW commandant, Pharaoh immediately hit the Israelites with an overwhelming barrage of abuse designed to obliterate the possibility of escape in their minds. He made them look, feel and think like POWs.

This is also Satan's strategy today. As soon as we compromise on the biblical truth of who we are in Christ and what we are meant to accomplish while on this earth, Satan moves in with full force. All kinds of mischief is heaped upon the Church—immorality, infighting, divorce, rebellious children, spiritual impotence. Satan's aim is to make us forget, once and for all, that we are meant to be spiritual marines. He afflicts us with hard labor so that we become bitter. His aim is to make us so preoccupied with our own misery that we will lose sight of the reason we are on earth.

How does he do it? By causing us to confuse trials, which always come from God, with the burdens that he imposes on us. When we subscribe to a POW mentality, we accept that the camp commandant has an implicit right to abuse us. Because we also believe in an omniscient and omnipotent God, we assume that God knows and approves of that abuse. This is how we find ourselves in the extremely dangerous position of thanking God for trials that, in reality, are burdens surreptitiously imposed on us by Satan (see 2 Cor. 2:7,10,11; 1 Pet. 5:7-9).

When a Christian thanks God for something the devil is doing to him, he finds himself "laboring rigorously" (see Exod. 1:13) and quickly heading for the mire of bitterness. Trials always bring with them the necessary grace to endure them. On the other hand, burdens are meant to destroy us. It is crucial to be able to distinguish one from the other. Because on the surface they are somewhat similar, Satan is able to take advantage of us, as in the case of the Church of Corinth where Paul discerned that Satan's scheme was to destroy the repentant sinner through excessive sorrow.

A trial is similar to undergoing surgery in the best hospital, while a burden is like being stabbed by a mugger in a dark alley. There are some superficial similarities: In both cases a foreign object cuts our flesh, bleeding occurs and there is potential for infection. However, what is the basic difference between these two? *The intent.* A surgeon—who is sworn to provide the best possible care for us—cuts our flesh to extract that which is damaging to us. His intention is to make us stronger. A mugger—who is bent on destroying us—uses a weapon on our flesh to weaken us and take advantage of us.

Deception always breeds domination. When Christians fail to see who they are in Christ, Satan takes advantage of them. This is why some Christians find themselves thanking God for what they consider trials, such as "the divorce that destroyed my marriage," "the rebellion that has overtaken my children" or "the bankruptcy that has deprived me of my daily bread." These are not trials from God! They are burdens Satan has imposed![1] God does not use divorce, rebellion, drug addiction or lack of daily bread to build us up. This is contrary to His Word. Of course, those things do happen to Christians, and God is able to use them for good (see Rom. 8:28). But they do not come from God. When burdens like this first appear, we are to resist and reject them, never to welcome them. Trying to find value in such burdens is like banging our heads against a wall to find out how good it feels when we stop. We already know how it feels!

When Christians submit to a mind-set that forces them to thank God, the Lord of hope, for hopeless situations, bitterness cannot be far away. This kind of situation is so biblically abnormal that anger immediately develops. In most cases we confine it to our subconscious level.

It is this anger that eventually causes us "to build cities of storage for Pharaoh" (see Exod. 1:11). What is a "city of storage"? It is a stronghold for the enemy to strengthen his position in time of war or need. This is precisely what the people of God did for Pharaoh. And this is what we do when we try to justify theologically our self-imposed impotence in the face of Satan's onslaught. We come up with man-made theological explanations for something that, biblically speaking, cannot be explained.

This is why the most damaging weapons in Satan's arsenal have been developed by Christian slave labor. Liberation theology, the theology of the death of God, situational ethics applied to the Bible, hyper-Calvinism, the "name-it-and-claim-it" theology and similar ones, are nothing more than the result of man's futile attempt to find a human explanation or solution for surreptitiously imposed satanic burdens.

Unfortunately, some of this damaging theological speculation has been produced on seminary campuses long after the shekinah of God's presence has departed. Through the excessive influence of Freudianism in our biblical curriculum, the term "overcoming" has been replaced by "coping." Consequently, the gospel has ceased to be good news and has become good advice. The difference between these two is as dramatic as the difference between day and night. Good advice is what you get from your banker when you cannot pay the mortgage on your house. Good news is going to that same banker and watching him smile while he announces that someone visited the bank, paid your mortgage in full and deposited one million dollars in your account for you to spend as you wish. *That* is good news!

Once we become Satan's captives, his objective is to weaken us to the point that escape will never be considered and that we will be happy with simply surviving.

3. *He began to destroy them.* "When you are helping the Hebrew women to give birth and see them upon the birthstool, if it is a son, then you shall put him to death; but if it is a daughter, then she shall live" (Exod. 1:16).

The genius of Pharaoh's scheme was that it combined death with life. Abuse with pseudograce. If all the babies would have been killed, the people of Israel would have never tolerated it. By giving them something, Pharaoh appeared gracious, much like a POW commandant who allows starving prisoners to celebrate Christmas with care packages sent to them from home.

Pharaoh's ultimate objective was to destroy their fruitfulness. Why were only baby boys killed? Because when boys grow up, they become soldiers. Similarly, Satan's strategy has been to remove every reference in our theology to spiritual warfare. Furthermore, many of the gifts of the Spirit that have been called temporary, or that some say ceased with the Apostolic Age, are vital in warfare against the devil. On the other hand, the promises we have kept emphasize the future life. We seem to say, "Don't bother about the fact that there are cities going to hell. There is nothing that can be done about the injustice, the deprivation, the mess around here. Just endure graciously. We have a new city coming up, the New Jerusalem." We have accepted defeat, and we are constantly suspect of victory.

General Patton, the colorful U.S. commander during World War II, once welcomed a batch of new recruits with these words: "Welcome to Europe and to the war. I am sure some high-ranking jerk back in the States has told you that the secret to winning the war is to die for your country. That is not so! The secret to winning the war is to make the enemy die for *his* country!" The same principle holds true today. It is all right to lose graciously—once or twice. But if the gospel is to be taken to the ends of the earth, we better begin to *win* graciously!

Deception, domination and destruction had created a picture of total chaos and despair for Israel. The people had been transformed from a privileged nation within the Egyptian empire into a nameless mass of slaves saddled with the most demanding task and headed for extermination. The compromising, self-serving speculations that eventually led them to accept Pharaoh's scheme had driven Israel into a corner. Hopelessness was beginning to set in. Something had to be done if the people of God were to avoid annihilation.

The Difference Prayer Makes

Backed into a corner, Israel discovered the power of prayer: "And the sons of Israel sighed because of the bondage, and they cried out; and their cry for help because of their bondage rose up to God. So God heard their groaning; and God remembered His covenant with Abraham, Isaac and Jacob. And God saw the sons of Israel, and God took notice of them" (Exod. 2:23-25).

Prayer turned deception, domination and destruction into divine deliverance. The power of Pharaoh was broken. God's power was fully released and two million slaves were set free! Do we realize that without that prayer, Exodus would be a two-chapter book? Because of that prayer, 38 chapters had to be added to report on God's answer!

This is where the parallel between Israel and the Early Church

---

THE DIFFERENCE BETWEEN PRAYER AS WE USUALLY CONCEIVE IT AND THE KIND THE EARLY CHURCH PRACTICED IS AS VAST AS THE DIFFERENCE BETWEEN SWIMMING IN THE BATHTUB AS OPPOSED TO SWIMMING IN THE OPEN OCEAN.

---

becomes clearer than ever. Israel's *only* weapon was prayer. No army, no economic power, no social status. Nothing. What set them free and gave them victory over Pharaoh's mighty army? Prayer. Likewise, the Early Church's *only* weapon was prayer (see Acts 1:14; 2:42; 4:24-31). The early disciples were third-class citizens (Galileans inside Israel, a country occupied by the invading Romans). They were unlearned and unwise as far as the world's standards are concerned. They had no military or political connections. In spite of all that, they established Christianity in Jerusalem, Judea and Samaria. By the time the disciples left this earth, the gospel was very much on its way to the ends of the earth. We are called to do the same, beginning with our own Jerusalem. Prayer is the key to successfully accomplish it.

Could it be that what we consider prayer today is not everything that prayer is from a biblical point of view? Often our view of prayer is so narrow as to render it totally unattractive. Prayer is more than just reading "I need" lists to God, hoping He will answer. Prayer, as the Early Church knew it, encompassed the Godhead, angels, the Church, Satan and his host of demons—all of them engaged in a struggle for the souls of men (compare Eph. 6:12 with Eph. 6:18-20; Rom. 15:30; Col. 2:1; 4:12). When the Early Church prayed, the earth shook (see Acts 4:23-31). They asked for boldness, and God obliged by granting signs and wonders. Actually, God worked with them, helping them. Prayer in the Early Church was dynamic, powerful and fun.

The difference between prayer as we usually conceive it and the kind the Early Church practiced is as vast as the difference between swimming in the bathtub as opposed to swimming in the open ocean. How long can you enjoy a swim in your bathtub? If you stretch your legs out under the water, your head sticks out. If you lower your head, your knees emerge. If you thrust your arms, you hit the sides. This is why we get in and out as quickly as possible. On the other hand, swimming in the ocean is exciting, unpredictable and exhilarating. This is the way prayer was for the Early Church. You never knew when an angel would show up or demons would present opposition or when the Holy Spirit might give a word (see Acts 10:2,3; 12:5-7; 13:2; Eph. 6:12,18-20; Jas. 4:7).

Once, I took an editor from a large publishing house to Argentina. He wanted to see the country and learn about God's movement there. We arrived in Cordoba when Omar Cabrera was having an all-night prayer meeting. It was winter and extremely cold. The editor asked me how many people were expected to attend. I thought that possibly 400 people would come. However, trying to play it safe, I said, "At least 200." He asked me if he could preach to them. That was easy to arrange because in an all-night prayer vigil you have 8 to 10 hours to play with. When my friend stood up to preach at midnight, instead of the 200 I had told him, he faced 12,000 Christians who had come out on a cold winter night to spend time with God and each other in prayer!

Why would so many people respond so enthusiastically on a bitterly cold night? Because it was the best show in town, so to speak. The Church was there in force, which means that all the gifts entrusted to individual members were able to operate in concert. The Lord Jesus, name above all names, was in their midst. The Father stood ready to answer "anything that they ask in His name" (see John 14:12-14; 15:16). Angels had secured the perimeter. The Holy Spirit was teaching them how to pray. As the prayer meeting got underway, the Church aggressively moved into the heavenly places, displacing the forces of evil. The fullness of Christ was on display. Anything could happen!

Prayer as a Vehicle to Exercise Spiritual Authority

What is the secret behind effective prayer? It is the use of the authority entrusted to the believer. Let us put it into perspective.

First of all, prayer is something that happens on this side of heaven only. It is something for which man is expected to take the initiative. Man pleads, God gives. Man knocks, God opens. Man asks, God answers. The initiative rests with man (see Matt. 7:7-11).

Second, prayer operates in the realm of God's self-imposed limitations. These are areas where God, for reasons unknown to us, chose to limit His options and, consequently, His freedom of action. One of those areas is preaching the gospel. God has determined that the gospel should be preached only by man. He could do a much better job than us, but He will not do it. Angels cannot do it, either. A classic example is Cornelius in the book of Acts (see Acts 10:1ff). If there was ever someone close to the kingdom of God, it was Cornelius. He even prayed and gave offerings before becoming a Christian! He leaned so much over the fence toward salvation that if someone sneezed behind him he would have tipped right over into God's kingdom. He was an easy catch as far as evangelism is concerned. God sent an angel to talk to him, but all the angel was allowed to do was to give him the name and address of a preacher: Peter (see Acts 10:3-6). It took a man to preach the gospel to another man. This is the way God has ordained it.

Another area where God established restrictions is prayer. He determined that certain things will happen only in answer to prayer (see Jas. 4:2; Eph. 6:18,19). And this is what makes prayer so central to the fulfillment of the Great Commission. Let us take a look at a progressive disclosure showing why God chose to delegate the ministry of prayer to believers:

1. God made the world and appointed Adam master over it.

2. When Adam, the master, sinned, he turned that dominion over to Satan.

3. Satan thus became the "de facto" ruler of the earth, God's creation.

4. Because Adam, God's deputy on earth, transferred his legal dominion to Satan, God became obligated to recognize Satan's legal standing in spite of the fraudulent way in which it was obtained.

5. God is all powerful, yet His power never operates in violation of His character. Before Jesus' victory at Calvary, God would not become a trespasser by challenging Satan directly in matters related to man and the world under his control. If he did so, Satan could have called God a trespasser.

6. Because the government of the earth was delegated to man and lost by man, it could only be legally recovered by another man.

7. However, because all men have sinned and thus came under Satan's legal dominion, man's condition and the future of the earth was hopeless.

8. God solved the problem through the incarnation of Jesus Christ. The fact that Jesus was conceived by the Holy Spirit prevented Satan from having any claim on Him. The fact that Jesus was born of the virgin Mary made Him a bona fide member of the human race. He became the last Adam and the second man (see Rom. 5:12-19; 1 Cor. 15:45-47).

9. The temptation of Jesus in the wilderness was a repeat of Satan's temptation of Adam and Eve. The outcome represents Satan's first major defeat on earth by man (see Matt. 4:1ff; Mark 1:12; Luke 4:1ff).

10. The Cross completed the victory and His resurrection categorically certified it.[2]

Deputies of the Court of Calvary

Satan is a sore loser, however. Even though the property was awarded to Jesus, Satan had no intention of vacating it. This is why Jesus told His disciples to wait in Jerusalem for the Holy Spirit. On the Day of Pentecost, they were finally given the badge that certified them as deputies of the court. Now their task was to go all over the world to confront and evict the intruders (see Matt. 16:18,19).

This is where prayer and the issue of authority come in! When we confront the intruders on issues where biblical evidence indicates they have no rights, and we relay that situation to God in prayer, God is then provided with the legal and moral justification to release His power to evict the intruders.

Like deputies of the court, we are empowered to serve an eviction notice. If the enemy resists, the Judge is morally and legally free to confront him directly. When a legal paper is served, the court deputy doesn't even have to raise his voice. He may even smile and say: "Be out of the premises by noon tomorrow." If it is ignored, tomorrow at 12:01 P.M. a carload of deputies moves in and takes possession by force. The key is not the power he possesses but the authority he has.

As Jesus said, "Behold, I have given you authority...over all the power of the enemy, and nothing shall injure you" (Luke 10:19).

What the first Adam lost through disobedience, the last Adam recovered through obedience (see Rom. 5:19; Phil. 2:8). Now the Church must repossess it through prayer and witness.

It is this element of authority that makes prayer such a dynamic enterprise. We have been given authority over *all* power of the enemy (see Luke 10:17-19). We can confidently resist the devil because authority overruns power (see Jas. 4:7; 1 Pet. 5:8,9). For instance, in our car, power is represented by the engine that sits under the hood. Authority is represented by the steering wheel. The engine makes more noise and indeed has more power than the steering wheel. But it is the steering wheel that determines where the car goes.

The Truth Shall Make You Free

Eventually, an allied airplane landed near the POW camp where General Wainwright was imprisoned. An American officer walked up to the fence, saluted and announced: "General, Japan has surrendered." Armed with that piece of truth, Wainwright limped all the way to the commandant's office. He opened the door and, without even raising his voice, asserted, "My commander in chief has defeated your commander in chief. I am in control now. You must surrender." Without firing a single shot, the emaciated, physically handicapped POW took over the camp from the well-fed, heavily armed commandant.

How was he able to do it? Because the truth had set him free. He also knew how to use authority to control power. The Japanese commandant's fear had finally materialized. His captives found out that they were mightier and decided to leave the land of captivity. Like Pharaoh of old, he eventually surrendered.

This is the kind of authority in prayer that is required to reach an entire city for Christ—"That the manifold wisdom of God might now be made known through the church to the rulers and the authorities in the heavenly places" (Eph. 3:10). The objective is to proclaim and exemplify the Lordship of Jesus to the forces of evil in the heavenlies and to set the captives free.[3] This is the bottom line: people coming to Jesus Christ. Spiritual warfare that does not result in setting the captives free is not warfare, but a military parade. These two are similar but not identical. In a parade, you show your weapons, but you don't fire them. In warfare, you load, aim and fire. This is why spiritual warfare must be conducted primarily on Satan's occupied territory, not just inside the four walls of our churches. To exercise authority over a rebellious power, you must engage it (see Cor. 10:3-5)!

In Revelation 12:11, we are told that we defeat Satan through the blood of the Lamb, the word of our testimony and because we do not love our lives so much as to shrink from death. We cannot improve on the first element: the blood of the Lamb. It was perfectly shed, once and for all, as a ransom for all. But we can improve on the word of our testimony. We have reduced it to merely witnessing to other human beings. Biblically speaking, the scope of our testimony is much broader. It reaches all the way into the heavenly places. According to Ephesians 3:10, we are to declare the manifold wisdom of God to the principalities and powers in the heavenlies.[4] We must confront them and remind them that they have no right to hang on to what Jesus paid for and bought with His blood. To do this effectively, we must be willing to die as the ultimate expression that we do not love our lives.

Carlos Annacondia, the Argentine lay evangelist mentioned in an earlier chapter, has led more than two million people to public professions of faith. According to C. Peter Wagner, Annacondia is perhaps the most effective mass evangelist of all time. Annacondia told a group of pastors how he was introduced to the issue of the spiritual authority of the believer. One day he was entreating God for more power. He was pleading with Him for a tangible dimension of the power he read about in the book of Acts. Then he heard God whisper to him in his heart, "I have already given you something more effective than power. I have given you authority over all power of the enemy."

A perplexed Annacondia asked, "Lord, if you already gave it to me, why is it that nothing happens?"

To this Carlos felt God reply, "Because authority must be exercised for things to happen. Go and use the authority that *you already have.*" Carlos felt vulnerable taking a stand against the enemy on account of words alone, but he did it and God backed him up. His ministry took off and multitudes have been added to the Kingdom, thanks to his understanding of this principle.

Anytime we courageously engage the enemy in the context of God's revealed will, God will back us up to the hilt. Angels will be dispatched to assist us. The powerful hand of God will certify the genuineness of our message (see Mark 16:20). The Holy Spirit will pray in us, for us and through us (see Rom. 8:26,27), and God the Father will grant our petitions (see Matt. 18:19; John 14:12-14). Nowhere is this truer than when it concerns the salvation of the lost. God wishes all men to be saved. Christ has given Himself in ransom for all. Now it is our duty to resist the god of this world who has blinded the lost to the light of the gospel (see 2 Cor. 4:4) and open their eyes through answers to prayer (see Acts 26:18).

When General Wainwright was flown to Japan in time for the surrender ceremony, he dreaded the moment he would face General MacArthur. In spite of having been liberated, he was still full of shame. He still felt like a failure. He was afraid of facing his commander. As MacArthur walked by, Wainwright could not resist the impulse to hide in a corner. MacArthur spotted him and called out to him. Wainwright obeyed, and as he faced MacArthur, he completely broke down. A flood of tears overwhelmed him. He stood before his commander in self-inflicted shame. He had failed him. He had surrendered Corregidor.

MacArthur reached out to him, embraced him and simply said, "It is okay. You fought well." At the surrender ceremony that followed shortly afterward, every general, admiral and brigadier assigned to the Pacific theater of operations was jockeying for position to stand next to MacArthur. In his classic style, MacArthur put all of them behind him as he sat at the table with Hiroshito's representatives. Only two generals were allowed to stand by him. To his left was the British General Percivale, who had surrendered Singapore at the beginning of the war. To his right was General Wainwright, who had surrendered Corregidor. As he put his signature on the document that certified Japan's unconditional surrender, MacArthur handed a pen to each one of them. By so doing, he was saying, "You did your best. Don't be too hard on yourselves. We have won."

Perhaps you feel as Wainwright did because of a past failure. Maybe you are still living in a POW camp. The enemy has lied to you and has deprived you of everything. Maybe you have lost your command; you have surrendered. Since then you have been punishing yourself. You have been living in a cloud of hopelessness. You watched the sun of hope set a long time ago, and since then you have lived in an interminable night of despair.

I encourage you to look up to your Supreme Commander, Jesus Christ, the Lord of lords and the King of kings. He is saying to you, "I will never leave you nor forsake you. Even when you are unfaithful, I remain faithful. I cannot deny myself. You may have surrendered a flag or two, but the war has been won. Be of good courage" (see Heb. 13:5-6).

On that final day, when Satan will be forced to acknowledge the facts as described in Revelation 12:11 as final proof of his total defeat, you are going to stand next to your Commander. You will be part of His triumphal parade. Until then, pick yourself up and charge against the strongholds of the enemy looming over your city. Serve eviction notices and radio for help. Tell the enemy that "my Commander in Chief has defeated your commander in chief." You are in charge now. Go and begin to set the captives free!

Notes
1. See Isaiah 30:18; John 10:10; James 1:17.
2. See John 12:31,32; Romans 1:4; Ephesians 1:19-23; Colossians 2:15; Hebrews 2:14,15.
3. Compare Ephesians 3:10 with Ephesians 6:12,17b,19; Matthew 4:4,7,10; Philippians 4:6; James 4:7; all of these suggest that verbal testimony may be included in resisting the forces of evil.
4. Compare 1 Timothy 5:21; Revelation 1:16; 2:1,8,12,18; 3:1,7,14.

Section II

The Strategy

THE FOLLOWING CHAPTERS ARE A DESCRIPTION OF THE STRATEGY we usually follow as we help pastors reach their cities for God. Please keep in mind that this strategy is imperfect and still very much in process. However, it represents the sum of what we know so far. It is our best attempt at implementing God's will.

Before I get into the details, I want to tell you a story that will set the stage for the information to follow. It's the story of a child who grew up in an abusive home. His father was a violent man and a practitioner of the occult. During his insecure and turbulent childhood, this boy watched many of his brothers die—burned alive by his father who offered them as human sacrifices. His father worshiped demons in the high places around his city. He did so until not a single hilltop was left undefiled. When he ran out of high places, he turned every green tree in the city and surrounding countryside into a satanic shrine. We can only try to imagine how awful this boy's childhood must have been. It is absolutely impossible for us to capture the full scope of the horror he experienced while changing from a child into a boy and eventually into a young man.

To compound the problem, his father, a head of state, was a frustrated man of war. He fought against every neighboring country and consistently lost. In a futile attempt to turn his war fortunes around, he made a treaty with a powerful king to assist him in staging a military revenge. Instead of helping him, his ally turned against him and inflicted great damage on the kingdom. With his troops at the gate of the city, he demanded ransom. To appease the traitor, the boy's father went into God's Temple, stripped it of much of its gold and offered it as a gift. But this did not pacify his tormentor, who proceeded to take many of the people captive, thus weakening the kingdom even further.

In trying to understand the reason for this series of defeats, the boy's father concluded that it had to do with the power of the gods assisting his enemies. He then began to pray to them and eventually made a pact with the devil. "Give me back my kingdom, and I will serve you," the king said. Again, the opposite of what he expected happened. The gods he prayed to also turned against him.

In total desperation, the boy's father decided to trust no one but himself. He made himself into a god. He entered the house of the Lord and used the precious-metal utensils there to build idols and altars, which he erected all over the capital of his kingdom. To his dismay, the situation did not improve. It got progressively worse. The king, his people and the nation became mired in spiritual, social and economic misery.

When he finally died, the king was so despised by his countrymen that he was denied the customary honor of a burial among former kings. Instead, a simple grave in the city where he had lived so miserably received his mortal remains.

For 25 years, the son of this evil king witnessed the consequences of his father's terrible deeds. Finally, the son succeeded his father as king and thus became the ruler of a broken nation. He resided in a capital city that was totally defiled. The moral, economic and social fibers of the nation were in shambles. The fact that he was still alive was a miracle in itself, given his father's record of burning his own children for human sacrifices. What was left of God's Temple was in total disrepair. Its doors were broken and the interior was defiled with all kinds of garbage and blasphemous paraphernalia.

The young king's name was Hezekiah. His chances for success in life, much less of living a godly lifestyle, were nil. He had succeeded one of Judah's most evil kings: his father, Ahaz. Their story is covered in great detail in the second book of Chronicles, chapters 28 through 33. If there was ever a picture of desolation and despair, this was it: an inexperienced young man in charge of a broken nation whose capital city had been turned into a demonic shrine and where God's name had been blatantly blasphemed.

However, in less than a year, the capital city was rebuilt, the countryside was restored and the kingdom regained a spiritual, social and economic stability, second only to the one experienced during the kingdom's golden hour under world-famous King Solomon. Hezekiah's life embodies one of the most dramatic examples of city and nation taking ever recorded anywhere.

I intend to use this story as the backdrop against which I present the strategy for reaching modern cities for Christ. Before I do so, allow me to elaborate on Hezekiah's life story and highlight his many accomplishments.

Hezekiah became king when he was only 24 years old. On that day, he must have been overwhelmed by the spiritual, social and economic misery in which his kingdom was submerged, all of which was the product of his father's folly. However, Hezekiah was a diligent person, and he decided to act swiftly to effect a radical change in the life of the nation.

As proof of that diligence, during the *first* month of the *first* year of Hezekiah's kingdom, he repaired the doors of the house of the Lord. This was his way of drawing a line in the sand and saying, "Enough!" With the doors repaired and in place, no more evil could enter God's house, nor could any of its remaining utensils be further defiled or removed.

Hezekiah then gathered the priests and the Levites into the capital city's main square. He challenged them to consecrate themselves and to cleanse the house of the Lord by carrying the uncleanness out from the holy place. After giving them a detailed summary of the nation's pitiful condition and identifying the nation's apostasy as the *only* reason for it, he publicly proclaimed: "Now it is in my heart to make a covenant with the Lord God of Israel" (2 Chron. 29:10). He followed this proclamation with an exhortation to the priests and Levites not to be negligent in doing the same: "For the Lord has chosen you to stand before Him, to minister to Him, and to be His ministers and burn incense" (2 Chron. 29:11).

This was quite a statement. No doubt, Hezekiah was a visionary. He told unemployed priests and Levites, who had lived in terror of his evil father in a city plagued with idols and with a totally defiled Temple, that they were about to minister to God and to become His ministers. And in order to put this in a tangible context, he told them that they would burn incense to the Lord. This was quite a challenge because the Temple was completely out of commission.

Somehow the Levites believed him. "They assembled their brothers, consecrated themselves, and went in to cleanse the house of the Lord, according to the commandment of the king by the words of the Lord" (2 Chron. 29:15). The priests also responded and they "went in to the inner part of the house of the Lord [they were the only ones allowed to enter the holy place] to cleanse it" (2 Chron. 29:16).

In just 16 days, the priests, working inside the Temple, and the Levites on the outside, accomplished the task. They announced to the king: "We have cleansed the whole house of the Lord" (2 Chron. 29:18).

The next day the king arose early and assembled the princes of the city and went up to the house of the Lord (see 2 Chron. 29:20). Once there, he proceeded to offer a sacrifice for the sins of the nation. The sins of the nation were many, and his father, King Ahaz, had been responsible for the bulk of them. Having offered that important sacrifice for the nation, he stationed the Levites with musical instruments all over the house of the Lord, and "when the burnt offering began, the song to the Lord also began" (2 Chron. 29:27), accompanied by trumpets and all kinds of instruments. As the smoke from the offering ascended, songs, music and worship filled the house of the Lord. This must have been quite a sight. All of this was happening in a Temple that, until a few weeks earlier, had been neglected to the point of having become a monument to the nation's blasphemy against God. What a dramatic change!

"Now at the completion of the burnt offerings, the king and all who were present with him bowed down and worshiped" (2 Chron. 29:29). Hezekiah knew that worship was possible once again because the sacrifice for the nation had finally ascended into the presence of God. For the first time in 16 years, the king bowed before God! Deeply moved by Hezekiah's example, "all who were present...bowed down and worshiped."

Not satisfied with this, the king now challenged the assembly to "come near and bring sacrifices and thank offerings to the house of the Lord" (2 Chron. 29:31). The people responded so enthusiastically and so generously that the number of priests was inadequate to handle the flood of sacrifices, and the Levites had to help them (see 2 Chron. 29:34).

In 2 Chronicles 29:35,36, two powerful statements are made. The first one is: "Thus the service of the house of the Lord was established again." A tremendous change—from an inactive, totally defiled Temple to a full and joyful restoration with such an abundance of sacrifices that the Temple storehouses were overflowing. The second statement is even more dramatic: "The thing came about suddenly." It happened so fast that no one was able to take credit for it. Undoubtedly, it was the king's and the people's consensus that God had done it.

After Solomon's death years earlier, the once-glorious united kingdom had been split in two: the northern kingdom was called Israel, and the southern kingdom was called Judah. Constant animosity and frequent wars had made the split irreversible. With the

Temple once again in operation, the sins of the nation atoned for, the priests and Levites reinstated, and the people of Jerusalem actively worshiping God, now Hezekiah embarked on one of the most ambitious enterprises ever attempted by a human being. He decided to invite the people of both kingdoms, Judah and Israel, to jointly celebrate the Lord's Passover in Jerusalem, the capital of the southern kingdom. This was quite a project. Since the time when Israel had split from Judah, the celebration of the Passover at the Temple in Jerusalem was the hottest political issue in Israel. So much so, that Israel's King Jeroboam, the one responsible for the split, had decreed that no one from Israel should go to Jerusalem to worship but instead should do it in one of the two shrines he built to pagan gods inside the northern kingdom.

Hezekiah was not intimidated by this. He was a visionary with missionary zeal. He had promised the priests and Levites that they would both minister to God and also be His ministers to the people (see 2 Chron. 29:11). However, the people he had in mind included more than just the dwellers of Jerusalem and the southern kingdom. He was thinking of *all* the people inhabiting *both* kingdoms, Judah and Israel. He was using as his model the splendor that permeated the land during Solomon's reign. He was determined not to settle for anything less.

To this effect, "Hezekiah sent to all Israel and Judah and wrote letters also to Ephraim and Manasseh, that they should come to the house of the Lord" (2 Chron. 30:1). His couriers visited every city in both kingdoms, even though in some places they were laughed at, scorned and mocked (see 2 Chron. 30:10).

While this was going on, God gave the people of Judah "one heart to do what the king and the princes commanded" (2 Chron. 30:12). This was good news for Hezekiah, because Jerusalem was still filled with idols and pagan places of worship. Shortly before the Passover, the people in Jerusalem spontaneously "arose and removed the altars which were in Jerusalem; they also removed all the incense altars and cast them into the brook Kidron" (2 Chron. 30:14). Now the Temple *and* the city where the Temple was located had been secured for God. It is evident that, as a result of the purification of the Temple and the consecration of the king, the priests and the Levites were affecting the masses in Jerusalem positively.

When the time came for the Passover to be celebrated, an unprecedented multitude gathered. To everyone's surprise, many of them were from the same cities where the couriers had been scoffed at and mocked as they delivered the invitations. In fact, so many came from those regions, apparently in a hurry, that they had not purified themselves properly. "For a multitude of the people, even many from Ephraim and Manasseh, Issachar and Zebulun, had not purified themselves, yet they ate the Passover otherwise than prescribed" (2 Chron. 30:18). King Hezekiah was forced to pray, "May the good Lord pardon....So the Lord heard Hezekiah and healed the people" (2 Chron. 30:18,20).

People from both kingdoms celebrated with great joy for seven days. It was such a happy occasion that "then the whole assembly decided to celebrate the feast another seven days, so they celebrated the seven days with joy" (2 Chron. 29:23). Nothing of this magnitude had happened "since the days of Solomon," and "there was great joy in Jerusalem" (2 Chron. 29:26). The crowning moment came when "the Levitical priests arose and blessed the people [of both nations]; and their voice was heard and their prayer came to His holy dwelling place, to heaven" (2 Chron. 29:27). What a contrast with the dark days of Ahab's reign, when the city of Jerusalem was defiled by satanic shrines and no public prayers were ever offered to God!

As the people returned to their cities, beginning in Judah and reaching as far as Ephraim and Manasseh in the northern kingdom, they began destroying the pagan altars "until they had destroyed them all" (2 Chron. 31:1).

The purification of Judah and Israel was quickly followed by tremendous prosperity, to the point that Azariah the chief priest declared, "Since the contributions began to be brought into the house of the Lord, we have had enough to eat with plenty left over, for the Lord has blessed His people, and this great quantity is left over" (2 Chron. 31:10). The abundance was of such magnitude that offerings lay in heaps throughout the Temple (see 2 Chron. 31:6). King Hezekiah commanded that storage rooms be built to keep the overflow (see 2 Chron. 31:11). God's hand was so much upon Hezekiah that "every work which he began...seeking his God, he did with all his heart and prospered" (2 Chron. 31:21).

The nation's recovery came full circle when the king of Assyria—the same nation that had inflicted great misery on Hezekiah's father by betraying the treaty with him—was soundly defeated in battle. It had been a long time since Judah had experienced any victory on the battlefield. Now, once again, as proof of God's hand upon the nation, the army of the powerful king of Assyria was totally annihilated. His warriors lay dead on the battlefield and he himself, upon returning to his capital city, was murdered by his own children as he entered the temple of his gods (see 2 Chron. 32:21).

What a tremendous story. First, a city was taken, then a nation, and, eventually, a divided kingdom was brought together in worship into the house of the Lord. The nation prospered as the house of God prospered. Eventually their former oppressor was totally defeated. What began as a picture of absolute despair evolved into the full sunshine of hope and victory. The principles responsible for this turnaround, and King Hezekiah's strategy to apply those principles are still valid in our struggle to reach our cities for God today. Let's examine them carefully.

6

Establishing God's Perimeter

"Then he [Hezekiah] said to them, 'Listen to me, O Levites. Consecrate yourselves now, and consecrate the house of the Lord, the God of your fathers, and carry the uncleanness out from the holy place....Now it is in my heart to make a covenant with the Lord God of Israel, that His burning anger may turn away from us.'" 2 Chronicles 29:5,10

HOW DO WE *BEGIN* TO REACH AN ENTIRE CITY FOR CHRIST? THE first step is to establish God's perimeter in the city. In military science, a perimeter is the outer boundary of an area where defenses are set up. The term implies a warfare context, real or potential. To attempt to reach a city for Christ is an act of war—spiritual warfare. God, through the Church, targets the strongman in the city so his camp can be raided and the captives set free. To use military terminology, a spiritual beachhead must be secured. To do this effectively, we must take a hard look at the city as it really is, physically and spiritually. In other words, we must acquire "military intelligence."

What does a city look like from a heavenly perspective? Try to picture your city as seen from above. Usually, a city consists of a mass of people of varying social classes, some struggling to live moral, refined and decent lives, while others follow a less disci-

---

IN MANY CITIES, THE CHURCH MEMBERS LOOK MORE LIKE POWS THAN MARINES IN A VICTORIOUS ARMY "MARCHING AS TO WAR." MANY BELIEVERS THINK OF THEMSELVES AS PEOPLE WHO ARE DESTINED TO ONLY SURVIVE RATHER THAN TO CONQUER.

---

plined lifestyle. All of these people are caught up in a maze of futility, most often accompanied by deep personal pain. Many cities are overwhelmed by crime and violence; others are overwhelmed by the anxiety to find meaning to life.

All cities are struggling against storms of evil, and many are stewing in a mess of social chaos. A thick cloud of spiritual darkness seems to envelop everything and everyone. But in most major cities, with few exceptions, if you peer carefully enough you will notice something else: the Church in the city.

What does the Church in a city look like from above? The Church—and by this I mean only one Church consisting of many congregations—at first may appear as myriad isolated lights illuminating strategic points, resembling beachheads, all part of a united military campaign. Too often, however, upon closer examination, what look like beachheads are really a disjointed collection of glorified POW camps—the sum of which constitutes the Church in the city. I know this is a strong metaphor; however, I am speaking only in general terms. I am not describing the *nature* of the Church, but rather the *state* of the Church. The Church is indeed God's most precious possession on earth, but often its condition does not match its essence. A child may be born to a king, but if he stumbles into a pigpen, he will look like a dispossessed peasant.

The strategy used to reach the city for Christ depends entirely on the performance of the Church already in place. That is why it is of paramount importance to determine its real condition. Let me ask you, what is the state of the Church in *your* city today?

King Hezekiah was extremely honest in his assessment of the city and the nation. He blamed the city's and the nation's misery first on "our fathers [who] have been unfaithful and have done evil in the sight of the Lord" (2 Chron. 29:6). This undoubtedly describes the evil of the city, Jerusalem, and the nation, Judah. But then he goes on to point out the responsibility and the fate of the ancient equivalent of the Church when he says, "They have also shut the doors of the porch and put out the lamps, and have not burned incense or offered burnt offerings in the holy place to the God of Israel" (2 Chron. 29:7). We must be equally honest in our own assessment today. We must avoid the classic mistake of cursing the darkness while holding an unlit candle in our hands. The state of the city is always the result of the Church's condition.

In many cities, the Church members look more like POWs than marines in a victorious army "marching as to war." They seem to go to services Sunday after Sunday, only to get the minimum possible spiritual ration so they can last until the following week. Being a POW is more of a mind-set than anything else. The determining factor is their attitude. Many believers think of themselves as people who are destined to only survive rather than to conquer. They seem to be waiting for the war to end and for their commander in chief to ship them home. This will not happen until the day they die or the world comes to an end. The latter, depending on theological perceptions, has a variation factor of seven to a thousand years!

Some of these POW camps have better services than others. Some offer more recreational time; others, better music or youth programs. Sometimes these improvements motivate some of the people to switch camps, and sometimes they misinterpret an increase in the bread-and-water rations as revival. However, as long as the objective is one of contentment with survival, rather than total commitment to overcoming the enemy, they will remain captives regardless of what they choose to call themselves.

What a contrast to the final objective of the Church as outlined by Jesus Himself in Matthew 28:18-20: "And Jesus came up and spoke to them, saying, 'All authority has been given to Me in heaven and on earth. Go therefore and make disciples of all the nations, baptizing them in the name of the Father and the Son and the Holy Spirit, teaching them to observe all that I commanded you; and lo, I am with you always, even to the end of the age.'" He did not call us to improve the condition of the camps, but to overrun the oppressors, flee the camps and repossess the land!

God did not save us to be POWs, but to be victorious spiritual marines. It is not God's will that "our fathers...[fall] by the sword, and our sons and our daughters and our wives [be] in captivity," as Hezekiah so aptly put it in 2 Chronicles 29:9. We are left in this world not to merely survive but to conquer. In fact, the *Heavenly Times* newspaper has the typeset ready for the victory headline to be published on V-day. It is described in Revelation 12:11: "And they overcame him [Satan] because of the blood of the Lamb and because of the word of their testimony, and they did not love their life even to death." This is quite a victory. In fact, this is total victory!

This final victory is the sum of many individual victories obtained by the saints in cities all over the world. There are three components to this victory: the blood, our testimony and our willingness to die, if necessary. The first component represents a constant, while the other two are variables. Because our success depends on using each component correctly, let's take a closer look at each one of them.

The shedding of Jesus' blood on our behalf is a fact that cannot be changed or improved on, because it represents a perfect sacrifice. Satan will not waste time trying to alter that constant. Instead, he will concentrate on the two variables, because this is where he sees potential for victory.

Our testimony can be effective or ineffective, depending on our understanding of who we are in Christ. This, in turn, affects our subsequent actions, which have to do with our willingness to risk or not to risk our lives for Christ. For instance, if we see ourselves with no hope other than enduring, we will conclude that our testimony, this side of heaven, is to be limited to graceful endurance. On the other hand, if we see ourselves as free in Christ, devoid of spiritual strongholds, filled with the Spirit and charged with taking the gospel to every creature on earth, we will then view the blood of Christ as the enabling element to defeat the spiritual darkness around us. We will do so by boldly testifying about the benefits emanating from the blood, and we will eagerly engage the enemy, even if that means losing our lives. In order to see Revelation 12:11 come to pass in our cities, people must flee the POW camps and trade their prison garments for the divinely powerful weapons of spiritual marines (see 2 Cor. 10:3-5).

The Faithful Remnant

The first step in taking a city for Christ is to build—or reestablish—God's perimeter in the city. This is exactly what Hezekiah did. In the midst of the devastating spiritual darkness enveloping the city, he called together the priests and the Levites, and, beginning with the house of the Lord, he established a perimeter of godliness. Likewise, in your city a spiritual beachhead must be established. This is usually done by the coming together of the "faithful remnant."

By "faithful remnant," I mean Christians who are already waiting for the kingdom of God to come to that city. (This is not meant as a put-down to other Christians who, even though they do not share that vision, are very faithful to the Lord.) Regardless of the pitiful conditions that exist around them, deep down these faithful Christians know that God will eventually break through. To them it is not a matter of "if" but rather "when." This seems to have been Paul's objective when he visited synagogues in unevangelized cities. He was looking for the faithful remnant. In every city in the world today, scores of people have abandoned the POW mind-set and are waiting for the call to come together to establish a perimeter of godliness for God's kingdom.

A member of the "faithful remnant" is someone who fits the following profile:

First, he is waiting for God to break through and manifest His power because of His love for the Church and for the lost.

Second, he is called to the city first and then to his local congregation. Even though he faithfully discharges his responsibilities to his congregation, his heart beats for the city and for the multitudes lost in it.

Third, he has a *lifestyle* of prayer. He knows in absolute confidence that God is the only source of power to solve the problems he faces daily, and that is why he talks to Him "without ceasing" (1 Thess. 5:17).

Fourth, he is a humble and effective team player. By this I mean that he is not domineering, for he knows he cannot do it alone.

Fifth, he is devoid of selfish ambition. He has no personal agenda, only God's agenda. He is a kingdom person. God and His kingdom are all that matter. A good litmus test is to ask the question, "Would you be willing to give it all in order to reach your city for Christ, even if that means your congregation will not grow?" If the answer is an unqualified yes, you have found a member of the faithful remnant.

The Elijah Syndrome

The coming together of the "faithful remnant" cures its members of what I call "the Elijah syndrome." Satan is always trying to neutralize those who stand for righteousness and revival by isolating them and deceiving them into believing that they alone are left (see 1 Kings 19:14). Like Elijah, they are tempted to retreat into a cave, enter into spiritual depression and become prophets without hope. However, when others with the same passion join them, they realize that God also has 7,000 others who "have not bowed to Baal" (1 Kings 19:18). By meeting other members of the faithful remnant, they are able to see themselves as *part* of what God is *already* doing.

I have seen this phenomenon take place, and its effect is exhilarating. In Resistencia, it occurred at the gathering of the seven pastors I described in chapter 2. In Calgary, Canada, it took place during a pastors' luncheon with the presidents of four ministerial associations. As these leaders chatted about their desire to reach Calgary for Christ, they realized how much they had in common, and they began to discover similar desires, visions and longings God had already deposited in each one of them. In Stockton, California, it began to happen when Tim Pollock, a local Bible Baptist pastor, invited 11 other pastors to lunch and asked me to speak on how to reach Stockton for Christ. Many of those pastors had never met each other or worked together before. Yet, as I shared from the Word of God and presented His heartbeat for the lost in the city, I was able to see the pastors' hearts begin to beat in unison. By the time the lunch was over, they *knew* that God had an army in Stockton, and they were a part of it.

Something similar happened in San Francisco. My friend Michael Brodeur, a local Vineyard pastor, invited my associate, David Thompson, and me to have breakfast with a group of his fellow pastors in the city. Nineteen pastors showed up—a much higher number than originally expected. We shared from 1 Timothy 2:1-8 and illustrated the biblical principles of unity, intercession and passion for the lost, providing examples from other cities where God is currently at work. All of a sudden, something dramatic took place. The presence of God fell on the group. Tears rolled down the faces of those battle-wise soldiers. Finally, one of them spoke.

"Brethren," he said, "I have been a pastor in the city for over 20 years. I have seen every conceivable spiritual fad come and go. I tell you, this is different. This is of God. Let's go for it!"

Right there, in a public cafeteria, we all held hands, repented of the sins of division and contention, and established a perimeter of godliness. Quite unexpectedly, these pastors planted the seed for "Pray San Francisco." Even though all of them had hoped for revival before, they had hoped alone. Now as they held hands and prayed, they saw the reflection of that hope in every-

---

ONCE GOD'S PERIMETER IS ESTABLISHED, SATAN HAS A BIG PROBLEM. HE MUST NOW CONCERN HIMSELF WITH A GROUP EQUIPPED WITH DIVINELY POWERFUL WEAPONS.

---

one else. Suddenly, they *knew* they were no longer alone and God was ready to move!

Once God's perimeter is established, Satan has a big problem. He must now concern himself with a group equipped with divinely powerful weapons, a group willing to risk their lives as they proclaim Christ's victory all over the city. This is bound to create chaos in Satan's domain. Other POWs may flee his camp and, worse yet, the masses of people Satan has blinded to the gospel may see the light and be saved!

By simply coming together, the faithful remnant can dramatically change the balance of power.

Unity Based on Christ
It is important to clarify that the coming together of the faithful remnant must be centered around Jesus and not a program, no matter how good that program might be. Even though Hezekiah instructed the priests and the Levites to clean the Temple, the heart of the matter was a covenant with God. All the subsequent

activity flowed out of that decision to meet with God on His terms.

Historically, pastors and leaders have always come together to *do* something (a crusade, a seminar, etc.), rather than to *become* someone *in* Christ. The problem with program-centered unity is that once the program is completed, the "unity" evaporates.

What I am describing here is radically different. It is unity *in* Christ. The remnant must come together not because they have common interests or doctrines but because they share the same life: Jesus.

Because Jesus is the Chief Shepherd, now His undershepherds come to meet with Him in order to receive instruction and edification. As a result, everything else becomes secondary and subservient to these endeavors. Thus, they do not come together to pursue another program but to listen and obey Jesus' directives. They begin to diligently "preserve the unity of the Spirit" (Eph. 4:3) and in so doing they hold fast to the head (Christ) from whom this microcosmic example of the body, being supplied and held together by the joints and ligaments, "grows *with a growth which is from God*" (Col. 2:19, italics added).

The Presiding Jesus

This approach is nothing more than the rediscovery of something the Early Church knew quite well: the presence of Jesus in their midst. In Matthew 18:19,20, we are told that when two or three believers gather together in Jesus' name, He is there in their midst. Anything that they ask in His name is done by the Father who is in heaven. What an intriguing passage, as nowadays we rarely see the Father answering *everything* we ask in Jesus' name. What's more, even though we always open our gatherings in His name, quite often Jesus is nowhere to be found (see Rev. 3:20). What is the *real* meaning of this passage?

From the text, we know that it takes a minimum of two people. "For where two or three have gathered together in My name." Those who so gather in His name already have Jesus in their hearts, but now, in addition to the indwelling Jesus, we are told that they will also experience the presence of Jesus Himself *"in their midst."* Why is it that we do not see this happen today when we open our meetings "in the name of Jesus"?

I suggest that there is something about gathering in Jesus' name that we do not quite understand yet. It is not merely stating it at the beginning of the meeting. It is something radically different. It is acknowledging Him as our Master, our Lord, our life. It is understanding that it is *His* meeting and not ours. He is in control, not us. For Him to be in control, we must deny ourselves and die to self so that the only life left in us is His life. We must empty ourselves to allow the fullness of God to overflow us. As we fellowship with each other in the Spirit, the *indwelling* Jesus becomes the *presiding* Jesus. He then becomes the center of the gathering. He teaches. He speaks. He corrects. It is no wonder, then, that all of the prayers coming out of a meeting such as this will be answered by the Father. Each one of those prayers has been prompted by and approved by the presiding Jesus. This kind of meeting represents an impenetrable perimeter!

Jesus Locked Out of His Church

The preceding explanation seems to shed light on Revelation 3:20: "If anyone hears My voice and opens the door, I will come in to him, and will dine with him, and he with Me." We tend to use this verse exclusively in evangelistic crusades and have apparent disregard for the fact that Jesus' words are directed not to unbelievers but to a Church—a citywide Church that, even though it had gathered in His name, had left Jesus out! Yes, I believe it is possible to lock Jesus out of the Church—His Church!

I submit to you that many of our meetings, especially those held inside our spiritual POW camps, are like that. We think He is there, but He isn't. What we have is a gathering of Christians *with each other*, but not with Jesus. He is outside waiting for "someone to hear his voice." Such meetings lack the glory and

---

WE OFTEN FAIL TO RISE PAST THE HUMAN LEVEL AND, THUS, FIND OURSELVES OPERATING IN THE FLESH, A POOR SUBSTITUTE FOR GOD'S EXCELLENCE DIRECTED BY THE PRESIDING JESUS.

---

the majesty of Jesus; they have a definite lack of power. For instance, in the following verse, Revelation 3:21, Jesus promised, "He who overcomes, I will grant to him to sit down with Me on My throne." What throne is this? It is the one described in Ephesians 1:20-22: "Far above...every name that is named." The phrase "to sit down with Me on My throne" is a direct reference to positional authority and the resulting authority over all power of the enemy.

In the absence of the presiding Jesus, quite often our prayers become aimless, full of qualifiers—in fact, quite similar to the prayers of the Pharisees. We feel powerless because we are by ourselves in our own house of mirrors, miles away from His throne and the authority that flows from it. As we see Satan close in on us, we pray more out of desperation than deep conviction. We lack what is necessary in order to persevere and eventually overcome; we are devoid of authority. We think we have gathered in

His name, but all we have done is routinely recite, "We open this meeting in His name." This is not enough. Jesus is not a formula but a Person who has *all* authority in heaven and on earth. When we have no clear understanding of the heavenlies, and when we're dominated by strongholds of self-confidence, we are totally vulnerable to Satan's schemes. More often than not, we fail to rise past the human level and, thus, find ourselves operating in the flesh, a poor substitute for God's excellence directed by the presiding Jesus.

When the faithful remnant in your city comes together, it must purposefully rediscover this combination of the indwelling and the presiding Christ. They must meet with, and wait on, the Lord until *He* chooses to move. The beauty of His presence must be such that no one will be in a hurry to do anything other than sit at His feet, unlike the days when superactivism was the preferred mode of escape for our stale meetings.

Bond Servants Wanted

One of the favorite expressions used by the apostles to describe themselves was "bond servant of our Lord." A bond servant is one who sits at the door of his master, not even daring to look at him in the eyes. He watches his master's hands. He never speaks unless first spoken to by the master. He always does what he is instructed to do—nothing less, nothing more. In light of this, I am appalled at the way we conduct our spiritual meetings. Many times we treat Jesus as if He were *our* bond servant. Our prayer meetings too often amount to nothing more than listing a set of errands for Him to carry out.

The thought of waiting on the Lord seldom occurs to us. We usually assume that we already know His will. There is no need to wait for Him to reveal it to us. We are in a hurry, and we'd better move on.

I remember a time when some Western visitors came to Argentina. I told them, "We are going to a prayer meeting where we will wait on God."

As soon as we got there they asked, "How long must we wait?"

I said, "I do not know."

"Why don't you know?" they said sharply. "Are we going to stay here forever?"

"I honestly don't know, and no one else here knows. This is Jesus' meeting. We have gathered in His name, and, as such, we have come under His authority. When He moves, we move. If He does not move, we do not move." Perplexity was the kindest response I got. Some of the visitors were visibly upset by this "waste of time."

Have you ever wondered what the 120 disciples were doing when the Holy Spirit first came upon them on the Day of Pentecost? Because Pentecost (see Acts 2) represents the most dramatic display of God's power on the Church, it would be interesting to find out what the disciples were doing when such a phenomenon took place. Acts 2:2 says they were *sitting*. Sitting is always associated with waiting. We must adopt today the waiting attitude that permeated the Upper Room when the greatest outpouring of God's power took place.

The beauty of this approach is that when Jesus *does* move, everything He tells us to ask of the Father is granted by the Father. Mark 16:20 tells us that God worked with the disciples. He told them what to say, and then He confirmed it with the signs that followed. That is why so many signs and wonders confirm the words spoken by the Church in Argentina. These words are not the result of speculation on the part of the speakers. They are direct commands from Jesus spoken through His bond servants.

To gather in Jesus' name is to meet in the name that is above all names. It is to come to the One before whom every knee must bow. He is the King of kings and the Lord of lords. It can never be done carelessly and flippantly. He is God!

A Circle of Light—Jesus' Light

When the newly founded Church in Acts 2 gathered for the first time in small, home groups all over Jerusalem, they came together around the person of Jesus. They devoted themselves continually to the teaching of the apostles, who taught them what the Holy Spirit was imparting to them. They partook of the Lord's Supper, which was a vivid reminder of His death and what they believed to be His imminent return. Fellowship happened at such a deep level of unity that the heavenly places over that meeting were in complete control of Jesus through His Church.

In that ideal context, they prayed. When they prayed "Let your kingdom come, let your will be done, on earth as it is done in heaven" (see Matt. 6:9-13), it actually happened. God's will was thoroughly done on earth! The myriad house meetings all over Jerusalem punched holes in the spiritual darkness. God's kingdom was indeed coming down to earth. This should be the Church's normal life today. What happened right after Pentecost was not an aberration but rather the new norm happening for the first time. This dynamic gathering of the Church needs to be rediscovered if we are to reach our cities for Christ. The first step is for the pastors to help establish God's perimeter in the city by gathering around the presiding Jesus!

This is the kind of spiritual perimeter that must be established by the faithful remnant. It becomes a circle of light on the edge of Satan's darkness. It is Jesus' light. It is a perimeter where Jesus manifests Himself to His followers, where He, the Chief Shepherd, gathers with the undershepherds in charge of His flock. He knows how to reach the city, and at the proper time, He will reveal the strategy. It is a gathering where no one promotes his own ideas on how to reach the city; rather, it's where a group of bond servants waits on their Master. Doing this, the faithful remnant will have established a spiritual beachhead on the edge of Satan's territory. As God's kingdom gets established inside that perimeter, it is only a matter of time before it expands and touches the entire city. As in Hezekiah's case, you will be surprised by how suddenly it may come to pass, "Because the thing came about suddenly" (2 Chron. 29:36).

The faithful remnant must hold firm to two foundational principles: they believe God for the city, and there is only one Church in the city, although it meets in many congregations. To the modeling of these they are totally committed. To that end, the first step is to establish God's perimeter in the city by identifying and calling together the faithful remnant.

7

Securing the Perimeter

*"Then King Hezekiah arose early and assembled
the princes of the city and went up to the house of
the Lord. And they brought seven bulls, seven rams,
seven lambs, and seven male goats for a sin offering
for the kingdom, the sanctuary, and Judah. And he
ordered the priests, the sons of Aaron, to offer them
on the altar of the Lord....Then they brought the
male goats of the sin offering before the king and the
assembly, and they laid their hands on them."*
2 Chronicles 29:20,21,23

ESTABLISHING GOD'S PERIMETER IN THE MIDST OF SATAN'S DOMAIN
is a very sensitive operation. It is not enough to simply set up a
perimeter; it must also be secured. This is the second step to taking your city for Christ. This is what Hezekiah did as soon as he,
the princes and priests and Levites gathered at the restored
Temple. They laid hands on the sacrificial animals for the sins of

the nation. Even though they had already made a covenant with God and with each other, they also knew that certain things inside the newly established perimeter required urgent action.

When pastors first come together with the clear objective of reclaiming a city for God, the souls of every person in that city are at stake. Satan, as the commander of the occupying army, is not pleased with the Church's new posture and will do everything in his power to prevent it from succeeding. Success depends on a secure perimeter. We must secure the perimeter against the devil and his schemes. This is an act of war.

Satan's preferred mode of operation is exploiting ignorance, our ignorance, because it allows him to move in our midst with impunity. Nowhere is this more lethal than when the Church believes that Satan is not at work in its midst. However, the Church is the main focus of Satan's attack, and he employs all kinds of devices to neutralize it. When the faithful remnant first comes together, it unknowingly brings into the newly established perimeter some of Satan's old schemes. To properly secure it, we must be aware of Satan's arsenal. What are his weapons?

Satan, our enemy, the one we are called to defeat according to Revelation 12:11, has three main weapons aimed at us, as we discussed in chapter 4.

The first weapon is sin. Satan is the tempter, and sin is the ultimate expression of this character trait. Like a bullet fired from a gun, sin is an active weapon. It seeks *us*. But we must not panic. God's counter weapon is grace. The beauty of grace is twofold. It cannot exist without the preexistence of sin, and the greater the sin, the greater the grace available to the repentant sinner to counteract it. We are well provided for by our loving Father.

Satan's second weapon is called accusation. This weapon reflects Satan's character as the accuser of the brethren. Using the awful record of our deeds in the flesh, he makes us feel hopelessly trapped by our sinful nature and by the magnitude of our sin. His objective here is to create uncontrollable anxiety. This weapon is a passive one, much like a trap that is set, waiting for the victim to fall into it. Satan waits for us to become vulnerable. When something goes wrong, he loses no time in telling us it's because of our terrible character or because of some past failure. Even though we have been forgiven, he tells us we are not. We are loved, but he insists that God has forsaken us. We are called, but he pronounces us unfit for spiritual service. God's counter weapon is His mighty hand under which we are told to seek refuge, especially when a fiery ordeal envelops us, or in moments of spiritual defeat. The admission ticket is humility: "Humble yourselves, therefore, under the mighty hand of God, that He may exalt you at the proper time" (1 Pet. 5:6). Once safely positioned under His mighty hand, we are told to cast all our anxiety upon Him because He cares (see 1 Pet. 5:7). As we resist the devil from this impregnable position, he has no choice but to flee (see Jas. 4:7).

The third weapon, and the one most likely to undermine the faithful remnant's newly established beachhead, is spiritual strongholds (see 2 Cor. 10:3-5). As stated previously, a spiritual stronghold is a mind-set impregnated with hopelessness that leads us to accept as unchangeable situations we know are contrary to the will of God. Strongholds represent the greatest threat to the Church today because of the prevailing ignorance about their nature, existence and usage.

Strongholds are built in the believer's mind by Satan so he can manipulate behavior without being detected. This reveals Satan's nature as the deceiver. God's counter weapon is the renewal of our minds (see Rom. 12:2; Eph. 4:22-24). This is a most radical operation. The new mind—Christ's mind in us (see 1 Cor. 2:16)—cannot be grafted onto the old one. It is either one or the other. The believer must die to self and come to life in Christ (see Gal. 2:20). That is why the type of gathering in Jesus' name described in chapter 6 is so essential. It is easier for us to overvalue our minds and their ideas when we are by ourselves. However, when we are in the *tangible* presence of the presiding Jesus, we immediately realize that it is He, and not us, who must increase. For instance, we may feel we have a good voice as we sing in the privacy of our bathroom. However, standing next to the world-famous tenor, Luciano Pavarotti, while he sings "O Sole Mio," dramatically convinces us that it's better to keep our mouths closed. The same is true when we are in Christ's presence.

The Three Deadliest Strongholds

The three deadliest strongholds that could undermine the mission of the Church in a city are disunity, spiritual apathy and ignorance of the schemes of the devil. The faithful remnant will not be in a position to inflict serious damage to Satan's position in the city until these three strongholds have been destroyed. This is why securing the newly established perimeter is an absolute must.

1. Disunity. Jesus stated in absolutely clear terms that for the world to believe, God's people must be one among ourselves as He and the Father are one. Jesus amplified this when he said, "By this all men will know that you are My disciples, if you have love for one another" (John 13:35). However, time and again, after surveying the spiritual landscape of a city, we wrongly conclude that spiritual unity as described in John 17:21 is unattainable. This is a stronghold created by a lie straight from the pit of hell.

Jesus prayed for unity (see John 17:20-23). Everything He did, including this prayer, was always according to God's will, and the

Father always heard His requests (see John 11:42). There is no doubt that the Father heard and answered Jesus' prayer as recorded in John 17. Evidence of this is Paul's exhortation to the Ephesians when he tells them not to *create* unity, but rather to be "diligent to preserve the unity of the Spirit [that already exists] in the bond of peace" (Eph. 4:3). Therefore, unity *already* exists in the Church. To preserve means to service something that already exists. It is like taking our car to the dealership for the required periodic services. Doing so will ensure proper performance. The Church is already united in the heavenly realm. Jesus is the head of the Church and the Holy Spirit indwells all the believers. The faithful remnant must deal with this stronghold by operating from the premise that unity already exists.

If this is so, what about some of the blatant demonstrations of disunity and strife among church leaders in the city? I am not minimizing this strife, but it is necessary to put it in the proper perspective. Suppose you are sailing in a small boat on the ocean, and a storm suddenly envelops you. Suddenly, you find yourself being swamped by 30-foot waves. Nobody will deny the menacing nature of those waves. A 30-foot wave compared to a tiny boat looks phenomenal. However, if you take a transversal look from the stormy surface all the way down to the ocean floor, perhaps a mile deep, that 30-foot wave will definitely look much less formidable. What is a 30-foot wave compared to a mile of ocean depth? It is only a tiny ripple.

This is the way our human feuds look when contrasted to the unifying presence of the Holy Spirit in all the believers. Many of those 30-foot waves represent self-appointed guardians of truth (as they understand it), who roar at each other over the media waves and fling grenades in the form of publications at each other. However, the work of the Holy Spirit is so deep and great that no one can divide Jesus' body. God did not allow any of His bones to be broken while He hung helplessly on the cross. His body remained whole even in death. How much more now that He is alive! The bones, muscles, tendons and ligaments are all there, though some of them may be stretched, bruised or torn. Therefore, we must approach the task at hand by believing and confessing unity as stated in God's Word in spite of the immediate circumstances.

As described in chapter 2, the stronghold of disunity was broken in Resistencia when the group of seven pastors partook of the Lord's Supper and washed each other's feet. That day, something previously considered unchangeable was, in fact, changed for the better. The perception of unshakable disunity must always be shattered by the faithful remnant standing on and modeling God's Word. There is only one Church in the city. As Christians confess and act on this premise, reality eventually lines up with the Word of God.

In Azul, Argentina, a town of 60,000 people, the stronghold of disunity was seriously disabled in August of 1993, when four of the eight pastors there decided to call the whole Church to a celebration of unity. They settled on a Sunday morning service, which included the Lord's Supper. By faith, they announced it as a celebration of unity for the whole Church, even though only half of the city's pastors were carrying the burden of the commitment. When that Sunday came, midway through the service they discovered that three of the other pastors had joined them. One of them, who had been adamantly opposed to the meeting, confessed that the night before, the Lord had spoken to him in a dream. The Lord told him to attend the celebration because it was His doing. By acting in faith—faith in the Word of God— the original four pastors brought reality in line with God's Word. In so doing, they pulled down the stronghold of disunity that until then had kept them separated.

2. *Spiritual apathy*. This stronghold is the one responsible for the Church's refusal to take the gospel to everyone in the city on account of lack of resources. Time and time again, we hear leaders say, "There is nothing we can do to win our city for Christ since we lack the money, the manpower and the means necessary to do

---

GOD WILL NOT RELEASE HIS SUPERNATURAL RESOURCES UNTIL WE ARE BROKEN BEFORE HIM, UNTIL WE HAVE ACTED ON HIS WORD AND HIS WORD ALONE. THE MIRACLE WILL NOT TAKE PLACE UNTIL THE NATURAL RESOURCES ARE SPENT.

---

so." However, Jesus commanded us to take the gospel to *all* people (see Matt. 28:18-20). The Bible declares that God wishes *all* men to be saved. The will of God is clearly spelled out. Therefore, it must be done regardless of what our present reality dictates. To be able to do it, a truth encounter is required. This occurs when people who are trapped in a hopeless environment built by lies are exposed to the truth of God's Word. As the truth of God's Word challenges the falsehoods about their circumstances, hope is introduced. Hope then eliminates the hopelessness that made those circumstances look unchangeable. Now people have a choice. As they embrace God's Word, its truth sets them free.

The first step in tearing down the stronghold of apathy is to expose the Church to this kind of truth encounter. This must be done by faith in prayer, in music, in gatherings, in publications. The faithful remnant must declare the will of God as expressed in the Scriptures, in spite of circumstances. As this is done, the mind of the Church in the city is progressively renewed.

When we first started to implement the plan in Resistencia, there were only 5,300 believers out of a population of 400,000. At first it was very difficult—in fact, almost impossible—to believe that so many hundreds of thousands of unbelievers could be reached by that tiny number of believers. However, the stronghold of spiritual apathy was finally broken when Christians all over the city—in response to God's Word—began to refer to the unsaved as people who had not heard the gospel *yet*. In that single word, "yet," there was embryonic faith. Faith in response to the Word of God, not the circumstances.

The second step, which has to be implemented concurrently with step 1, is for the faithful remnant to become *totally* vulnerable by publicly standing on the Word of God in spite of circumstances. They must publicly declare that God will touch the entire city even though at the time of the proclamation there is no tangible proof of it. For instance, Jesus ordered His disciples to tell a hungry crowd of 5,000 men to "recline to eat" (Luke 9:14). He had them sit down in groups of 50, most likely so that aisles would be left between groups for the servers. Can you picture the disciples' vulnerability at that moment? They had told a hungry mob to sit down to eat when there was no food in sight! They made aisles for those bringing the food trays when all they could see was five loaves of bread and two fish. Nevertheless, on the strength of Jesus' word, they did it.

At what point was the bread and the fish multiplied? Not until Jesus broke them. Then *and only then* did the multiplication take place. God will not release His supernatural resources until we are broken before Him, until we have acted on His word and His word alone. The miracle will not take place until the natural resources are spent. No miracle will happen until a miracle is *absolutely* necessary. Like the young man who brought the five loaves and the two fish, we must give everything we have to the Master and then tell the people that a miracle is on its way. Then, and only then, will the stronghold of apathy be shattered forever. The principle of faith can only become a personal con-

---

SATAN'S SCHEME AGAINST THE CHURCH IS CENTERED AROUND THE VULNERABILITY OF ITS LEADERSHIP. THE LEADERS' WEAKNESSES ARE ALSO THE CHURCH'S WEAKNESSES.

---

viction after it has been thoroughly tested in the most adverse circumstances. Then, and only then, faith makes the transition from the academic chambers of our minds to the life-changing boiler room of our souls.

Hezekiah was bold to the point of total vulnerability when he told the unemployed priests and dispirited Levites, "The Lord has chosen you to stand before Him, to minister to Him, and to be His ministers and burn incense" (2 Chron. 29:11). There was no natural indication that anything of that sort was going to take place. In fact, the record from the past 25 years indicated the exact opposite. Hezekiah was totally dependent on God as he stepped out in faith and made such a bold proclamation.

3. *Spiritual ignorance*. This particular kind of ignorance has to do with Satan's schemes against the Church in the city (see 2 Cor. 2:11). I often ask pastors, "Is Satan your greatest enemy?" When they answer affirmatively, I ask them, "What is Satan's scheme against your church?" Repeatedly, I hear the same

answer, "I do not know. Should I?" Well, Paul was not ignorant of Satan's schemes. He knew exactly what Satan was up to. Likewise, it is extremely important that, without taking our focus off Jesus, we become knowledgeable of Satan's strategy against us and our congregations.

Many pastors say, "How can I know that? I have hundreds of members in my congregation." Using the principle of authority, we can easily discern Satan's schemes against our congregations. When a king errs or sins, the entire nation suffers. When parents fail, innocent children are affected by the consequences. The leaders' weaknesses are also the Church's weaknesses. In war, for example, if one is able to eliminate the top commander, the whole army under his command is affected. This is also true in spiritual warfare. Satan's scheme against the Church is centered around the vulnerability of its leadership. This is why I suggest the following steps to expose and eventually destroy the stronghold of spiritual ignorance:

• *Obtain a deeper, more biblical understanding of grace.* Be aware that grace is always extended in greater measure than the sum of the sins committed *and* confessed. We must shake off the religious spirit that leads us to believe that the more spiritual we become the less sin we will have to deal with. The opposite is true. The closer we are to God, the more aware we are of our sinfulness and, consequently, the more dependent we become on His grace.

• *Go away by yourself and let the Holy Spirit do a "CAT scan" of your soul.* Let him show you everything that is wrong with you.

First, look for a pattern of sin in your life. What are the sins you have been vulnerable to through the years? Do not be afraid to look at your sin. Grace cannot exist without the preexistence of sin, and the greater the sin, the greater the grace available to the repentant sinner. Go for the maximum possible grace by digging up the maximum possible sin in your life.

Second, look for pressure points in your life. At the other end of those pressure points you will always find Satan's handiwork. Now put these two pieces of information together—your habitual sins and your pressure points—and you will have a road map to Satan's schemes against you. This is your vulnerability profile. Because of your sphere of influence, many of these schemes will also involve the church.

• *If you are a pastor, repeat steps 1 and 2 with your staff and elders.* (If you are a lay leader, suggest this to the pastoral staff and other leaders.) Make yourself vulnerable by sharing about your weaknesses and God's provision to help you deal with them. Encourage the others to prepare a similar profile. Then combine your profile with theirs. This composite profile usually parallels Satan's scheme against the Church. If such an exercise produces a profile characterized by bitterness or greed or temporal values, you will find that this is also true of the congregation at large. This is because the principle of authority dictates that what the leader does—be it good or evil—affects the followers accordingly.

It is absolutely essential that the Church secure the newly established perimeter. To do so, there is no substitute for the pastors to "come together and in one accord" regularly (see Acts 2:1). The pastors in the city are equal members of the same team, whose head coach is Jesus. As such, they must work in harmony "in a manner worthy of the calling with which you have been called, with all humility and gentleness, with patience, showing forbearance to one another in love, being diligent to preserve the unity of the Spirit in the bond of peace. There is one body and one Spirit, just as also you were called in one hope of your calling; one Lord, one faith, one baptism, one God and Father of all who is over all and through all and in all" (Eph. 4:1-6).

For instance, in Resistencia pastors met every week for prayer and body life. In Salem, Oregon, pastors meet twice a month on the second and fourth Tuesday. In San Jose, California, where "Pray South Bay" has been launched to reach the entire area for Christ, participating pastors meet every two weeks to pray during the lunch hour, but without the lunch! The key characteristic of these examples is that of leaders meeting with Jesus. These are not administrative meetings but rather prayer meetings in the fashion described in Matthew 18:20. It is in the context of these gatherings that the leaders begin to see the strongholds break down. There is no substitute for it.

Once the perimeter is secured, the faithful remnant is in a position of strength. Hezekiah was not satisfied with having cleaned the house of the Lord. Even though that act alone was a formidable one, he knew the whole assembly of princes, priests and Levites was highly vulnerable unless the sin of the nation was dealt with (see 2 Chron. 29:21). Only when the burnt offering for such sin ascended to the heavenlies were the king and the people able to worship. In so doing, they brought the strength of God's presence and His communion with them to bear on their perimeter. They knew then that they were indeed on holy ground.

Likewise, unity, holiness and passion for the lost represent the ideal environment of which the Church must avail itself and begin to use the divinely powerful weapons issued by its Supreme Commander (see 2 Cor. 10:3-5). Once you have a secure perimeter, you have no reason to fear the evil one because he no longer has a claim on you. On the contrary, he now fears *you*. By securing the perimeter, you have initiated the war he fears so much. Angels now stand ready to join you as you prepare to fight Satan to cause his captives to depart from the land. Now you are ready for the next step.

8

Expanding God's Perimeter

"Then Hezekiah answered and said, 'Now that you have consecrated yourselves to the Lord, come near and bring sacrifices and thank offerings to the house of the Lord.' And the assembly brought sacrifices and thank offerings, and all those who were willing brought burnt offerings....Now many people were gathered at Jerusalem to celebrate the Feast of Unleavened Bread in the second month, a very large assembly. And they arose and removed the altars which were in Jerusalem; they also removed all the incense altars and cast them into the brook Kidron."
2 Chronicles 29:31; 30:13,14

GOD FIRST USES THE FAITHFUL REMNANT TO ESTABLISH A MODEL. Once that model is in place, others, whose hearts God has been preparing, feel led to join in. Expanding the perimeter is essential in order to build the largest possible expeditionary force that will eventually launch the attack on the forces of wickedness in the heavenly places over the city.

King Hezekiah modeled repentance as he and his princes offered sacrifices for the nation and worshiped. He then spoke to the people who had been watching this, saying, "Now that you have consecrated yourselves to the Lord, come near and bring sacrifices and thank offerings to the house of the Lord" (2 Chron. 29:31). By doing this, Hezekiah expanded the perimeter beyond himself, the princes, the priests and the Levites to include the people of the city. Later in 2 Chronicles 30:13,14, these people expanded the perimeter further when they spontaneously removed the pagan altars that used to be all over Jerusalem.

Paul did something similar in Ephesus (see Acts 19:1-10). First, he began with 12 men and a few God-fearing believers inside the local synagogue. Later, he withdrew with a much larger group to a storefront church by renting the "School of Tyrannus." This eventually led to the evangelization of the entire area (see Acts 19:10).

In San Jose, California, God used four pastors to establish and secure the initial perimeter. As God's grace was bestowed on them, a fifth pastor asked to join them. When the first celebration of unity was held in the form of a banquet, another church—a large one—was inspired, and it also launched a similar thrust. Awhile later, at an areawide pastors' prayer retreat, as the original group of pastors shared testimonies of God's grace on them, two other churches were touched and also decided to join in. God will continually add those that He wishes to be part of the plan, and the perimeter will expand accordingly.

The expansion must be both inward and outward. Inward expansion affects the life of the local congregations. In chapter 2, I shared how my friend Phil Nordin instituted a program to pray for a different congregation every Sunday and how this resulted

in a dramatic reconciliation among two formerly unfriendly con-
gregations. This is a classic example of inward expansion. Phil
Nordin's action impacted his local congregation, as Sunday after
Sunday people were reminded in an objective way that the

IN STOCKTON, CALIFORNIA, THE
PASTORS LEADING "PRAY STOCKTON"
HAVE AGREED THAT WHENEVER THEY
TALK TO NON-CHRISTIANS THEY WILL
INTRODUCE THEMSELVES AS PASTORS OF
THE CHURCH IN STOCKTON, PURPOSELY
AVOIDING ANY REFERENCE TO THEIR
DENOMINATIONAL AFFILIATION.

Church in the city was bigger than their local assembly. As other
pastors heard about this, they, in turn, imitated Phil's approach.

In 1992, in Azul, Argentina, Jose Garcia, a Pentecostal minister, had major surgery and was unable to conduct his weekly television program. He asked Daniel Martinez, a Christian
Missionary Alliance pastor, to host the program. As Garcia's
parishioners watched Martinez minister to them, they experienced the reality of being one in the same flock. Later, when a
terrible storm destroyed the roof of Garcia's church building, the
congregation moved to Martinez's building for a number of
months until repairs were completed. This became a powerful
lesson in unity and trust for the Church in Azul. As believers
from both congregations shared quarters, the inside wall of the
perimeter was expanded.

In Stockton, California, the pastors leading "Pray Stockton" have agreed that whenever they talk to non-Christians they will introduce themselves as pastors of the Church in Stockton, purposely avoiding any reference to their denominational affiliation. They have instructed their church members to do the same. Now nonbelievers are beginning to use the same expression—the Church in the city—rather than denominational or individual names. But the most significant impact is on the believers themselves, who see one Church all over the city. It first began with the pastors, and now it has trickled down to the members. This is what inward expansion is all about.

As for outward expansion, that happens as the Church begins to project itself into the life of the city through new people and avenues of ministry that reflect the attitude already present among the members of the faithful remnant. In Resistencia, we were perplexed by the expression found in Acts 2:47, "Having favor with all the people." As we surveyed the homes in the immediate proximity of the local congregations, we found that very few of these people, if any at all, attended the nearby congregation. If the Church is Jesus' Body on earth, and it represents God's voice in the city, why is it that those in close proximity to the place of regular meeting did not attend? Obviously, the Church had no favor in their eyes.

The Search for Favor in the Eyes of the People

In Resistencia, the general impression was that the Church was corporately ineffective in dealing with the daily problems faced by the people in the city. Together with the pastors, we began to pray for the Lord to show us how to find favor in the eyes of the unsaved. The answer came in the form of an invitation to visit the mayor of the city. As a result of that time with him, we were asked to build 16 water tanks in slum areas where there was no running water. God provided the funds, and a Christian civil engineer volunteered to manage the project. All of a sudden, the original perimeter, which was made up exclusively of pastors, began to expand to include those involved with the water tank project.

When the first two water tanks were completed, the mayor asked me to "bless them"—which is what a Catholic priest would be expected to do. I told him that as long as I had my Bible, and he provided a microphone, I would be glad to "bless the water tanks." We rode with the mayor, members of city council and the press to the area where the tanks had been built. Earlier we had asked the mayor if he would place a plaque by the water faucet quoting Jesus' words from John 4:13,14, "Everyone who drinks of this water shall thirst again, but whoever drinks of the water that I shall give him shall never thirst." As we approached the newly built tanks, we expected to see a small five-by-seven-inch plaque next to the faucet.

However, when we were still about 150 feet away, we were able to read "the plaque." To our total surprise and delight, the mayor had hired a professional letter painter who, using 16-inch-high characters, painted Jesus' words on the tanks. When my time came to "bless the tanks," I did not even have to open my Bible. I told the mostly nonchurched audience, "Would you turn with me to the water tank, and read Jesus' words out loud, please?" I proceeded to compare religion to a water tank, and Jesus to a wellspring. The former must be refilled continually; the latter springs up from the source. It never runs out. That is the way Jesus is. When I gave the invitation, almost everybody in the audience made a profession of faith in the Lord. What an explosive expansion of the original perimeter!

Something similar happened to a Christian lawyer in Resistencia. Her heart's desire was to see God's kingdom come to the legal community. She established and secured a perimeter of godliness in the legal system, and, when the time came, the gospel was presented to the members of the Supreme Court, the Provincial Bar Association, and at one point, we found ourselves in chambers with seven appellate court judges, *five of whom professed to be born-again Christians!* Likewise, you should look in your city for people strategically placed by God within the Church *and* throughout the city who will facilitate the expansion of the perimeter.

In Salem, Oregon, the pastors are pursuing a three-pronged strategy, combining prayer, doing good and caring for the needy. In order to carry out the last two elements, they have encouraged an organization called "Love, Inc." to network with participating congregations to recruit church volunteers. These volunteers make themselves available to help with a wide variety of needs such as fixing leaky roofs, changing the car oil for elderly citizens, driving people to the doctor, taking groceries to shut-ins and so on. The city of Salem has been made aware of the free services, and, through a local telephone number, people can call to find out if a Christian volunteer is available to help with a particular need. The response has been very positive, and it has expanded the original perimeter far into the heart of the city.

The pastors in Salem are also arranging to have every public official prayed for. Prayer groups are being organized to eventually cover every governmental department, using believers who already work there. Intercessors are being recruited among Christians who are retired to position themselves on the balcony of the state legislature building and pray during the sessions. This represents a significant expansion of the original perimeter.

In San Jose, California, churches have launched a program

called "Adopt-A-Cop." Congregations in the city are being encouraged to spiritually adopt one or two police officers, and then pray and care for them. The chief of police was positive about the idea and lent his support to it, to the point that he wrote the manual on how churches should spiritually adopt cops. When I first learned that he had written the manual, I feared the worst. I was afraid he might have watered down the spiritual aspect of the program. To my surprise, he did the opposite. He stated clearly that each church should pray for the adopted officers daily, make weekly contact by phone or letter, and at least once a year invite the police officer to church to pray for him or her in person. The key contacts for this major breakthrough were the president of the Christian Police Officers Association and the police chaplain. Thanks to these two Kingdom-minded Christians, the Church in the city found itself expanding its perimeter by coming in touch with police officers who patrol the city day and night.

Another San Jose example involves the high school population. In California's Santa Clara County, there are 36 high school campuses. Steve Taylor, a Youth for Christ leader, brought together most of the youth pastors in the area and challenged them to plant a "praying church" on each one of the 36 campuses. By the beginning of 1994, they had succeeded, and today more than 1,000 high school students have joined one of the 36 "congregations" that make up the Church on Campus. Steve Taylor and his associates are training the students to pray three specific prayers on the way to school and during each of their in-between class breaks. The first one is a prayer for themselves. The second one is a prayer for at least three fellow Christians on campus, and the last one is a prayer for 10 unsaved students and three teachers. If everybody does it, more than 20,000 prayers will go up each day on the high school campuses of Santa Clara County. Students on campuses all over are beginning to come together, and the faithful remnant perimeter keeps expanding. Tremendous!

WHEN THE CHURCH IN THE CITY
DRINKS OF THE CUP TOGETHER AND
SHARES THE SAME BREAD, SOMETHING
HAPPENS IN THE HEAVENLY PLACES THAT
UNDERMINES SATAN'S POWER OVER THE
CHURCH AND, EVENTUALLY, THE CITY.

Once the original perimeter has been established and secured, God will bring together like-minded people from all walks of life in order to expand the perimeter even further. Be on the lookout!

Celebrations of Unity

The most effective way to connect people who eventually will help expand the perimeter is through periodic celebrations of unity involving the participating congregations. What are these celebrations? At least once a quarter, Christians of all denominations should come together to celebrate Jesus and who they are in Him. Rather than inviting a speaker or a performer, I suggest that they gather to do two things: partake of the Lord's Supper and nurture the vision for the extension of the kingdom of God in the city. The first one is familiar to everybody. When the Church in the city drinks of the cup together and shares the same bread, *something* happens in the heavenly places that undermines

Satan's power over the Church and, eventually, the city. "And day by day continuing with one mind in the temple, and breaking bread from house to house, they were taking their meals together with gladness and sincerity of heart, praising God, and having favor with all the people. And the Lord was adding to their number day by day those who were being saved" (Acts 2:46,47).

The second endeavor—nurturing the vision—can be done a number of ways. Perhaps the most visual illustration is a candle ceremony. This ceremony is a simple but powerful one. During the celebration of unity, a big candle is lit in the center of the platform. That candle represents Jesus, the Chief Shepherd. As the artificial lights are dimmed, the local pastors—Jesus' under-shepherds in the city—light their individual candles from the big one. While the congregation sings "Shine, Jesus, Shine" and similar songs, they in turn light the candles of those positioned at the end of each row. Gradually the whole place lights up as one Christian passes the light on to the other. It is a vivid picture of what will eventually happen in the city as Christians gather around Jesus and pass on His light to the unsaved around them. It is a faith seeding event, and it makes a powerful impression on everybody present.

Hezekiah effectively used similar symbolism when he "stationed the Levites in the house of the Lord with cymbals, with harps, and with lyres" (2 Chron. 29:25).

> And the Levites stood with the musical instruments of David, and the priests with the trumpets. Then Hezekiah gave the order to offer the burnt offering on the altar. When the burnt offering began, the song to the Lord also began with the trumpets, accompanied by the instruments of David, king of Israel. While the

> whole assembly worshiped, the singers also sang and the
> trumpets sounded; all this continued until the burnt
> offering was finished. Now at the completion of the
> burnt offerings, the king and all who were present with
> him bowed down and worshiped. Moreover, King
> Hezekiah and the officials ordered the Levites to sing
> praises to the Lord with the words of David and Asaph
> the seer. So they sang praises with joy, and bowed down
> and worshiped (2 Chron. 29:26-30).

For the multitude in attendance to see a formerly deserted and
defiled Temple, full of music, praise and worship must have been
a powerful incentive to believe that God could do the same in
the city and eventually in the nation. They saw in the microcosm
of the Temple what Hezekiah had already seen by faith in the
macrocosm of both kingdoms. Faith was injected into the people
and consequently the perimeter was expanded.

What About Those Who Don't Join In?

In expanding the perimeter, you must plan for and hope that
everybody will eventually join in. However, not everybody will
do so, and this is also part of God's doing. He will purposely keep
out those who would compromise the security of the emerging
perimeter.

We find an illustration of this principle in Acts 5:1-14. The
Early Church had been infiltrated by people such as Ananias and
Sapphira who were driven by selfish ambition. When Peter con-
fronted them, both dropped dead. Immediately, fear fell upon
everybody, inside and outside of the Church (see Acts 5:11).
Following that, the Scriptures make reference to three distinct

groups: (1) the Church, united and in one accord, through which God performed many signs and wonders (see Acts 5:12); (2) the unsaved people, in whose eyes the Church had great favor; and (3) "the rest" (Acts 5:13), who dared not to gather with them because of the fear that came upon them. The Bible does not elaborate on who made up "the rest." However, from the context, I believe that "the rest" was made up of people such as Ananias and Sapphira: double-minded, politically astute status seekers with a selfish ambition disguised under the false appearance of godliness.

Sooner or later, this third group will emerge in your city. Do not try to bring it inside the perimeter. If you do, you will compromise its security. Satan uses perfectionism to slow us down and, if possible, to stop us. Perfect unity does not exist this side of heaven, and trying to bring "the rest" inside the perimeter may distract you or even destroy the perimeter. How can you tell who they are? Fear seems to be the driving force behind them. They are consumed by fear. Fear of false doctrine. Fear of criticism. Fear of church splits if their flock is exposed to outsiders. Even fear of "missing God's best." Sanctimoniously, they declare that they prefer to "wait out" the emerging unity because they are afraid that if they join in they will miss something better that God may bring about in the future. When fear is the main distinctive, you can safely assume that you are dealing with a member of "the rest."

Just to keep us humble, we have also found that some congregations, without being part of either the faithful remnant or "the rest," have benefitted from the plan. Dave Thompson, a fellow team member who directed "Plan Resistencia," had an experience that illustrates this point.

Dave went to visit the pastor of a small Pentecostal assembly, which was fundamental in doctrine and closed-minded in regard to cooperating with others in the city. At the time of the first visit, the pastor, although friendly, remained firm in his position not to join the plan but assured us of his prayers.

A year later, when Dave visited the pastor again, he was surprised to discover that the congregation had practically doubled in attendance. When he asked the pastor the reason for such dramatic growth, he was at a loss for words and simply said, "I guess it's just the faithfulness of God for our many years of hard work." Dave asked him if he had changed his strategy during that time. He responded, "No, we've just kept on doing the same thing."

For his part, the pastor was right. What he did not know was that the spiritual environment over the city in which he labored during that year had changed dramatically. Though he offered little to build that environment, God in His sovereignty chose to bless him anyway.

All of this is consistent with the "Gideon principle" as described in Judges 7, which shows us that even though a handful did the most dangerous and demanding task, once victory was assured, all the people participated in the looting of the enemy's camp.

During this third step, the key is to expand God's perimeter in the city as much as possible without compromising its safety. Once the maximum possible expansion has been reached, you are ready to move on to the fourth step. Before you do, let's review how far you have already come. Previous to the establishment of God's perimeter, the Church in the city was struggling in a mire of hopelessness. Since then, a committed group has come together and a safe perimeter has been established. Now it has been expanded to the safest point possible with many new leaders and congregations joining in. At this juncture, Satan has a major problem with which to contend. The Church is now poised and ready to strike out at his domain, shaking it at its very foundation.

9

Infiltrating Satan's Perimeter

"Now Hezekiah sent to all Israel and Judah and wrote letters also to Ephraim and Manasseh, that they should come to the house of the Lord at Jerusalem to celebrate the Passover to the Lord God of Israel."
2 Chronicles 30:1

FROM A SECURE AND EXPANDED BASE OF OPERATIONS NOW COMES the crucial task of turning the tables on the enemy in order to make *his* base of operations insecure. This must be done by astutely "parachuting behind enemy lines."

Once Jerusalem was secured, Hezekiah sent messengers to infiltrate the darkness enveloping both the northern and southern kingdoms with a message of hope: "For if you return to the Lord, your brothers and your sons will find compassion before those who led them captive, and will return to this land. For the Lord your God is gracious and compassionate, and will not turn

His face away from you if you return to Him" (2 Chron. 30:9). The messengers blanketed every city in both kingdoms with that message. "So the couriers passed from city to city through the country of Ephraim and Manasseh, and as far as Zebulun" (2 Chron. 30:10). Hezekiah left no area untouched.

The best way to infiltrate Satan's perimeter in our cities is by turning every Christian home into a prayer cell. This is exactly what happened in Jerusalem when the Church was first founded! "And day by day continuing with one mind in the temple, and breaking bread from house to house, they were taking their meals together with gladness and sincerity of heart" (Acts 2:46). This is also what Paul instructs Timothy to do in 1 Timothy 2:1-8, as discussed in chapter 1: the Church praying for all men everywhere with holy hands without wrath or dissension. Prayer cells must be established throughout the city so that no neighborhood is left without a spiritual lighthouse.

In military science, when attempting to infiltrate enemy territory, success depends on how inconspicuous the infiltrators are. Nowadays, there is a prevalent temptation in spiritual warfare for pastors and evangelists to be personally involved in the infiltration. If they could, they would love to be the ones who personally seek out and bring down the prince over the city. However, generals do not parachute behind enemy lines. Furthermore, it is the Church acting as a whole, and not an individual, or group of individuals, who must "bring to light what is the administration of the mystery which for ages has been hidden in God, who created all things; in order that the manifold wisdom of God might now be made known through the church to the rulers and the authorities in the heavenly places" (Eph. 3:9,10).

How did General Norman Schwarzkopf infiltrate enemy territory during the Gulf War? He chose allied soldiers who looked like Iraqis and spoke their language—people who had what it took to blend in. When it comes to infiltrating Satan's perimeter, it is of strategic importance to have the Church's rank and file carry out this step. Hezekiah did not personally go all over the kingdom inviting people to the Passover. He sent couriers (see 2 Chron. 30:6). Church members should be organized into neighborhood prayer cells until every block in the city is being prayed for. In this manner, we will be deploying the largest possible number of troops, with the least possible logistical disruption where they can inflict the greatest possible damage to the enemy with the minimum possible risk.

In the cities where our team has assisted local pastors, we have suggested the following procedure.

First, we conduct a training seminar on the principles covered in chapters 2 to 5 for the participating congregations. Following the training seminar, the first wave of prayer cells—sometimes called lighthouses—is established. Their locations are carefully and systematically identified on a map of the city. At the quarterly citywide celebration of unity, this map is displayed and testimonies from the existing houses of prayer are shared with the audience. This prompts others in the audience, whom God has already been preparing, to volunteer their homes to become houses of prayer.

The prayer house deployment plan consists of motivating, training and mobilizing each participant to do the following:

1. *Establish and secure the spiritual perimeter in your neighborhood.* Do it along the lines of steps one through three, as discussed in chapters 6 through 8.

2. *Determine the target area.* For how many neighbors are you going to pray? One hundred is a good number. Draw a map reflecting the target area, and choose a time to pray for those who live inside the target area. Make a covenant with your family to become "spiritual block parents."

3. *Walk the neighborhood with your family or with a prayer partner, and as you do, talk to God about each neighbor.* Take time to listen to what He tells you through the indwelling Holy Spirit (see John 10:27; 14:26; 16:13,14). Don't be surprised if, as you walk by a certain house, the Holy Spirit leads you to pray in a very specific way (see Rom. 8:26; Eph. 6:18).

4. *Once the area has been saturated with the first wave of silent prayers, proclaim the Lordship of Jesus over the target area and serve an eviction notice to the forces of wickedness that are blinding the unsaved neighbors to the gospel* (see Matt. 4:10; 16:23; 2 Cor. 4:4; Eph. 3:10; 6:17b; Jas. 4:7). Stand your ground in the heavenly places as you remind those evil forces of Christ's victory over them (the blood of the Lamb) and of the authority delegated to you by Jesus (your testimony), and do it boldly (loving not your life even unto death, see Rev. 12:11).

5. *The next step is to leave a doorknob hanger to let your neighbors know that you are praying for them regularly and that you would like to know their specific prayer requests.* Be sure to list your name and telephone number on the doorknob hanger.

6. *Soon afterward, follow up by visiting every targeted home to collect prayer requests.* Make reference to the doorknob hanger you left previously. Tell your neighbors that God does care for them and that He is eager to reveal Himself to them. Propose to them that they identify their greatest need for which you are to pray. Also, ask them to report back to you as soon as the need is met or the problem is resolved.

7. *Go boldly before the throne of grace and prepare for an avalanche of answers.* You're tapping into the grace of God that has been reserved for the one hundredth sheep!

When we first tried this approach in Argentina, some intercessors carried a prayer book in which they jotted down their neighbors' prayer requests. Each page in the notebook had three columns. In the first column, they wrote the date. In the second, they wrote down the prayer request in great detail. The third column was left blank in order to enter the date when the prayer was answered by God. While collecting prayer requests, this book was shown to the neighbors and special emphasis was placed on the third column, the blank one. "The only thing we

---

THE PRINCIPLE OF THE ONE HUNDREDTH SHEEP SHOULD CAUSE A SIGNIFICANT NUMBER OF ANSWERS TO PRAYER. THESE ANSWERED PRAYERS BECOME SPIRITUAL IOUs—DEPOSITS GATHERED NOW AGAINST FUTURE WITHDRAWALS.

---

ask of you," the intercessors would say to the neighbors, "is that you report to us when God answers. When that happens, we will enter the date here and transfer this petition to the back of the notebook as a praise report." At that point, the intercessors would show the neighbors two or three praise reports from the back of the book, if possible, involving people in the same neighborhood. All of this had a dual effect: For the unbelievers, it acted as a "primer" for their faith as they heard of prayers that had *already* been answered. Second, by agreeing to notify the intercessors of when God answered, they had entered into a covenant relationship.

My good friend Vance Hardisty, president and founder of Renewal International, has developed an excellent booklet entitled *Houses of Prayer*, which has many practical ideas about how to turn homes into prayer cells.[1]

Spiritual IOUs

Because of the principle of the one hundredth sheep discussed in chapter 2, you should expect to see a significant number of answers to prayer right away. These answered prayers become spiritual IOUs—deposits gathered now against future withdrawals. Let them pile up to be cashed in during the next step.

In Stockton, California, local Christians have seen dramatic, and oftentimes instantaneous, answers to prayer. Becky and Cecilia, two members of the church pastored by Tim Pollock—the pastor who first conceived "Pray Stockton"—regularly walk their neighborhood while asking God on which doors they should knock to offer prayer. On a certain day, they felt led to call on a house where there was some sort of a commotion. When the front door opened, they saw a group of Vietnamese positioning a mattress on the living room floor. When the two women inquired about it, they were told by a young man that his mother had been involved in a car accident, and she was on her way home from the hospital. Because they had no medical insurance, the local hospital had refused to treat her beyond the initial care. They were extremely distressed over this and were expecting an ambulance to bring the injured lady to the house at any moment. Just as he finished talking, the ambulance arrived and the lady was transferred to the mattress on the floor. What a tragedy!

The two Christian ladies identified themselves as representatives of "the Church of Stockton" and offered to pray. The offer was accepted, and they knelt down and interceded for the lady. A few days later, the woman had totally recovered, and some members of the family are now attending church. In fact, at the time of this writing Pastor Pollock had just baptized three members of that family.

On another occasion, these same two intercessors knocked on

a door, and a man answered, his body language projecting frustration. The Christian ladies again identified themselves as members of "the Church of Stockton" and asked if prayer was needed.

SATAN KNOWS THAT IF THE CHURCH SUC-
CESSFULLY ESTABLISHES PRAYER CELLS ALL
OVER THE CITY, HE WILL FIND HIMSELF
OUTGUNNED, OUTMANNED AND OUTMA-
NEUVERED. HE WILL FIGHT TO THE BITTER
END TO PREVENT THAT FROM HAPPENING.

The man's mouth dropped open. He turned around and pointed to the family room where his family was gathered. He said, "This is incredible. At this very moment, my family and I are crying out to the God of heaven that He send someone to help us." And God did—right on time!

Satan's All-Out Counterattack

Infiltrating Satan's perimeter is where the Church makes it or breaks it. This is the most decisive moment in the whole process. Based on my experience in many cities, I believe that this is when Satan will launch a cruel and fierce counterattack. He knows that if the Church successfully establishes prayer cells all over the city, he will find himself outgunned, outmanned and outmaneuvered. He will fight to the bitter end to prevent that from happening. During this particular stage, we consistently have felt the full force of Satan's attack against the Church, against us, against our families. We even suspect that Satan reassigns demons from secular targets to church targets.

At this crucial point, Satan zeros in on the Church's most vulnerable members. Sin explodes all over. Anxiety tempts believers to move out from under God's mighty hand. It seems that every remaining stronghold in the mind of the believers is activated. Satan is on a rampage, and it shows. Accidents happen. Finances dry up. Domestic disputes erupt. Immorality is exposed. This is the most difficult time. Many believers quit at this point.

Satan's strategy aims to cause the Church to long for "the onions and the garlic of Egypt"—that is, to make the Church miss the "normal," uneventful days of captivity. Weaker believers begin to complain out loud. Many regret that they ever heard the term spiritual warfare and seem ready to negotiate for peace at any cost. Satan's clever scheme rests on a premise that is appealing to the double-minded believer: a conforming POW will always enjoy safety, while an attacking marine will constantly be under enemy fire. However, this fiery ordeal provides the Church in the city with an exceptional quality-control tool. Each one of the new challenges is nothing more than the outward manifestation of a deeper problem, which until that point has remained undetected. In his attempt to corner the Church by exposing the problem, Satan stands to lose the element of surprise. No matter how imposing Satan's counterattack is, remember at all times that everything Satan intends for evil, God *will* use for good. By taking proper care of every new challenge, the Church in the city ends up stronger than ever.

When we found ourselves at this stage in Resistencia, our team was buffeted by internal mistrust. We had to go on half salaries for more than six months. For the first time in my life, I suffered from panic attacks. These attacks were so disabling that I had difficulty keeping my mind on the task at hand. Two of our children became very ill. My wife struggled with discouragement and physical infirmities. People in whom we had confided betrayed our trust. It was all-out warfare indeed. Roberto Troia, the man who led me to Christ and who was my first personal intercessor, was severely disabled and put out of commission for a time.

Something similar happened in La Plata. At the end of 1992, nearly 2,000 houses of prayer had been established. However, six months later most of them had disappeared as a result of confusion among those in charge of the project. The pastoral leadership came under attack. One of the largest churches in town suffered a split. A key pastor became very ill, almost to the point of death.

In Azul, adultery was exposed among the leadership of one of the participating churches. At the same time, a secular city official who was key to the ministry died suddenly.

In a Canadian city, right before launching the houses of prayer, the leadership team was shaken by misunderstandings. A parachurch organization barged into town, promoting its own program and causing additional strife. The minds of many were clouded and at the training session for houses of prayer only a fraction of the church membership showed up. The mark of Satan was all over the place. Confusion is his trademark.

It is at this stage of the struggle that the value of intercessors becomes most evident. In fact, success depends entirely on their effective deployment. An intercessor is a person who stands before God, pleading for His will to be done on earth while actively resisting the devil in the heavenly places until he flees. To do this effectively, an intercessor is equipped with spiritual gifts in the area of wisdom, discernment and faith. These gifts enable the intercessor to accurately determine God's will from Scripture and from insights that the Holy Spirit provides in the heat of battle. The shield of faith enables the intercessor to "extinguish all the flaming missiles of the evil one" (Eph. 6:16). Intercessors are called and empowered by the Holy Spirit to pray for all the saints at all times. The primary targets of the enemy are leaders with an apostolic calling. This is why Paul requested prayer, saying, "And pray on my behalf, that utterance may be given to me in the opening of my mouth, to make known with boldness the mystery of the gospel" (Eph. 6:19). Key leaders in a city-reaching thrust *must* have a "prayer shield," as C. Peter Wagner calls it in his book by the same name.[2]

In the midst of the chaos and strife, we must remember at all times that our objective is not merely to hold on to our perimeter but to successfully infiltrate Satan's perimeter. Houses of prayer must be established all over the city, and we must hold on to them. Our response to Satan's onslaught must be perseverance that eventually leads to the establishment of prayer beachheads in *every* neighborhood in the city. This is the ultimate objective, and it must be reached at *any cost*. Hezekiah's couriers were laughed at, scorned and mocked (see 2 Chron. 30:10), but this did not stop them. They "passed from city to city" until the entire kingdom of Israel was covered. They did not care if people opposed them. Their objective was to touch every square inch of the enemy's territory. And they succeeded.

Eventually, when Satan's perimeter is successfully infiltrated, his stronghold on the unbelievers weakens considerably. Do not let the devil distract you from your primary objective of infiltrating his territory. Often we find the strongest resistance where Satan's greatest vulnerability lies. Hezekiah's messengers were opposed by people in Ephraim, Manasseh and Zebulun (see 2 Chron. 30:10). However, when the Passover was finally celebrated, "a multitude of the people, even many from Ephraim and Manasseh, Issachar and Zebulun...ate the Passover" (2 Chron.

30:18). The greatest response came from the area that initially offered the strongest resistance!

Once Satan's perimeter has been infiltrated by the establishment of houses of prayer in each neighborhood, the Church begins to gain favor in the eyes of the unsaved by virtue of the spiritual IOUs generated through prayer. This, in turn, favorably predisposes them for salvation. With a unified and secured perimeter, and with houses of prayer all over the city, now the Church in the city is in a position to begin the destruction of Satan's perimeter. This is the next step.

Notes
1. To order *Houses of Prayer*, write to: Carodyn Publishers, 1569 Rancho View Rd., Lafayette, CA 94549.
2. C. Peter Wagner, *Prayer Shield* (Ventura, CA: Regal Books, 1992).

10

Destroying Satan's Perimeter

*"Now when all this was finished, all Israel who were
present went out to the cities of Judah, broke the pillars
in pieces, cut down the Asherim, and pulled down the
high places and the altars throughout all Judah and
Benjamin, as well as in Ephraim and Manasseh, until
they had destroyed them all. Then all the sons of Israel
returned to their cities, each to his possession."*
2 Chronicles 31:1

NOW THAT THE CHURCH IS ON THE MOVE, RELENTLESSLY APPLYING
pressure to Satan's perimeter in the city and weakening his stronghold through the neighborhood prayer cells, a trumpet call must go
out signaling the beginning of the Church's all-out attack. The
objective of this attack is to bring down the walls that have kept
the unsaved people in Satan's captivity and to open their eyes to
the light of the gospel (see Acts 26:18; 2 Cor. 4:4). This is it!

It is impossible to overemphasize this simple truth: The objective is to set the captives free. "To open their eyes so that they may turn from darkness to light and from the dominion of Satan to God" (Acts 26:18), as Paul explained to King Agrippa. Remember, no one in your city has a choice until you open their eyes. Then, and only then, will they have a choice—the choice of turning from darkness to light.

Hezekiah's initial covenant with God led to people in both kingdoms being blessed, their voice being heard on high and their prayer coming to His holy dwelling place in heaven (see 2 Chron. 30:27). The eyes of the people were thus opened to the degree that, on their way back from the Passover, "When all this was finished, all Israel who were present went out to the cities of Judah, broke the pillars in pieces, cut down the Asherim, and pulled down the high places and the altars throughout all Judah and Benjamin, as well as in Ephraim and Manasseh, until they had destroyed them all" (2 Chron. 31:1). Hezekiah opened their eyes to the reality of God through the celebration of the Passover. Once their eyes were opened, the people "turned from darkness to light," and in so doing, they destroyed Satan's altars (strongholds) all over Israel. This was an all-out attack.

In military terms, the difference between a parade and an amphibious landing is in its overall objective. A parade is designed to show the weapons and to salute the commander. The weapons are not loaded, and the enemy is nowhere in sight. Unfortunately, some of the so-called spiritual warfare breakthroughs going on today seem to be nothing more than nostalgic parades. A lot of feeling is expressed, great speeches are made and a sense of awe is displayed over the weaponry inside the church. This kind of spiritual parade makes good copy, but it amounts to very little in advancing God's kingdom. If the enemy is not engaged, his camp cannot be overrun.

An amphibious landing is a dangerous and decisive operation. By dangerous, I mean that loss of life and property may occur. By decisive, I mean that it can never end in a draw. You either win or you lose. Although a parade is held on friendly grounds, an amphibious landing is carried out in enemy territory. The time has finally come for us to bring an end to the parades inside the four walls of our buildings. Let's take the living Church to the city. That's where it belongs. The objective is to push the enemy back in order to set the captives free.

At this point, we must incorporate into our strategy the intel-

---

ANY EFFORT TO REACH THE CITY WITH-OUT A WELL-THOUGHT-THROUGH PLAN TO ADEQUATELY CARE FOR THE NEW BABES IN CHRIST IS AN EXERCISE IN FUTILITY.

---

ligence gathered through the spiritual and social mapping of the city. Demonic strongholds, properly identified, must become primary targets. Their mode of operation has to be studied for both offensive and defensive purposes.

In Resistencia, knowing that Satan's main strongholds on the people were fear of death and a divisive spirit, we planned accordingly. To deal with the former, we preached a message of life and victory over death. Practically everything we did and said was "packaged" in the context of Jesus' victory over death. In combating the divisiveness, pastors brought their congregations together prior to the evangelistic outreach and, in plain view of the membership, they chose the evangelists from among themselves for the neighborhood crusades and laid hands on them. It was a tremendous blow to the mistrust that had simmered for years in congregations all over the city!

For further insight into this, consult C. Peter Wagner's book on spiritual mapping, *Breaking Strongholds in Your City* (Regal Books, 1993). It contains a chapter by Victor Lorenzo, a member of our team who specializes on the subject, with excellent examples from Resistencia and La Plata.

Be Wary of a Fascination with the Occult

I must issue a warning here. In our attempt to identify the enemy's modus operandi, we must be careful not to fall prey to fascination with the occult. Time and again, I have found that when Satan's schemes are finally exposed, he tries one last trick: tempting the leaders to become intrigued with how he works. Do not pause to write a book on his looks. Do not analyze it. Paralyze it! An old warfare maxim provides a good antidote: once the enemy is within shooting range—shoot to kill! Do not fall prey to the devil's fascinating schemes.

Because the bottom line is raiding the enemy's camp—and this means leading people to the saving knowledge of Jesus Christ (see Acts 26:17,18; 18:9)—provision must be made for the care of the new converts. Any effort to reach the city without a well-thought-through plan to adequately care for the new babes in Christ is an exercise in futility. If the principalities and powers are bound and cast out of the house (the city), the clean house must now be filled with enough congregations to care for the new converts lest the principalities and powers come back and the outcome is seven times worse than when we first began (see Matt. 12:43-45).

The Church in the city must participate in intentional, preplanned church planting. One way to do this is to combine 10 houses of prayer operating in the same area to give birth to a new congregation. Ideally, there should be a Bible-believing, Bible-preaching, Spirit-led congregation for every 1,000 people in the city. In other words, if your city has a population of 100,000 souls, you should plan on having at least 100 congregations to care for them.

How to Go About Destroying Satan's Perimeter

The first move toward destroying Satan's perimeter should be a house-to-house, door-to-door approach. In Resistencia, the pastors organized a visit to every house in the city on a given day. The week prior to this, the city was blitzed with television ads announcing, "Next Saturday, a package of good news is coming to your home!" A large, attractive envelope was shown on the screen. It seems that the entire population heard this announcement. When Saturday came around, practically everyone in the city knew that something special was coming their way. Finally, on the appointed day, operating out of command posts spread all over the city, an army of believers fanned out into every neighborhood. The entire population was visited, and 63,000-plus homes were touched with a written portion of the gospel in less than four hours.

It was an exciting event. When doorbells were rung and the "package of good news" shown, many people recognized it from the television ads. The unsaved were then told, "This is the favorable year of the Lord." When they asked what that meant, they were told, "God is ready to do you favors. What do you need that we could pray for right now?" On that historic day, marriages were mended, rebellious children were brought back into the family fold, demons were cast out and sick people were made well by the power of effective prayer. It was indeed the Favorable Year of the Lord!

Those visited were invited to come to a public arena that same evening to thank God for His goodness. So many people came that many of them had to be turned away due to lack of space!

North America has developed good evangelistic initiatives such as the "WHY" movement in Canada and the *Jesus* film in the United States. The "WHY" movement attempts to deposit an attractive coffee table type of book, containing exciting testimonies, in every home in Canada. This is preceded by systematic prayer on behalf of everybody listed in the city's phone book. This thrust, as well as the distribution of a videotape copy of the *Jesus* film, could have greater effectiveness if those evangelistic materials were distributed through the houses of prayer in each neighborhood, after the initial wave of prayer described in the preceding chapter. The contact would then be neighbor to neighbor, and the follow-up would be done by someone in close and constant proximity. This is something we hope will eventually come to pass.

Praying and distributing literature is not enough. Enemy lines must be penetrated and eventually obliterated. A well-planned major evangelistic thrust must be organized sometime after this initial blitz. I suggest that a few weeks later, neighborhood crusades be held. It is always safer to make a gradual transition from small to big.

In Resistencia, the 600-plus lighthouses of prayer combined among themselves to produce 34 neighborhood crusades. This means that approximately 18 lighthouses joined forces to sponsor each one of the area crusades. Three months later, these mini-crusades were followed by 10 larger crusades. Each one of these crusades combined the resources and manpower of approximately 60 lighthouses each. Finally, a citywide crusade was held with the support and participation of all the lighthouses and congregations in the city. By the time we got to the citywide crusade, preaching for converts was like fishing for whales in a swimming

---

ONCE SATAN'S CAMP IS INFILTRATED, HE WILL STAGE A DIVERSIONARY COUNTER-ATTACK BY ORCHESTRATING WEIRD DEMONIC MANIFESTATIONS ALL OVER TOWN, ESPECIALLY INSIDE THE CHURCH. THIS IS THE SPIRITUAL EQUIVALENT OF A DEFEATED ARMY THAT REFUSES TO SUR-RENDER BY SWITCHING TO GUERRILLA WARFARE AND SUICIDAL MISSIONS.

---

pool. It was hard to miss. There was tremendous freedom in the Spirit to minister because of the extraordinary prayer covering and also because the eyes of the unsaved were wide open to the gospel.

A word of caution: It is our experience that at this point Satan will stage a diversionary counterattack by orchestrating weird demonic manifestations all over town, especially inside the Church. This is the spiritual equivalent of a defeated army that refuses to surrender by switching to guerrilla warfare and suicidal missions. Because a frontal attack is no longer a possibility, the only way left is a diversionary attack. Those demons must be dealt with, but the Church should not become focused on them.

At this stage of the operation, the objective is setting the captives free, not writing an essay on the systems and procedures used by the captors. Do not become captivated with the enemy's camouflage and war paint. Don't succumb to the temptation to put down your rifle in order to pick up your camera or your notebook and pen. This is not the time to take pictures or jot down notes. Destroy the enemy! Remember, spiritual warfare without freeing the captives is nothing more than a glorified parade. During this phase of the struggle, the bottom line is: Set the captives free! By doing this, you are truly and effectively destroying Satan's perimeter.

11

Establishing God's Perimeter Where Satan's Used to Be

"And Hezekiah appointed the divisions of the priests and the Levites by their divisions, each according to his service, both the priests and the Levites, for burnt offerings and for peace offerings, to minister and to give thanks and to praise in the gates of the camp of the Lord....And every work which he began in the service of the house of God in law and in commandment, seeking his God, he did with all his heart and prospered."
2 Chronicles 31:2,21

NOW THAT THE ENEMY'S CAMP IS IN TOTAL DISARRAY, TROOPS must be repositioned so that God's perimeter is established over the city. The Church must occupy the heavenlies over the city as well as establish greater physical presence in the city itself. This enables the Church to move from an offensive to a defensive position, similar to what Paul describes in Ephesians 6:12-18. This maneuver involves two simultaneous thrusts: routing the enemy and healing the wounds inflicted by the occupying army.

The first one requires that you inflict the greatest possible damage on Satan's camp, which is already in shambles. You should do this by moving into his strongholds. For instance, seize the media and sign long-term contracts for radio and television programs, if possible. Start evangelistic Bible studies in government offices, public schools and among the political leaders of the city. Minister to the gangs, the prostitutes, the pimps and the drug dealers. Move in force and with spiritual authority to declare inside those formerly impregnable strongholds that the day of salvation is at hand. Now that the angel of the Lord has visited the enemy's camp and terror has overtaken it, raid that camp. Loot it. Do not be satisfied with a successful crusade or with large numbers of converts. Go for the city—the whole city! Set the captives free. God has delivered them. Lead them to freedom. Now is the time. Go for it!

Second, look for the marks of Satan on the Church and the city and heal those wounds. Heal the wounds by using a strategy that is the exact opposite of what Satan used to inflict on them. In Resistencia, the mark of the devil on the Church was division and mistrust. In order to treat this with the opposite spirit, the pastors did something unprecedented at the end of the plan. They planned a joint baptism for all the new converts, as described in chapter 2. It was an exercise in premeditated trust. Baptist pastors were baptizing converts who would eventually join a Pentecostal congregation, and vice versa.

This visible expression of unity blessed the multitude of people watching and also exposed the new believers to a practical manifestation of unity. The impact rippled through the heavenly realms, sending a loud and clear message to the satanic hosts: Move over! The Church has taken over! The Church thus moved from an offensive to a defensive position as it occupied the heavenlies over the city. In so doing, the Church established its perimeter where Satan's used to be.

WHEN A CITY IS EFFECTIVELY REACHED, THE CHURCH MUST SWITCH FROM AN OFFENSIVE MODE TO A DEFENSIVE MODE BECAUSE IT MUST NOW DEFEND THE NEWLY ACQUIRED TERRITORY.

Hezekiah recognized that Satan's mark on the kingdom—a legacy from his evil father's reign—was the poverty and disrepair of God's Temple, and the absence of priests and Levites. He now moved to appoint divisions of them (see 2 Chron. 31:2). He also built storehouses for the abundance of offerings that lay in heaps all around the temple (see 31:5-11).

Make a thorough survey of "Satan's former occupation of the city." Where are the marks of his evil paws? Then invest extra time and effort to erase those marks. For instance, if sexual immorality had been rampant, launch a major Bible-teaching thrust to expound on the beauty of chastity. If people in government had been hostile to the gospel, initiate a strategy of good works by offering volunteers to assist them. If families had been in disarray, emphasize by teaching and by example what Christ can do for a family. If no Christian school existed before, plant one or more. If the media used to be antagonistic, begin to cultivate and pray for them. In essence, overcome the evil that characterized Satan's perimeter by using God's good.

Look Out for a Second Counterattack

It is definitely easier to reach a city than to rebuild it after it has been reached. Moving into what used to be enemy territory is a vulnerable move. There are no defenses in place, and now you become an easy target. This is why the Church must maintain a warfare mentality at all times. Even though the enemy's camp has been raided, the Church is still at war and should prepare for a counterattack. When a city is effectively reached, the Church must switch from an offensive mode to a defensive mode because it must now defend the newly acquired territory. Being on the defensive is a definite advantage because, in military science, you need three attackers for every defender to be assured of victory. Notice that when Sennacherib, king of Assyria, attacked Judah, he was forced into an offensive move "that they might take the city" (2 Chron. 32:18). By rebuilding the city and organizing the defenses, Hezekiah had the home advantage.

The elders of the Church must now "sit at the gates of the city." Because there is only one Church in the city, the leaders of the many congregations should come together regularly "at the gates," which in the Bible always refer to the most sensitive area of security. The gates control what comes in and what goes out. The elders of the Church must sit at those gates to protect the city through prayer and by dispensing wisdom. This is what the apostles did: They spent time in prayer and teaching the Word (see Acts 6:4).

When Satan tried to divert the apostles with complaints regarding less crucial matters, they refused to become distracted (see Acts 6:2). As a result of this decision, "The word of God kept spreading; and the number of the disciples continued to increase greatly in Jerusalem, and a great many of the priests were becoming obedient to the faith" (Acts 6:7). Prayer and the Word exercised in a context of spiritual warfare (at the gates) always results in successful, ongoing evangelism. Hezekiah also took immediate possession of the gates: "And Hezekiah appointed the divisions of the priests and the Levites...in the gates of the camp of the Lord" (31:2). If the gates are secured, the city is secure.

You must not let the enemy tempt you into putting this operation on hold until you have taken care of the new converts. Both must take place concurrently. Although we must make every effort to incorporate new believers into the Church, we must also realize that Jesus, the Chief Shepherd, will take care of them. He is the head: "From whom the whole body, being fitted and held together by that which every joint supplies, according to the proper working of each individual part, causes the growth of the body for the building up of itself in love" (Eph. 4:16).

Our mission is to walk and work together in unity ("the whole body, being fitted and held together by that which every joint supplies") so that Jesus (the head) can cause "the growth of the body." New believers, more than a follow-up course, need a healthy body into which to be assimilated. The Holy Spirit, and His fullness, are the key. He is the *paracletos* who will lead us to all truth and righteousness (see John 16:13-15). Very little follow-up is needed if we follow through with a clear introduction of the new believers to the Holy Spirit. When a properly taught, Spirit-filled, prayerful Church in the city is focused on winning the lost, God will take care of the daily maintenance details that seem to consume the bulk of our time, resources and energy.

A good example of this is Hector Gimenez, a former drug addict and criminal, who pastors a congregation in Buenos Aires, Argentina, that reports approximately 150,000 members. The church has up to 13 daily meetings, 7 days a week. The first meeting begins at 1:00 A.M. and the last one ends at midnight. From midnight until 1:00 A.M., the building is closed for cleanup and maintenance. Hector and his associates claim to add approximately 3,000 new converts each month. How can they do it?

KEEP IN MIND THAT WE CAN NEVER *FULLY* TAKE A CITY FOR CHRIST—NOT UNTIL THE MILLENNIUM, AT LEAST, WHEN SATAN WILL BE CHAINED AND JESUS WILL RULE WITH A FIRM HAND.

Very simple: They remain focused on the lost and are continually raiding Satan's camp. As long as they do this, God will take care of their supply lines because they are doing what they are supposed to do: warring with Satan for the souls of men.

Remain Mobilized for War

When the allied troops were shipped to the Persian Gulf, no soldier had to worry about food, clothes, medical care or lodging. Their commander in chief took care of those details because they were mobilized for war. However, once the war was over and they returned home, they had to pay for their own food, lodging, transportation and clothing. Why? Because they had been demobilized. They were no longer at war. This is also true of the Church. When the Church does what it is supposed to do—that is, to take the gospel to everyone—the Lord takes care of *all* of its needs. This is an important principle to be observed during this last step. Do not get distracted with the minor details. Set up

God's perimeter in the city not so much to merely consolidate your gains but rather to maximize them further.

It was unity that brought you this far, and it is unity that will carry you beyond. Now more than ever the pastors must spend time together in prayer and in teaching the Word. They must appoint deacons to set the tables. They must never compromise their seat at the gates in the company of their fellow undershepherds. This is the key to being able to extend God's perimeter to the entire city.

Let us also keep in mind that we can never *fully* take a city for Christ—not until the millennium, at least, when Satan will be chained and Jesus will rule with a firm hand. This side of the millennium, the most we can aspire to is to struggle victoriously. Struggle we will. That is a nonnegotiable. The only difference is whether our struggle leads to victory or defeat.

Go Beyond Your City

Finally, because the best defense is an aggressive offense, take this axiom to the ultimate level. Do not make your city the final objective of your spiritual warfare. Keep the enemy off balance by devising a strategy that will enable you, and the now-expanded faithful remnant, to reach neighboring cities for Christ. Implant a missionary vision in the Church—especially among the new converts—to reach "the regions beyond." There is a powerful temptation deeply rooted in our old lifestyle to become too focused on ourselves, our ministry and our city. God wants you to go to the ends of the earth, and your city is nothing more than the starting point. You must begin with your city, but once you have reached it for Christ, you must go on to Judea and Samaria and to the uttermost parts of the earth (see Acts 1:8). If you

don't, God may send a persecution as described in the book of
Acts (chapter 8) to force you to do it.

This tendency to be focused on ourselves proved to be true in
Resistencia. When the plan was over and a successful prototype
for citywide evangelism was available, God began to use it in
cities all over the world. However, some of the local pastors
missed that blessing. While trying to "organize the results" and
analyze the procedures, they became self-absorbed. We, at
Harvest Evangelism, also failed to keep the big picture before
them. Anytime you focus on yourself and your work—even if it
is your work for God—you lose God's perspective. At that
moment, it is very easy for the enemy to make us focus on the
many less-than-perfect details in order to ruin our victory celebration. It was not until one of those pastors traveled overseas
and saw what God was doing through the pioneer work of Plan
Resistencia that the vision to keep pressing on began to return.

So many times we are like Jacob; he wanted a wife so badly
that, by trying to get her on his own strength, he got himself into
all kinds of trouble. However, God had something bigger in
mind: a nation. Through Jabob's pain and disappointments, God
reached His objective. Out of the often frustrating marriage to
Leah and Rachel, the heads of 12 tribes came into being.

Do not let a perfectionistic drive prevent you from seeing the
big picture and moving outward to Judea and Samaria. This side
of heaven, the Church will never get perfect scores. Like an
army in the trenches, it looks less than perfect, but as long as it
stays in those trenches and fires in the right direction, God will
sustain it and provide for it. We should save the details for the
millennium when we'll have plenty of time. Right now a war
rages on, and we are called to fight it! The best way to protect
God's perimeter in your city is to open up other fronts in neighboring cities.

Hezekiah's story is recorded in the Bible for our encouragement. God chose a young man who was raised in a corrupt home and used him to establish His kingdom on earth. It all began with a covenant with God. You might wonder where he found the inspiration for such a sublime act after growing up in such a corrupt environment. We are told that Abijah, his mother, was Zechariah's daughter (see 2 Chron. 29:1). Why would the Bible record this fact when nothing is known about this Zechariah, who was Hezekiah's grandfather? Zechariah means "remembrance of the Lord." It is possible that, in spite of his evil father, Hezekiah had a godly mother and a godly grandfather who taught him to remember God, a God who remembered His promises and covenants in spite of His people's rebellion. This is exactly what Hezekiah did in the *first* month of his *first* year as king; he made a covenant with God that allowed him to retake his city, his nation and even the northern kingdom. Remember the Lord's words to you and act upon them.

You are a bond servant and your Master has already stated His orders: Beginning in your Jerusalem, take the gospel to all the neighboring cities until you have reached the remotest parts of the earth. And then the end will come. Yes, Lord Jesus, come!

12

How Far Can You See?

WHERE DO YOU GO FROM HERE? YOU DEFINITELY HAVE A BURDEN for your city and now more than ever you *know* that God wishes none of its inhabitants to perish but for all to come to repentance. God has led you to that special spot where you have no choice but to go for it. The question now is: Where do you begin?

I suggest that you take an inventory of your spiritual condition.

First of all, do you have a passion for the lost? Have you caught the heartbeat of God that cries with all its might "that none should perish"? If the answer is no, or even a qualified yes, you need to heed *now* the tender voice of the Holy Spirit bringing conviction to your heart. Fully yielding to the prompting of the Holy Spirit now will spare you a sea of regretful tears at that moment when eternity is only one second away and the rest of your life is one second behind. At that time, to know that you have lived for Jesus and that you have fully devoted yourself to Him and His kingdom will joyfully usher you into the presence of the Lord as you hear His words, "Well done, good and faithful servant" (Matt. 25:21, *NIV*).

Second, do you understand the dynamics of the heavenly places? Are you familiar with the realm of the Spirit, where the real battle is waged? Have you voided every known jurisdiction that, through unresolved anger, you may have created for the enemy to have authority over your life? Your sensitivity and your response to this important question will determine whether you stand by your Master the way General Wainwright gratefully and proudly stood by his commander in chief at Japan's surrender ceremony as we discussed in chapter 5, or whether your life is being wasted the way the brilliant commando from chapter 3 was destroyed for having entered a war zone unawares and unprotected.

Third, have you pulled down the strongholds that Satan has surreptitiously built in your mind through the years? Are you truly free in Christ, or are you struggling with a double mind? Remember Jesus' admonition to Peter, "Get behind me, Satan! You are a stumbling block to Me; for you are not setting your mind on God's interests, but man's" (Matt. 16:23). From God's perspective, there is no intermediate ground. It is either black or white. It is either God's way or the enemy's way. Be single-minded all the way for Jesus!

Fourth, have you learned to pray with authority? As a deputy of Calvary empowered by the Holy Spirit, are you exercising your God-given authority as you confront violations of God's will in your life? Do you realize that the power now working in you and through you is the same power that raised Jesus Christ from the dead (see Eph. 1:19,20)? Use it for His glory!

Finally, how far can you see? Can you trust God for the entire city, now? If not, can you trust Him for your neighborhood? Or the block where you live? Or perhaps the school you attend or the place where you work? The Lord Jesus Christ is the most brilliant and caring commander in chief in the whole universe. He will never leave you stranded in enemy territory without proper supplies and support. There is already a faithful remnant near you. You may not see it, but it is there. Sound the trumpet, and they will rally to you.

A Possible Sequence of Events

To give you an idea of how much may be involved in a city-reaching thrust, let me share how events have unfolded in the many cities where we are currently assisting the Church in reaching the lost through prayer evangelism.

When we are invited by the faithful remnant to go to a city, our first visit is a short one that usually happens in the context of a pastors' breakfast or lunch. At that gathering, we "cast the vision." We share from the Scriptures and from our treasure chest of testimonies how to reach that entire city for Christ.

This first visit usually leads to a second one in which we do a four-hour workshop. The purpose of this workshop is to present the biblical principles while the local pastors choose the best strategy to implement those principles in their city. Time and time again, I tell pastors, "We do not have a plan to reach cities. What we have is a set of principles and copious notes on how those principles are being applied all over the world. It is up to you to discern how God wishes you to use them in your city." If everything goes well, at the end of the four-hour workshop, the local pastors will have produced the first draft of *their* plan to reach *their* city for Christ.

The next step—if the pastors agree—is for us to do our Life Encounter Seminar. This seminar is designed to equip pastors, leaders and church members on the principles behind prayer evangelism. It extends from a Friday evening to a Saturday afternoon. Members of all the participating churches come together

to study the principles. The seminar ends with a majestic celebration of unity, the Lord's Supper and the candle ceremony I
mentioned in chapter 8.

As the pastors begin or continue to pray together, they choose
the date to launch the prayer cells. The objective is to have a
prayer cell in every neighborhood until the entire city is prayed
for daily. A prayer cell can take several forms. It may be made up
of a family that regularly and systematically prays for a given
number of neighbors. Or it can be a gathering of several individuals from the same congregation who come together on a weekly basis. Or it could be a meeting of Christians who attend different congregations but who live in the same neighborhood.
Using personal visits and doorknob hangers, they gather prayer
requests from the people.

I suggest that you consider the possibility of linking all the
prayer cells in your city through local radio or television once a
week. This kind of program becomes a trumpet calling the people to war. On the same day each week, all the prayer cells should
tune in to the radio or television broadcast. For a half hour, two
leaders, acting as anchormen, should lift prayer requests for the
felt needs of the city, which can be found in the local newspaper.
Why the local newspaper? Because it is the best source to discover the felt needs in your community. For instance, if there was
a riot at the local prison, or if a factory is facing bankruptcy with
the consequent job layoffs, the prayer cells are led in intercession
for these needs through the radio or television program. Once
the half-hour program is over, each prayer cell then prays for
their neighborhood. Doing it this way provides the dynamic that
was at work in Acts chapters 2 through 5, where we see the Early
Church continually praying in homes and, once a week, praying
and ministering together at the Gate of Solomon.

As the city becomes covered with prayer cells and every home has been contacted and prayed for, a day is chosen to visit every house in the city. Easter or Christmas are ideal times. Operating out of the myriad of prayer cells, every house in the city is visited with a "package of good news." This package might include anything from gospel tracts to the *Jesus* film.

How long does it take to visit every home in the city? Not as long as most people think. We have visited 200,000 homes in less than five hours, using a task force of 4,000 workers. This allows for a six-minute average visit to each home!

This massive visitation should be followed by a regular "Gate-of-Solomon" kind of service in a public place. By this, I mean the kind of activity in which the Early Church was engaged in Acts 5:12. It was able to meet the felt needs of the people as the Lord confirmed the validity of the Church's message through answers to prayer.

This gathering is a service for the exclusive benefit of the unsaved. It includes no offering, no church lingo, no announcements. It is a coming together of the Church in the city to proclaim the good news of Jesus for those who don't know Him. Ideally this should be done every fifth Sunday evening. There is a fifth Sunday each quarter. Holding this meeting on the fifth Sunday will not affect the income or the programs of the local congregations, which usually count on four Sundays each month. This will provide a regular inlet for the lost in the city to experience the power and the love of God. People in the city will know that at least once a quarter the Church in the city will meet in a public place to minister to them.

How Far Can You See?

Maybe the first step is to call a group of pastors together as Michael Brodeur did in San Francisco. What was billed as a fellowship breakfast became the beginning of an unexpected, yet successful, amphibious landing in the heavenlies over the Bay Area, as the Spirit of God was poured upon that gathering.

Maybe you need to invite other pastors to lunch and share your heart for unity and for the lost. This is what Tim Pollock did in Stockton, California, and "Pray Stockton" was born.

Maybe you should call the pastors in your city to a four-day prayer summit as Murray Moerman, Paul Johnson and others did in Vancouver, British Columbia, Canada, in April 1993. One hundred and twenty pastors and leaders responded. Out of that summit, came a servant leadership team that eventually issued a call to explore how to reach Vancouver for Christ, and 288 leaders responded to the invitation. "Pray Vancouver" is already a reality.

Or you may want to follow the example of Dr. Cliff Daugherty, superintendent for Valley Christian Schools in San Jose. In 1991, his schools had been buffeted as never before by all kinds of problems: negative cash flow, strife among the administrators, lack of vision among the teachers, alcohol and pregnancies among the students, and so on. As soon as Dr. Daugherty became aware of the biblical principles outlined in this book, he encouraged the board of directors of the school to go away for a retreat and study these principles. As I am the chaplain to the board, I had the privilege of playing a part in that retreat. As the board pondered the reality of the heavenlies and identified the jurisdictions from which Satan was assailing the school, they repented and eventually voided those jurisdictions.

Two weeks later, the administrators and the faculty joined the board for a spiritual retreat to deal with similar issues. This action significantly expanded the spiritual perimeter established by the board. Eventually, the students were challenged to "take their schools for Jesus." At the right moment, intercessors began to descend on the Valley Christian campus. Nobody called them, but rather, God sent them. They asked for the use of a classroom, and they have been meeting there every Monday evening ever since. Students were also called to intercede for one another. As a result, "Pray South Bay" was launched by several San Jose churches in cooperation with Valley Christian Schools. As of this writing, close to 50,000 homes have been targeted for prayer. The evangelization of the entire city of San Jose is not far away. It all began with a frustrated superintendent who wondered out loud, *What should I do now?*

How far can you see? Maybe you can see quite far, but you are not sure if you can go the distance. The most important step in a journey of 1,000 miles is the first step. You can never take the second step until you have taken the first one. Make sure you are facing in the right direction and take that first step!

My Own Pilgrimage

When I was a brand-new believer, my pastor told me I should share Christ with everyone I came in touch with at all times. No exceptions. He emphasized that if I did not do it, I was responsible for their eternal demise. I believed my pastor, and I wanted to obey him, but during my first days as a Christian I was painfully shy. Shyness had been a problem since my childhood. God eventually cured me, but, in the infancy of my faith, I was paralyzed by it.

I was so shy that I had to practice in front of the bathroom mirror before talking to my father about any serious matter. I would say, "Hello, Father. How are you?" Then, imitating my father, I would respond, "Fine. What is it, Son?" To this I would reply, "I was wondering if I could go to such and such place." On and on it went. Everything was fine as long as I was in charge of the whole dialogue. But the minute I came out and faced him, if he failed to follow the script I had imagined, I would freeze and run back into the bathroom. Shyness was my greatest obstacle in trying to talk to strangers about Christ.

When I first got saved, I rode a public bus for about 20 minutes each day. Repeatedly, I was tormented by my inability to share Christ with the 30 passengers that rode the same bus. At the end of my daily ride, I would feel like a total failure, but not for lack of trying. I constantly tried to speak to strangers, but my mouth was welded shut. I used to have nightmares in which I saw myself approaching the Judgment Seat of Christ. While I stood before the Lord, some of my fellow bus riders would yell from hell to Jesus, saying, "Don't let him in! He rode the bus with us, and he never told us about You or heaven or hell!" I felt as though I was in hell myself. What could I do?

It was then that I came across Ephesians 2:10. I was impacted by the last part of the verse: "God prepared [good works] beforehand, that we should walk in them." It was clear to me that sharing Christ with strangers was part of God's list of good works for me. I already knew I had been called to evangelism, but I also knew that I was greatly handicapped by my shyness. So I asked the question: How far can I see?

Could I preach the gospel to a busload of people? No! Could I pass out tracts to the people riding the bus? No! What could I do? How far could I see? I settled for the very minimum. I decided to silently pray every day for the person seated next to me. So for a number of weeks I quietly sat next to someone while silently praying for his or her salvation. After doing this for a season, it occurred to me that I could bring some gospel tracts from home and sneak them behind my back before I stood up. Like a terrorist trying to activate a bomb, I found myself surreptitiously sliding the gospel tracts between my back and my seat on the bus, hoping that my fellow riders would find them after I had left.

After doing that for several weeks, I felt courageous enough to give the tracts to my neighbors at precisely the moment I was getting off the bus. It was a very safe move. If he or she asked any questions, I could truthfully say, "I'm sorry. I am getting off here." A few weeks later, I felt confident enough to go a little further. Rather than handing out the tracts the moment I was ready to descend, I decided to do it one block before my destination. I still felt safe. If any question was asked, I could still excuse myself on account of my imminent descent.

Before long, I began to feel more courageous and decided to give out the tracts five blocks before my final stop. Then I moved that up to 10 blocks. Later on, 15 blocks. Finally, the day arrived when I was able to distribute the tracts the moment I boarded the bus. "Here," I would say, "this is for you. Please read it. If you have any questions, I will be glad to answer them."

Today, I look at entire cities and do not feel the least tinge of apprehension as I strategize how to reach them for Christ. By going as far as I was able to as I rode that bus, God enabled me to gradually increase the distance. This is also true for you. How far can you see? Go as far as you can, no matter how minuscule that first step appears to be. Take it and continue to move along the path ahead of you. At the end of the journey, an entire city waits for you. Go for it! God wishes "that none should perish!"

Appendices

6 Steps for Reaching a City for Christ

Step 6: Establish God's New Perimeter Where Satan's Once Existed

Loot the enemy's camp. Entirely dispossess him of his most prized possession—the souls of men. Unless spiritual warfare results in solid, tangible conversions which are incorporated into a growing number of churches, nothing of consequence has happened.

(Repeat the Cycle)

Step 1: Establish God's Perimeter in the City

Look for people who make up the "faithful remnant," those who are waiting for the Kingdom of God to come to their city. Such a group forms a microcosm of God's Kingdom in the midst of Satan's dominion.

Step 5: Attack and Destroy Satan's Perimeter

Begin the "frontal assault." Launch the spiritual "take-over" of the city, confronting, binding, and casting down the spiritual powers ruling over the region. Proclaim the message of the gospel to every creature in the city. Disciple the new believers through the established "Lighthouses."

Step 2: Secure God's Perimeter in the City

Recognize that the enemy has infiltrated not only the city, but also the Church through sin, anxiety, and strongholds. Counter Satan's schemes and tear down the strongholds. Practice "keeping the unity of the Spirit in the bond of peace."

Step 4: Infiltrate Satan's Perimeter

From a secure base of operations, make the enemy's base insecure by parachuting behind enemy lines through a massive "air assault" of specific and strategic intercessory prayer. This is done by establishing hundreds of prayer cells throughout the city to weaken Satan's control over the unsaved, and produce a favorable disposition to the gospel by finding favor with the people.

Step 3: Expand God's Perimeter in the City

God uses the faithful remnant to establish a model. With that model now in place, now others whose heart God has been preparing must gradually be brought inside the perimeter to build up the army of saints that will eventually launch the attack on the forces holding the city in spiritual darkness.

The Concept:
Preparing an Atmosphere for Effective Evangelism

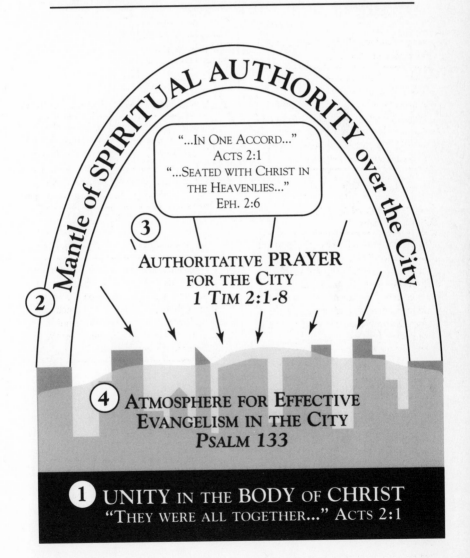

"It's God's Time for YOU!" Prototype

First Year: Preparation-"...Together in One Accord..." (Acts 2:1)

Columns (months): SEP, OCT, NOV, DEC, JAN, FEB, MAR, APR, MAY, JUN

THE PASTORS IN ONE ACCORD — Commit to "...be of one mind..." regarding the city.

THE PASTORS TOGETHER IN ONE ACCORD — Begin to meet 2 times a month for prayer and ministry to one another.

THE CONGREGATIONS IN ONE ACCORD — The Congregations commit to unity, to prayer for one another, and to hold united meetings. Pastors may interchange pulpits.

THE CONGREGATIONS TOGETHER IN ONE ACCORD — Regular program of "Unity Celebrations":
- 1st Celebration of Unity
- 2nd Celebration of Unity
- 3rd Celebration of Unity
- 4th Celebration of Unity
- 5th Celebration of Unity

THE CHURCH PRAYING — The "Prayer Cells" begin to function.

THE CHURCH PREPARING
- Seminar I: "Inner Healing"
- Seminar II: "How to Pray for the City"
- Seminar III: "Intercession and Spiritual Warfare"

THE CHURCH PROCLAIMING
- Evangelistic Crusade(s) House-to-House Literature Distribution

THE CHURCH REPRODUCING
- Discipleship / Church Planting

The 6 Steps to Reach a City for Christ
1. ESTABLISH God's Perimeter in the City
2. SECURE God's Perimeter in the City
3. EXPAND God's Perimeter in the City
4. INFILTRATE Satan's Perimeter in the City
5. DESTROY Satan's Perimeter in the City
6. ESTABLISH God's New Perimeter in the City

ACTS 2:1 "...THEY WERE ALL TOGETHER IN ONE ACCORD."

What Does That Mean? Together refers to their physical proximity: near to each other in the same upper room. In One Accord refers to the attitude of the heart: one in Christ, having the same mind and purpose. This diagram suggests a sequence of events that begins with "Being Together" and ends with "Being of One Accord." First among the Pastors, then among the Congregations, and finally throughout the whole City!

For more information, write to or call:

Rev. Ed Silvoso, Director
Harvest Evangelism
P.O. Box 20310
San Jose, CA 95160-0310
408-927-9052